Super Rich

Super Rich

The Rise of Inequality in Britain and the
United States

GEORGE IRVIN

polity

First published in 2008 by Polity Press

Polity Press
65 Bridge Street
Cambridge CB2 1UR, UK

Polity Press
350 Main Street
Malden, MA 02148, USA

ISBN-13: 978-0-7456-4464-6
ISBN-13: 978-0-7456-4465-3(pb)

A catalogue record for this book is available from the British Library.

Typeset in 11.25/13 pt Dante
by Servis Filmsetting Ltd, Stockport, Cheshire
Printed and bound in Great Britain by
MPG Books Ltd, Bodmin, Cornwall

For further information on Polity, visit our website: www.polity.co.uk

Contents

List of Figures

Introduction

Equality is part of the quality of our life, like income, the environment and public services . . . Equality makes diversity possible, and makes it possible for everyone to count as a person.

Massimo Cacciari, quoted in Bobbio (1996: xiv)

The theme of this book is that it is not just poverty but growing inequality that should concern us; a less equal society is a less civilized society. I have chosen to write on inequality in the rich countries, particularly in the UK and the USA, where, following the neo-liberal revolution of the Reagan-Thatcher period, economic growth has made top income earners vastly richer while much of the population has struggled to maintain its standard of living. In both countries, too, there are signs that the issue of inequality may return to the political agenda, particularly if a prolonged recession occurs. The broad goal I suggest in the concluding chapter will seem revolutionary to some, but in reality it is both modest and feasible: namely, a return within a generation to the lower degree of income inequality which prevailed in the 1970s, taking the Nordic countries as exemplary of desirable levels of social provision.

Three qualifications should be added immediately. First, this book is written for a general audience, not just academics and researchers; I have tried to minimize economic jargon, though I cannot pretend to have eliminated it completely. Second, I hardly touch on inequality and poverty in the developing countries of Africa, Asia and Latin America; nor do I examine the complex interaction between economic growth, distribution and global climate change. I don't wish to minimize the critical importance of these issues. Indeed, I hope that my focus on the growth of inequality in the world's richest countries will help illuminate the wider picture. Third, some readers may feel that I have stressed the similarities of the UK and US experiences at the expense of highlighting the differences. There is a difficult balance to be struck here between the different historical trajectories, particularly as concerns the growth of left-of-centre political parties and institutions in the past century, and the convergence of the two countries both during and after the Reagan-Thatcher period. Suffice it to say that one cannot write about growing inequality without stressing this convergence.

After Tony Blair became leader in 1994, if the 'new' Labour Party in Britain could be said to have any policy towards inequality, it was one of emphasis on reducing poverty amongst society's most vulnerable groups, children and the aged. Such an aim is admirable, and it is undeniable that under Blair and Brown, many of the very poor in Britain are today less poor. Equally, had a Labour government not come to power in 1997, interpolating the trend of the previous decade suggests that many more would be in poverty today. Nevertheless, whatever Blair and Brown's intentions, it is also true that Britain's rich have grown very much richer under Labour. Poverty may have fallen, but inequality clearly has not. If we focus on the top end of the distribution of household income (say, within the top decile), inequality has actually increased.

The US picture is bleaker and, in contrast to the UK, there has been no ideological ambiguity about poverty on George Bush's watch; he has simply ignored it. Since the Reagan era, the divide between rich and poor has continuously deepened; in the world's richest country, some 36 million people live below the poverty line. (The figure would be over 70 million were the EU definition of 'relative poverty' used.) A further 57 million are estimated to be 'near poor', bringing the total either in poverty or at risk of it to nearly one-third of the total population. Not only is climbing out of poverty more difficult in the USA, but swathes of 'middle-class' families are struggling to make ends meet. Moreover, there is a growing body of evidence drawn from Britain, America and elsewhere that suggests it is *relative* deprivation, not simply absolute deprivation, which matters in the rich countries of the West. There are fundamental implications here, I shall argue, for the way in which we think about designing social policy to achieve a 'fairer' society.

I started researching this book in 2006, a year in which the *Guardian* reported that London's investment bankers had made record-breaking profits.[1] Investment banks, hedge funds and private equity firms paid out nearly £9 billion in bonuses at the end of 2006 – just over 4,000 employees in the City (London's Wall Street) received an extra £1 million each! As I finished the book, total City bonuses had nearly doubled; indeed, when added to 'performance pay rewards', the total for 2007 is likely to be £26 billion, enough to raise the income of the poorest-paid 20 per cent of British workers by £5,000 a year or to lift nearly everyone out of poverty.[2]

Headlines about extravagant bonuses no longer count as 'news'; such pieces appear on a daily basis. Since the 'Big Bang' reform of London's

Stock Exchange in late 1986, the growth of the financial services sector has been precipitous. The evidence of Britain's newfound fortune is everywhere: from the towers of Canary Wharf to the Victorian warehouses of dockland now transformed into luxury apartment blocks, to the astronomical property prices in London and the south-east of England. In the past two decades, the City has 'generated wealth' in the sense of attracting banks, brokerage houses and a host of talented young people from all over the world. This inflow of foreign capital has made it possible for Britain to leave behind its notoriously frail economy, plagued by fiscal and financial stop–go cycles, greatly easing Gordon Brown's job when he was Chancellor and making him appear something of a magician. Doubtless the success of the City is one reason why New Labour has been deeply reluctant to do anything about the rise of the super rich. Witness the Chancellor, Alistair Darling, plugging a few tax loopholes in Britain's laws affecting the non-domiciled rich while raising the inheritance tax threshold to assuage 'middle England', an act of such blatant opportunism that Polly Toynbee declared it to be 'the death of social democracy'.[3] New Labour has to date not countenanced raising the top rate of income tax or creating a new higher tax band, nor does it ever seem likely to do so.

There are a variety of reasons why inequality has grown so much since the 1980s in the United States and Britain – one should add that inequality has not grown to any comparable extent in continental Europe. An obvious starting point is the conservative political and economic revolution (or restoration if you prefer) under Thatcher and Reagan. The roots of the conservative revolution lie in the crisis of the 1970s. As corporate profits were squeezed and inflation rose, the foundations of the post-war social-democratic settlement began to crumble. Internationally, the fixed exchange-rate regime collapsed and the US trade-deficit pumped dollars abroad, setting the stage for a huge expansion in financial services. By the 1980s, deindustrialization and inflation undermined the bargaining power of organized labour and accelerated the casualization of the workforce. The crisis was particularly severe in the UK and the US. The conservative answer was to shrink the state and to 'roll back' the post-war institutions of social democracy and welfare. Capitalism appeared to find new dynamism in the 1980s and 1990s with the explosive growth of corporate mergers, private equity buyouts, the rise of the 'high tech' sector and of finance, particularly in the UK where finance overtook the manufacturing industry in generating GDP and employment. In the USA, the share of financial sector profits in total corporate profits rose from 14 per cent in 1981 to nearly 40 per cent at the turn of the new century.[4]

Financial sector growth brought an explosion in executive rewards. The earnings of Britain's chief executive officers (CEOs), although they have grown less dramatically than in America, are far ahead of CEO earnings in the rest of Europe. In 2005, directors' pay in Britain's top companies rose by 28 per cent, more than seven times the average rate of pay and eleven times the rate of inflation. In the prior three years, directors' pay rose by 16 per cent, 13 per cent and 23 per cent, while average earnings rose at around 3.5 per cent per annum. The average pay for a CEO in Britain's top 100 companies was £2.4 million in 2005. Across the Atlantic, the average CEO of a Standard & Poor's 500 company received $15 million in total compensation in 2006.[5]

Peter Mandelson famously remarked to an American audience that New Labour was 'intensely relaxed about people getting filthy rich' as long as they paid their taxes. His comment has never been contradicted by anybody in the Labour Party leadership. Indeed, starting with the Commission on Social Justice set up under John Smith in the early 1990s, New Labour has moved away from seeking a more egalitarian distribution of income and wealth (i.e., 'outcomes') towards one of equalizing 'opportunities'. Meritocracy, not equality, has been the rhetorical – and indefensibly shallow – flavour of the decade. Any suggestion that Labour should attack unjustifiably high levels of remuneration has been derided as old-fashioned and dismissed as the 'politics of envy'; wealth creation and enterprise are sacrosanct and must be rewarded. Ideological support for the rise of inequality, once the preserve of the extreme right, seems to have colonized the full political spectrum. Nevertheless, there is some evidence that the tide may turn; e.g., a 2007 report for the Rowntree Foundation says: 'There is considerable public concern regarding economic inequality, and certainly no evidence that people see the income gap in the UK positively.'[6]

The chapter sequence runs from the current situation and its historical roots to a section on the costs of inequality, an examination of what various authors proposed to do about it, the sustainability of financing US and UK consumption by means of foreign savings and, finally, to a defence of greater equality which is both theoretically rooted and practically feasible. The first two chapters summarize the empirical evidence on the distribution of income and wealth in the UK and the USA. There is a plethora of specialist material on this matter; I have tried to make the evidence accessible while providing relief to the reader by sprinkling the text with illustrative anecdotes. Chapters 3 and 4 are intended to provide a historical framework to the argument by looking at the following questions. What is neo-liberalism? Why was the conservative reaction greater in the USA and the UK than in continental Europe? What is the future of the European welfare state? Broadly speaking, I view neo-liberalism as a response to the vulnerability of American and British capitalism in the 1970s, and argue that the welfare state, far from being an unaffordable luxury, is vital to the success of a modern economy.

Do we need more growth? Chapter 5 looks at the 'science of happiness', the subject of much recent attention amongst social scientists. A number of these have reflected on the apparent paradox that, as America and Britain grow wealthier, their citizens seem not to grow happier; instead, they suffer in ever great numbers from anxiety and depression, as reflected for example in the alarming growth of binge drinking, road-rage and other symptoms of social malaise. For reasons which will become apparent, I consider the happiness literature to be something of a curate's egg; the micro-analysis of happiness is in places useful, even if the overarching social theory implied is less than satisfactory.

I devote chapter 6 to the declining socio-economic fortunes of the middle class; more precisely, to that part of the middle class which finds itself slipping into the lower half of the 'hourglass society'. Here I draw heavily on US evidence, partly because the American middle class is so (subjectively) large and because the mythology of upward mobility and meritocratic advance is so pervasive. In Britain, New Labour has sought to appropriate and implant this ideology. In fact, the evidence runs almost entirely in the other direction; in the USA, at least, the middle class swims against far more treacherous currents in the job market than it did two generations ago, and the prospect of disappearing beneath the waves into proletarian obscurity is correspondingly higher. Marx's view that a communality of interests exists between 'workers by hand and by brain' seems apposite, even if the political alliance he supposed would result seems as distant as ever.

Chapter 7 considers the cost to society of growing inequality. There is a burgeoning literature on the subject, ranging from the traditional social sciences including social psychology, to social epidemiology and evolutionary biology. Here again, I mix academic evidence with anecdotal material, hoping this will help more than hinder. In discussing inequality, it is the importance of *relative* socio-economic status which stands out. In chapter 8, I move back to my own domain of economics where I try to tie together the themes of income and consumption growth, financial deregulation, diminishing household savings, global economic imbalance and looming recession. America's propensity to spend more than its income is mirrored by a huge and growing current account deficit. This is not intended as a moral tale about profligacy. Rather, to the extent that global financial markets perceive the US deficit (and that of its UK cousin) to be unsustainable, there is a real danger that we are drifting into a financial and economic crisis of global proportions. Just as in the 1930s, to respond to the crisis by stringent economic belt-tightening would only make matters worse. Economists recognize the dangers, but policy-makers appear to believe that the problem is best resolved by trusting in the beneficent working of the free market. I argue that such a response is incoherent and irresponsible.

The final chapter puts the case for socio-economic equality. It is argued that the claim for meritocracy is empty unless young adults face a reasonably level playing field; in truth, the growth of inequality has tilted the playing field so violently that the veneer of legitimacy sustaining neo-liberal ideology is being stripped away. To stabilize the tilt, much less to redress it, requires a major extension of social provision, particularly to pre-school children, as well as the redistribution of income and wealth. I am hardly alone is proposing redistribution; Robert H. Frank, Juliet Schor and others have argued for a progressive tax on consumption. I argue that a far more radical redistribution is needed than what has been proposed by any of them.

It is worth recalling that the notion of 'greater equality' was once central to political discourse in Britain and shared across much of the political spectrum, from Butler to Gaitskell, in the post-war years. In the USA, although the notion of meritocracy has always held greater sway than in Britain, reducing inequality was one of the aims of FDR's inter-war 'New Deal', and that goal was shared by the main parties until the 1980s. Indeed, income and wealth inequality fell steadily in both countries during the post-war period. Doubtless, political support for equality has been weakened by the neo-liberal restoration, and some would argue that globalization has made the welfare state an anachronism. In my view, the challenge of globalization and the 'knowledge economy' can only be met by moving towards much greater socio-economic equality; to do so will require the sort of social transfers and investment which the Nordic countries have undertaken for several generations. The reader who has travelled the full length of the book will hardly be surprised to learn that I am unapologetically 'old' Labour and deeply sceptical about the 'new egalitarianism' favoured by some of New Labour's academic advisers.

In writing this book. I wish to express my thanks to the International Centre for European Research (ICER) in Turin where I spent several months in early 2007 enjoying the support necessary to write the bulk of my first draft, as well as to my academic colleagues at the University of London, SOAS, who have helped me hone some of the main ideas.

Particular thanks goes to those who read and commented on the manuscript at different stages: Norman Dombey, Barbara Ehrenreich, Laurence Harris, Alejandro Izurieta, Stuart Lansley, Michael Rustin, John Schmitt, Elaine Sharland, Jenny Shaw, John Grieve Smith, Bob Sutcliffe, Robert Wade and Richard Wilkinson. My editors at Polity Press have been hugely helpful, particularly Sarah Lambert and the copy-editor, Helen Gray. There are others I should add; inevitably, though, a list of names is marred by omissions, particularly of those who helped shape my views on inequality. My own father, the journalist Warren Irvin, was passionate about social justice; he died many years ago, but his influence is embedded in this work. I want to thank my own family, too: my adult children, Marc and Leonora, and my wife, Lindsay Knight. In particular, it is Lindsay – herself a journalist – who has provided not just loving support and encouragement, but long hours of proofing copy and invaluable suggestions about how the text might be improved. The usual caveat about errors applies. As in the past, it is to Lindsay, Marc and Leonora that this book is dedicated.

George Irvin
Brighton, December 2007

1

Neo-liberalism and the Return of Inequality

Not since the Roaring Twenties have the rich been so much richer than everyone else . . . [the] nation needs an administration that will offer solutions for the scourge of income inequality.

Editorial, 'It didn't end well last time', *New York Times*, 4 April 2007

Is Criminality Redundant?

Max Hastings, a former editor of London's respectably conservative *Daily Telegraph*, is not known for holding strongly socialist views, but the extent of inequality in Britain has led him to write:

Today's filthy rich are wealthier, healthier and more secure than ever . . . It seems remarkable that any high roller these days resorts to fraud to enrich himself. It is possible to bank such huge sums legally that criminality seems redundant.[1]

There is now a voluminous literature on growing inequality in Britain and the USA, not to mention an avalanche of newspaper articles on City bonuses and 'fat-cat' salaries. For many years the conventional wisdom was that as countries grow richer, inequality at first rises but ultimately tends to fall when countries become fully industrialized.[2] Over the past thirty years, however, inequality appears to have worsened for the OECD countries taken together. This result is most strongly influenced by what has happened in Britain and the United States where income inequality today has returned to levels last seen in the 1930s. Squaring this trend with conventional economic theory has required telling a story about the growing premium placed on highly educated labour (including top entrepreneurial talent) in the 'new economy' while bemoaning the lack of dynamism of 'old Europe'. An alternative story is traced in this book which looks more closely at the changing political and economic landscape of the period.

The rollback of the 'welfare state' – particularly in the UK, but also of its weaker US version set up under Roosevelt's New Deal – is the main legacy of the Reagan-Thatcher years, underwritten by subsequent governments in both countries and whose international expression is the Washington Consensus.[3] The neo-liberal revolution of the 1980s had two critical implications for the way we think about economics. Not only did it coincide with the decline and demise of the 'socialist' (USSR-style) centrally planned economy, but in Europe neo-liberalism signalled the re-emergence of unfettered free-market capitalism as an alternative to the dominant post-war social democratic consensus. Social democracy was no longer seen as a 'middle path' between unfettered capitalism and state socialism; instead, it became a hindrance to capitalist hegemony.

Underlying the Reagan-Thatcher political project were structural changes in both the USA and the UK; notably, the decline of industrial capital and the trade unions, the rise of the international financial sector and the growing importance of the two-tier service economy; i.e, low-wage and low-skill (e.g, McDonald's and Wal-Mart) and high-tech (e.g, Microsoft and Goldman Sachs). The much-hyped 'new economy' has helped to fragment labour markets, change the structure of remuneration, weaken job security, undermine the bargaining power of trade unions and spread neo-liberal ideology. Growing inequality fed back into the political consolidation of neo-liberalism in a variety of ways, ranging from the shift towards individual and corporate donations in the funding of political parties, the concentration of media power in the hands of fewer owners and the commoditization and repackaging of politics into sound-bites and spin. In short, the modern Anglo-American model has challenged the European 'welfare state' version of the market economy under which a relatively strong, democratically financed state mediates conflicts between capital and labour and guarantees political and social cohesion and high levels of public provision.

It is crucial to emphasize that the Reagan-Thatcher project was itself a response to the decline of US and British industrial hegemony in the post-war period. Having been dominant globally for half a century, by the 1970s Britain was the 'sick man of Europe' and the USA was rapidly losing its manufacturing dominance, in part because of an inflation-financed war (Vietnam), but crucially because it faced stiff competition from reconstructed Europe and emerging Asia – what today we would call a 'globalization' effect. As the rate of profit fell[4] and share prices stagnated, Wall Street complained increasingly that the fault lay with stodgy corporate executives whose salaries were paid regardless of performance; the mantra of 'maximizing shareholder value' began to be heard. Spurred on in the early 1980s by the appearance of corporate raiders and junk-bond finance, America's corporations began to restructure by selling off entire divisions, becoming 'lean and mean' and looking for new 'synergies' through mergers. Above all, 'maximizing shareholder value' meant tying CEO remuneration to market performance, crucially through the use of share options, thus laying the basis for a quantum leap in executive rewards and the rise of a new class of super rich whose influence soon spread to Britain.

The Reagan-Thatcher period also saw the introduction of important legal milestones which would change the distribution of wealth and power. In the UK, the explosive growth of financial services accelerated after the large-scale deregulation and streamlining of City transactions under the 'Big Bang'[5] legislation of late 1986; this boost in comparative advantage gave London a decisive edge over Frankfurt and New York. The end of national wage bargaining and a variety of anti-union measures – symbolically capped by the defeat of the miners – constrained union activity; Britain's strong exchange-rate policy favoured the financial sector and helped underpin long-term deindustrialization. Moreover, Britain's relatively lax tax residency law, coupled with the absence of the direct taxation of land or financial assets and low rates of tax on income, helped make the country a leading tax haven.

The assault on welfare in the UK was not just a matter of bashing organized workers. Government statistics for the period 1980–2000 show the number of children in poverty having risen from 1.4 million to 4.4 million, and the number of pensioners with less than half the average income doubled.[6] By the end of the century, not only was Britain less equal than other EU states at a comparable average income level, but its social and economic infrastructure was in tatters. Although, since 2000, a Labour government in the UK has made modest progress in alleviating poverty amongst pensioners and children, a 2005 Report from the Office of National Statistics (ONS) suggests that the growth in inequality that Britain experienced under Thatcher has not been reversed. The same Report notes that, when both direct and indirect taxes are counted, the poor in Britain pay a larger share of their income in taxes than do the rich. In the words of Francis Jones, the Director of the Office of National Statistics (ONS):

> Inequality of disposable income increased rapidly in the second half of the 1980s, reaching a peak in 1990 . . . After 1995/96 inequality began to rise again reaching a peak in 2001/02 – actually at a level very similar to that seen in 1990. From 2001/02, there was a small reduction in income inequality, although the latest figures for 2005/06 show an increase over the previous year, and *the latest evidence suggests that inequality may be increasing again* [my emphasis]. [7]

What also seems to be true is that there is greater geographical clustering of poverty and wealth in Britain. A recent study by Dorling et al. (2007) shows the poor and wealthy becoming increasingly physically segregated from each other; moreover, the study suggests that in recent years, while the proportion of very poor households has fallen in Britain, the proportion of 'breadline poor' has increased.[8]

In the United States during the 1980s, airlines, trucking, banking and some utilities were deregulated while industrial concentration – as reflected in growing corporate mergers – would grow explosively in the 1990s. As top corporations became more concentrated, CEO pay grew disproportionately, aided by favourable tax legislation. Reagan's Economic Recovery Act of 1981 greatly reduced the top rate of personal tax while extending corporate tax write-offs and easing depreciation rules; further tax reductions followed in 1986. Corporate tax before Reagan accounted for nearly one-third of total US tax revenue; today's figure is less than 8 per cent. Income inequality grew strongly under Reagan and G. H. W. Bush, a trend that Bill Clinton in the 1990s did little to reverse. Indeed, the 1997 'Taxpayer Relief Act' produced another bonanza for the wealthy: it is estimated for every $1 in tax savings going to the bottom 80 per cent, the top 1 per cent of income earners saved over $1,000 in tax. While swathes of unionized skilled workers lost their jobs as traditional industries disappeared, the remuneration of top CEOs grew. As the president of the New York Federal Reserve Bank, William J. McDonough, noted in a speech to mark the first anniversary of 9/11, in 1980 America's top executives on average earned about forty times as much as the average worker; by 2000 the ratio was 400:1. Such a jump, he said, was impossible to explain by corporate performance.[9] The situation has been summarized more recently by the *Guardian* journalist, Jonathan Freedman:

> You can pick your stat[istic], ranging from the claim that just two men – Bill Gates and Warren Buffett – have as much money between them as 30% of the entire American people, to the findings by a federal reserve study that the top 10% of Americans now own 70% of the country's wealth, while the top 5% own more than everyone else put together. There was a time when a company boss earned perhaps 10 or 20 times the salary of his lowliest employee. By 2004, that ratio between average chief executive and average worker had leapt to 431 to one, and the gap has got wider. It means that the average worker takes more than a year to earn what his boss brings home in less than a day. The result is grand houses on New York's swankiest avenues that were, until recently, multiple apartments but which are now restored to the private homes they were a century ago. Makers of 200ft yachts report record sales.

Economists say the last time such a yawning chasm separated rich and poor was in the Great Gatsby years, on the eve of the crash of 1929.[10]

London's 'Wealth-creating' Square Mile

London today is booming, and the square mile of the City (London's financial centre) is at the heart of the boom. Hardly a day goes by without a new story about how workers in the City's major banks and financial houses are receiving huge bonuses. The average salary for somebody working in the financial sector in 2006 was reckoned to be £100,000, up by a fifth from the previous year. Nor has the current credit crunch stopped the rich (with a few exceptions) getting richer.

The impact on London's economy is highly visible as these new entrepreneurs queue up at exclusive restaurants, and buy diamonds and luxury cars for their partners. It is a world of 'you deserve it' and 'gorgeous gets what gorgeous wants', apparently without limit, and nowhere is it more visible than in the property market where burgeoning demand and constrained supply have combined to raise the average house price in London to £300,000, nearly three times as high as in the north-east of Britain.

Those who wonder why New Labour is so relaxed about this state of affairs need look no further than the Treasury. With nearly one-third of the capital's workforce in the financial or business services sector, London accounts for more than 20 per cent of the UK's total income tax receipts, while receiving only 15 per cent of government spending. A study by Oxford Economic Forecasting suggests that London's net contribution to public receipts is running at around £13 billion a year, enough to finance, say, the entire bill for replacing Trident missiles in two years. It is hardly surprising that Ed Balls, formerly Gordon Brown's right-hand man at the Treasury, has been called 'Minister for the City'.[11]

And it is not just financial traders and deal-makers who earn big money. London is home to many who have come to the UK to avoid higher tax regimes in other EU countries. A recent study by the accountancy firm Grant Thornton concluded that Britain's fifty-four billionaires, with assets of £126 billion between them, paid only £14 million a year in income tax.[12] The City is also perceived to be less tightly regulated than in other leading centres – including New York and Frankfurt – which is one reason why, since the Big Bang, London has prospered. Of course, London is not just about new wealth. Aristocratic fortunes made centuries ago continue to thrive. Take the 6th Duke of Westminster, who in 2005 was reported to be the third richest man in the UK and whose family fortune derives from the 17th-century inheritance of a large chunk of what is today Mayfair, Belgravia and Pimlico. Or take the Cadogans, Portmans and Howard de Waldens (or for that matter the Windsors), all of whom own prime chunks of urban real estate and who have made a vast amount out of rising property values in the past decade.[13]

Does London really 'generate wealth'? The answer depends on whether one thinks 'wealth generation' is simply about making money – or, more precisely, making money out of other people's money. It is certainly difficult to claim that those who make fortunes from rising property values are 'generating wealth'. For classical economists like David Ricardo, the landowning classes, far from generating wealth, were an impediment to economic development. Ricardo famously argued that they benefited from the Corn Laws, a form of agricultural protection, which served to keep food prices high and squeezed industrial profits. Indeed, Adam Smith – writing half a century before Ricardo – argued decisively against the Mercantilist notion that the accumulation of gold (through trade or otherwise) could be counted as 'wealth creation'.

The boom in London's financial sector since deregulation in 1986 has been remarkable, it is true. But the financial boom is a *worldwide* phenomenon. Half a century ago, much of the money flowing around London served to lubricate the wheels of trade, whether providing insurance for ships, fees for merchants or finance for cargoes. Today, the flow of money around the world in general – and through London in particular – greatly exceeds what is needed to make or transport goods. On an average day, financial transactions in London are estimated to be in excess of $1 trillion. The power of 'finance capital' has grown out of all proportions to that of industrial capital. In essence, London's financiers are not in the business of producing real wealth in the sense of adding to the world's productive capacity; rather, they make money out of money. This is a crucial distinction which classical economists like Smith and Ricardo wrote about, but which Britain's political elite today has chosen to ignore.

At the other end of the scale sits London's underclass; has the wealth trickled down to them? If one excludes jobs in the City, London's unemployment rate stands at 8 per cent, well above the national average; in boroughs like Hackney and Tower Hamlets, unemployment is typically twice that rate. Five of the ten most deprived boroughs in the UK are reported to be in London. Moreover, because the cost of living is so high in London relative to the rest of the UK, the poor are poorer than elsewhere. The capital's Living Wage Campaign – backed by London's mayor, Ken Livingston – has helped to spotlight the plight of cleaners, catering staff and other low-paid workers. The Transport and General Workers' Union has championed a

'Justice for Cleaners' campaign and argues that the minimum wage in London needs to be at least 30 per cent above that in the rest of Britain if the low paid are merely to survive. 'We are working hard for companies earning millions of pounds but we can't afford to feed our children. Cleaners, come out of your cleaning cupboards and fight for justice!', said cleaner Abiola Arowolo, getting the campaign for justice under way outside KPMG's offices in the City of London in March 2006.[14]

A piece in the *Observer* illustrates the contrast between rich and poor with particular poignancy.[15] On one side of the page is the picture of the City banker, Bob Diamond, who is head of Barclay's Capital, the bank's investment banking arm. He lives in the ultra-chic area of Kensington, where the average family home is said to cost several million pounds. In 2005, his basic salary was a mere £146,000, but he received a $4.4 million cash bonus and £1.9 million in share awards. He is reported to have been promised a bonus of £15 million if Barclay's Capital met its end-of-year targets in 2006.

On the other side of the page is a picture of Charlie Sawyer, a fifty-eight-year-old cleaner who works for the London Underground. Charlie says:

> I start at 11pm, finish at 6:30am and earn £6.05 an hour. I live in southeast London, in Peckham – I'm a council tenant. What they pay me is not sufficient: I do another job as a porter. . . . I came from Sierra Leone nine years ago. Most of the cleaners are migrants. People don't respect us, but without cleaners the Queen couldn't live in Buckingham Palace. . . . We only get 12 days' holiday pay. We don't get a tube pass, and we're cleaning the tube.

And it is not just the low paid who struggle. Teachers, nurses, civil service clerks and other public service workers who once thought of themselves as 'middle class' now struggle to survive, with rent and travel costs eating up their take-home pay. As house prices continue to rise (albeit more slowly in 2007), it is clear that most of these same people – never mind the unskilled and semi-skilled – will never manage to get on to the property ladder within 10 miles of central London, and that many will never be able to afford property anywhere in London. The middle class is being hollowed out. London's entrepreneurial spirit and 'wealth creation' may be good for some and admired by the political classes, but for the growing number who are being left far behind, there is real pain.

What of the American Dream?

What is true of Britain is even more so of the USA. Numerous authors have noted that in the United States it is not just the poor who are growing

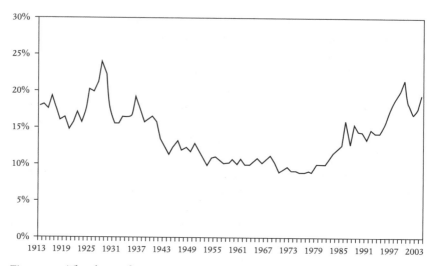

Figure 1.1: The share of income going to the top 1 per cent, including capital gains, 1913–2004
Source: Figure 1M from: L. Mishel, J. Bernstein and S. Allegretto (2007)

poorer, but the middle class too. The American Dream – the notion that anyone willing to work hard enough can go from rags to riches – was always a convenient ideological myth serving the interests of the few. Even at the height of post-war prosperity in the 1960s, when America was growing richer and somewhat more equal, some social scientists disputed the extent of upward mobility in the USA.[16]

Today, as US inequality grows, the dream is receding – even if a majority of Americans still cling to its promise. For many Europeans, the television images of Hurricane Katrina were revelatory, stripping away the gloss to reveal the underside of the 'American way of life': an underclass of poor whites, blacks and Hispanic migrants living in dire poverty and largely neglected by their political representatives in Washington. Several recent studies suggest that before Katrina struck, poverty amongst the families it displaced was far greater than previously imagined.[17] The official poverty rate in the USA is about 14 per cent (2005) for all families, but 18 per cent for children and 30 per cent for blacks; these are the worst figures for any OECD country.

Figure 1.2 provides a graphic illustration of income inequality in the United States and is based on Congressional Budget Office research data released in December 2005. In 2003, the top fifth of earners in the USA received over half of the national income while the bottom fifth received only 5 per cent. In fact, the top 1 per cent took in more of the pie than the

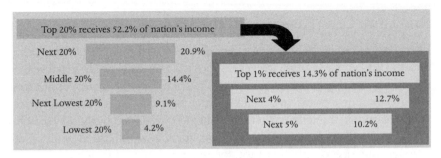

Figure 1.2: 2005 Distribution of income in the USA
Source: <http://www.cipa-apex.org/toomuch/inequality.html>

bottom 40 per cent. According to an editorial in *The New York Times*, 'In 2005, the latest year for which figures are available, the top 1 percent of Americans — whose average income was $1.1 million a year — received 21.8 percent of the nation's income, their largest share since 1929. Over all, the top 10 per cent of Americans . . . collected 48.5 per cent, a share last seen before the Great Depression.'[18] Moreover, it is not just under the presidency of George W. Bush that average wages in the United States have fallen; official figures show that the share of labour remuneration (compensation of employees) in GDP is lower than at any time since 1947. Since CEO salaries are part of the share of labour remuneration in GDP, this means that ordinary workers have been squeezed very hard indeed.

Just like in Britain, growing inequality in the USA is producing what is called an 'hourglass economy'; i.e., one in which there are lots of lower-paying (though not necessarily low-skill) jobs and higher-paying jobs, but fewer of the middle-class, middle-income jobs that used to span the gap between skilled blue-collar and high-level, white-collar professional jobs. During the heyday of the American middle class, the USA had a diamond-shaped economy: growing middle-income jobs with fewer low- and high-end ones. In the words of one observer:

> The most significant aspect of our emerging hourglass economy is that, even as the economic top is pulling farther away from the bottom . . . Stockbrokers, money-managers and CEOs become superrich while college professors, doctors and other professionals struggle to stay in the upper middle class. This ultimately ends in the classic pyramid economy of the pre-democracy era: a small group of the superrich organizes politics and economics to continue to feed wealth to them at the expense of everyone else.[19]

Runaway CEO Rewards in the USA

Every spring, media and business research organizations in the United States release CEO compensation surveys of pre-tax executive pay levels over the preceding year. The numbers must be treated with care because sample sizes and the exact groups of corporations surveyed differ. Equally, discrepancies arise because of the different ways in which bonuses and perks are treated. The accompanying figure 1.3 shows results for 2005 as published by different US research organizations. With the exception of Forbes, which puts average remuneration at $10.9 million, the five data sources show results in the $5–7 million range. Given that US median income in 2005 was about $46,000, the average of top pay shown ($7.42 million) here exceeds median income by a multiple of 161. Moreover, top CEO salaries in the USA have been growing much faster than has median income.

Similar survey figures exist for Britain or other OECD countries, but precise international comparisons are difficult to make, in part because of the differing nature of remuneration, the different exchange rate that can be used and so on. Nevertheless, the broad picture is that the gap between median and top earnings in Britain, though less wide than that in the USA, is considerably wider than the earnings gap in continental European countries (see chapter 4).

The Reagan Revolution

A quarter of a century ago in August 1982, Ronald Reagan signed the Economic Recovery Tax Act of 1981. This Act slashed top rates of tax in the United States, reversed the egalitarian consensus in place since Roosevelt's New Deal and set into motion a conservative fiscal revolution which would affect much of the rest of the world. Reaganomics incorporated the 'supply side' principle that high taxes act as a disincentive to wealth creation and, therefore, that cutting rates would raise both GDP and tax revenue, a view formalised by the economist, Arthur Laffer. The Reagan 1981 Tax Act did more to benefit America's 'successful' than any single piece of legislation in modern history. The Act indexed tax brackets for inflation and reduced the corporate income tax rate. Crucially, it sliced the top tax rate on most income over $200,000 from 70 to 50 per cent and, in the process, set the United States on a course that would see the top rate fall to the current level of 35 per cent for incremental income above $336,000.

These principles, not surprisingly, were warmly applauded by the US financial sector in general and by the *Wall Street Journal* in particular.

Figure 1.3: Selected US surveys of top CEO annual remuneration, 2005

Source	Methodology	Median CEO Annual Pay	Worth Noting
The Corporate Library March 20, 2006	Covers 554 large U.S. corporations that had filed their required pay data through March 13, 2006.	$5.7 million	The biggest of the year's CEO pay winners: Capital One Financial's Richard Fairbank. His $280.1 million 'exceeded the annual profits of more than 550 Fortune 1000 companies.'
New York Times, April 9, 2006	Covers 200 major U.S. companies that had filed data by March 31. Includes salary, bonus, as well as the value of restricted stock and other long-term incentives. Does not include profits on options exercised in 2005. Does include value of new option grants.	$8.4 million	Top CEO on the list: Occidental Petroleum CEO Ray Urani took home $63 million in total pay. He also realized an additional $37.6 million in stock option profits.
Wall Street Journal April 10, 2006	Survey by Mercer Human Resource Consulting covers pay data from 350 large companies. Total direct compensation includes salaries and bonuses, plus the value of restricted stock at the time it was granted, gains from stock-option exercises, and other long-term incentive payouts.	$6.1 million	On top of 2005 earnings, the typical CEO in the *Wall Street Journal* survey is sitting on another $10.2 million in unrealized gains from previously awarded stock options.
Bloomberg News, May 3, 2006	Survey by pay analyst Graef Crystal, based on data from Equilar Inc., covers the 2005 pay of 492 CEOs at firms worth $3 billion or more. Pay includes salary, bonus, the value of stock options granted during 2005, the	$6 million	Five of the 16 highest-paid CEOs owed their fortunes to the oil industry. These five oil 'roughnecks of remuneration,' charges Crystal, raked in a collective 361 percent more in pay than

Figure 1.3: (continued)

Source	Methodology	Median CEO Annual Pay	Worth Noting
	value of free shares awarded during 2005, long-term incentive plan payouts, and miscellaneous other compensation.		legitimate market factors would warrant.
Forbes, May 8, 2006	Covers CEO pay in the last fiscal year at America's 500 largest companies, as measured by a composite ranking of sales, long-term incentive payouts, profits, assets, and market value. Pay includes salary and bonuses, grants of restricted stock that have vested, perks, and gains realized by exercising stock options.	$10.9 million	Forbes also ranks CEOs by their cumulative pay over the last five years. Leading the pack: Oracle CEO Larry Ellison with over $868.9 million in take-home. A $80,000-a-year software engineer would have to work over 10,000 years to bring home as much as Ellison did in five.
Average of 5 Sources		**$7.42 million**	

Source: S. Pizzigati, S. <http://www.cipa-apex.org/toomuch/articlenew2006/ExecPayin2005.html>

According to a recent piece celebrating the anniversary of the Act, the cuts totally reframed America's national discourse over taxes and wealth. Even the nation's most 'ardent liberals', the *Journal* claimed, no longer dare to 'propose to return to the top pre-Reagan income tax rate'.[20] Moreover, much of the rest of the world followed Reagan down the tax-cut curve. Indeed, the top tax rate on high incomes has dropped, since 1980, in every industrial nation in the world. Significantly, it has been cut by a larger percentage in the USA and Britain than in the other OECD countries; even Ireland, regularly heralded as a low-tax haven, retains a higher top rate than Britain.

The Rich Reclaim Their Share

The distribution of income in the USA today is the least egalitarian of any of the major industrialized countries.[21] This was not always true. The

Down the Laffer Curve

Top income tax rate

	1980	2004
Australia	63%	47%
Canada	60	39
France	60	48
Germany	65	46
Ireland	60	42
Italy	72	47
Japan	75	50
Korea	89	40
Spain	66	35
Sweden	87	54
Switzerland	31	26
U.K.	83	40
U.S.	70	35
OECD Average	67	43

Figure 1.4: 1980 and 2004 Top income tax rates for selected countries
Source: TaxProf Blog, August 13, 2006

policies introduced under Roosevelt's New Deal in the 1930s improved the lot of the poor, the Second World War brought full employment and the post-war period saw further strides in reducing the extreme inequalities that characterized US capitalism in the early twentieth century. However, over the past three decades the distribution of household income in the USA has become as unequal as it was before the Great Depression.[22] Broadly speaking, this shift is explained by the fact that the rich – the very top percentiles (1 per cent slices) of the household income distribution – have become very much richer than before. By contrast, income has stagnated for the vast majority of Americans, while the bottom 20 per cent (the lowest quintile) is actually worse off than in 1970.

In the years 1970–2000, the pre-tax income share of the top 10 per cent of households – the 'top' decile – rose from 23 to 44 per cent. This is a startling figure. It means that the lion's share of the increase in US national income over the past thirty years has been captured by the richest 10 per cent. Moreover, within the top decile, the inequality in income distribution is as striking as for the population as a whole. The 11-point gain in the share of national income going to the top decile has not been shared out equally.

Rich pickings

Income share in US, excluding capital gains, %

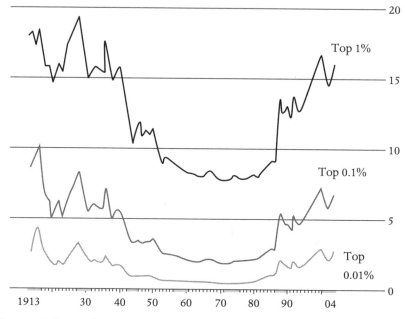

Figure 1.5: Forward to 1913
Source: The Economist 'Inequality in America', 17 June 2006

Far from it; the share of the lower half of the top 10 per cent – from the 90th to the 95th percentile – has remained nearly flat, with the gain concentrated in the top 5 per cent, and amongst those in the top 1 per cent.[23]

This trend is confirmed by US Census Bureau data showing that, despite a GDP growth rate of 3.8 per cent in 2004, only the top 5 per cent of households experienced real income gains; incomes for the remaining 95 per cent were flat or falling.[24] Moreover, the combination of rising remuneration in the form of share-options, capital gains and other forms of asset appreciation, plus lax inheritance tax, means that America's wealth distribution looks worse than its income distribution. An unequal distribution of wealth helps propagate the transmission of income inequality from one generation to the next, thus re-enforcing the hierarchy of privilege.[25] Krugman's warning is worth quoting:

> The United States did not start as a society that you could describe as middle-class. We were a society with a dominant economic elite. We became a middle-class society and thought we had reached a stable state.

Household income can be ranked from 'poorest' to 'richest' and then sliced into percentiles (100 slices of 1 per cent), deciles (10 slices of 10 per cent), quintiles (5 slices of 20 per cent) and so on. In speaking of deciles, for example, the poorest 10 per cent is the 'first decile' and the richest is the 'tenth decile'.

Figure 1.6: Percentiles, deciles, etc.

> We were wrong because we have now moved right back to where we were before. . . . We can no longer dismiss income distribution as a minor issue. In the United States it is now of the same order as economic growth in determining the standard of living of ordinary families. (Krugman, 2004: 79, 88)

The same author has argued that the trend in income distribution in any period is closely associated with the dominant political current. Hence, after Roosevelt and under Truman, Eisenhower and Kennedy until the 1960s, America became steadily more egalitarian. By contrast, since Reagan, the two Bushes and even Clinton, growing inequality has prevailed. While politics may not drive income distribution, it is clear that deregulation of labour markets and tax breaks for the rich have been part of the neo-liberal political agenda for a generation. Most Europeans would take this as self-evident; nevertheless, Krugman's piece was met by a barrage of hostile comments when it appeared.[26] Krugman's conclusion is supported in an article by Levy and Temin who argue:

> The early postwar years were dominated by unions, a negotiating framework set in the *Treaty of Detroit* [a five-year contract negotiated in 1950 between the 'big-three' automobile makers and the union], progressive taxes, and a high minimum wage – all parts of a general government effort to broadly distribute the gains from growth. More recent years have been characterized by reversals in all these dimensions in an institutional pattern known as the *Washington Consensus*. Other explanations for income disparities including skill-biased technical change and international trade are seen as factors operating within this broader institutional story. (Levy and Temin, 2007)

I emphasize the political roots of inequality precisely because it is important to avoid the notion that there could be only one response to the crisis of the 1970s. As the Oxford economist Andrew Glyn has put it:

> The [reduction] of domestic conflict does not necessarily have to take inegalitarian forms. In principle inflation may be reduced at high employment levels through acceptance by the trades-union movement of the

real-wage trend made 'feasible' by productivity and terms-of-trade movements together with the profit requirements for adequate investment. Even if an increase in profitability is called for, the extent to which this leads to extra consumption for higher-income groups may be curtailed through discouragement of dividend increases and the taxation of capital gains. Budget deficits could be closed by an increase in taxation falling hardest on top income groups. Strikes could be reduced if these policies were seen as the resolution on labour's terms of the conflict generated by slow growth. The alternative, inegalitarian pattern would involve higher unemployment, together possibly with legislation to weaken trade unions, in order to impose the unwinding of inflation whilst profitability was improved. The number of strikes, perhaps after a period of defensive conflicts, would fall despite lower real wage growth. Profit increases would be reflected in rapid increases in (lowly taxed) capital gains on shares, whilst consumption from unearned incomes was further boosted by high (real) interest rates. Budget deficits would be closed primarily by cuts in welfare spending with top income groups benefiting from tax cuts. It is the latter inegalitarian pattern of response which dominated the OECD in the 1980s. (Glyn, 1992: 78)

Decoupling Wages and Labour Productivity

The conventional economic explanation of why income distribution in the USA (and to a lesser extent in the UK) has worsened is that the new economy puts a greater premium on high levels of education and entrepreneurship. Doubtless there is some truth in the 'skill-biased technological change' view, but recent studies confirm that the change in labour productivity patterns does not explain the very high degree of inequality now observed in the UK and the USA.[27] After all, the Nordic countries also enjoy high levels of productivity growth and have produced some of the world's most technologically advanced and dynamic industries, yet there is no sign that inequality has increased significantly in these countries over the past three decades. Crucially, 'skills-based technological change' does not explain the huge increase in rewards at the very top of the pyramid.

Economists have traditionally seen economic growth and average productivity growth as two sides of the same coin. If labour productivity growth is high, one would expect the average real wage (including service provision) to be growing. In effect, labour productivity growth and wage growth have become 'decoupled' from one another. An influential paper by Ian Dew-Becker and Robert Gordon (2005) of Northwestern University shows that in the USA, over the period 1966–2001, only the top 10 per cent of the income distribution enjoyed a growth rate of real wage and salary income equal to or above the average rate of economy-wide productivity growth. Median real wage and salary income barely grew at all. Half of the income gains in the USA went to the top 10 per cent of the income distribution, with little left over for the bottom 90 per cent. Moreover, only half of the increase in inequality is attributable to gains of the 90th percentile relative to the rest. The other half is due to the increase in inequality within the top 10 per cent.

Dew-Becker and Gordon (2005) argue that too little attention has been paid to the latter; i.e, to the growth of inequality *within* the top decile. They attribute this growth in large measure to two complementary factors. One is the growth of 'winner-take-all' markets; markets in which enormous rents go to a few super-stars. The other is to the escalating earnings of corporate CEOs. Between 1966 and 2001, the median wage in the USA has hardly increased in real terms. By contrast, average earnings of the top decile (the top 10 per cent) increased by 58 per cent. More striking still is the fact that over the period 1966–2001, real earnings of the top 1 per cent increased by 121 per cent; the corresponding figure for the top 0.1 per cent is 256 per cent and for the richest .01 per cent is 617 per cent. In their view:

> Growing inequality is not just a matter of the rich having more capital income; the increasing skewness in wage and salary income is what drives our results . . . This source of divergence at the top, combined with the role of de-unionization, immigration, and free trade in pushing down incomes at the bottom, have led to the wide divergence between the growth rates of productivity, average compensation, and median compensation. [28]

Three factors are of particular importance in explaining the explosive growth of CEO compensation since the early 1980s: share options, leveraged buyouts and the growth of financial corporations. Granting low-priced option-to-buy shares (which can be exercised at some future date as the market rises) became a favoured way of rewarding top executives in the 1980s, initially because of their tax advantage.[29] During the long boom of the 1980s–90s, as the use of share options became ubiquitous, CEO rewards grew hugely. In the words of *The Economist*: 'the story behind the growth of pay in the 1990s is really the story of the option. In 1992 S&P 500 companies issued options worth $11 billion . . . in 2000 the number reached $119 billion.'[30]

The growth of super-rewards is associated, too, with the buyout-and-merger mania[31] of the past two decades. A leveraged management buyout is merely a debt-funded takeover in which a specialist company – aka 'corporate raider' – gains control of the assets of a limited liability corporation, changes its status from public to private, uses its cash flow to service debt, sells off assets (typically greatly profiting the new owners) and ultimately sells the shell back to shareholders. Major swashbucklers in this business include Morgan-Stanley and Kohlberg-Kravis-Roberts, the firms behind the infamous RJR Nabisco buyout in the USA, and financiers such as James Goldsmith and Philip Green in the UK.[32] Most importantly, in the USA, it is estimated that executives of non-financial companies represent only some 20 per cent of the highest-paid CEOs (and even fewer in Britain). Riding on the back of the 1990s boom, financial consultants, senior investment bankers, fund-managers and other top people in the financial services sector have become prominent in the US rich-list. 'To qualify for Institutional Investor's Alpha magazine rankings of top hedge-fund managers in 2005, you had to earn $130m [annually].'[33] I examine this matter in greater detail in the chapter that follows.

Unequal Taxation

Equally, over the same period the incidence of total taxation in the USA has become less progressive. The work of Thomas Piketty at the *Ecole Normale Supérieure* and Emmanuel Saez at Berkeley is seminal with respect to income distribution in the USA as it is based on a very detailed study of US tax data.[34] A recent paper by the authors (Piketty and Saez, 2006) summarizes their conclusions as follows:

> The progressivity [*sic*] of the U.S. federal tax system at the top of the income distribution has declined dramatically since the 1960s. This dramatic drop in progressivity is due primarily to a drop in corporate taxes and in estate and gift taxes combined with a sharp change in the composition of top incomes away from capital income and toward labour income. The sharp drop in statutory top marginal individual income tax rates has contributed only moderately to the decline in tax progressivity.

During and immediately after the Second World War, the top marginal rate of income tax in the USA ranged from 84 per cent to 94 per cent. From the early 1950s to the mid-1960s, the top rate was 91 per cent – levied on income in excess of $400,000 (the equivalent of about $2.64 million at 2006 prices). In 1971, under Nixon, the top marginal rate was reduced from 71 per cent to 60 per cent on taxable income in excess of $996,000 (at today's prices); shortly thereafter it dropped to 50 per cent and remained there until

1987. Under Reagan in 1988, it was reduced to 30 per cent. 'These large reductions of the top marginal rate during the 1970s and 1980s were an open invitation to astonishing increases in executive compensation, and the invitation was widely accepted.'[35]

A study by Frydman and Saks (2005) at Harvard notes the remarkable stability of executive compensation from 1936 to 1969. During this thirty-three-year period, the average 1.3 per cent annual increases in executive pay were less than the wage gains made by the average American worker. By 1969, the inflation-adjusted value of executive pay had just barely returned to its pre-Second World War level. Frydman and Saks also note that between 1969 and 1992, average total executive compensation increased by 75 per cent, and that during the period 1993 to 2002 executive pay rose at an astounding rate of more than 14 per cent per year so that at the end of the twentieth century, 'the real value of executive compensation was more than seven times its level prior to World War II'.[36]

Although a similar trend can be observed in the UK, the same is not true for most other EU countries. In France, for example, effective tax incidence has become *more* progressive over the past thirty years. Indeed, within the EU-15, the UK currently ranks twelfth out of fifteen in the progressiveness of overall tax incidence and thirteenth in the income distribution tables.[37] And although a nominally progressive government has been in power since 1997, a study in 2004 by the Institute for Fiscal Studies shows that inequality had not improved since that date.[38]

The Distribution of Assets

The skewness described above also holds true for the distribution of assets, which strongly influences the distribution of earnings, and is in general even more unequal – and more difficult to measure because of inadequate data. One estimate puts the combined net worth of all millionaires and billionaires in the USA at $30 trillion, more than the GDPs of Brazil, China, Japan, and Russia combined.[39] The richest 10 per cent of Americans own 70 per cent of the country's wealth; the remaining 90 per cent own what remains. More instructively, the asset share of the bottom 50 per cent of Americans is only 2.5 per cent. The distribution of wealth is slightly less skewed in Britain where (based on 2002 figures) the top 1 per cent owns 23 per cent of all assets and the share of the bottom 50 per cent is 7 per cent. However, a higher proportion of UK asset concentration is explained by land ownership and, as land prices have escalated, so has wealth concentration.[40] Between 1990 and 2002, the top 10 per cent of the population

> *The Gini coefficient is one of several measures of inequality; a country having a Gini value of 0.00 indicates that each household had the same income (perfect equality); by contrast, a Gini value of 1.00 indicates perfect inequality. In practice, Gini values for income distribution in egalitarian countries cluster in the 0.20–0.30 range while countries with a Gini of over 0.40 can be considered very unequal. For an excellent explanation of different inequality measurement statistics, see Sutcliffe (2002).*

Figure 1.7: The Gini coefficient

increased its share of total wealth from 47 to 56 per cent. The Gini coefficient for wealth distribution in 2002 was 0.70, compared to 0.36 for disposable income.[41] And because the Land registry in England records only transactions, forming a clear picture of the ownership of land assets is nearly impossible.[42]

In sum, the evidence for the USA and the UK – but not for the EU – suggests a return towards levels of inequality last observed in the 1930s. The gains from growth have accrued largely to the richest 10 per cent, and disproportionately to the very rich within this decile. The same is true for the distribution of assets, which is even more skewed than the distribution of income and which strongly influences the distribution of earnings. Taxation, the main mechanism for redistributing wealth and income, has steadily become less progressive. Those who believe that a more egalitarian society is a desirable end of social policy will find this state of affairs deeply troubling.[43]

Decreasing Social Mobility

Even more distressing is the evidence on social mobility showing that working-class Americans growing up today cannot expect to get very far up the social ladder. The best predictor of an individual American's economic fortunes today is still the socio-economic status of his or her parents. Moreover, this appears truer today than it was, say, two generations ago.

A recent study by the Economic Policy Institute (EPI) in Washington[44] reckons, for example, that it would take an average poor family with two children nearly 200 years of economic climbing to attain middle-class status. The figure shows income mobility for OECD countries for a three-year period, using data taken from the late-1980s to the mid-1990s. The United States, far from offering greater income mobility than other countries, has the lowest share of low-income workers that exit their low-income status

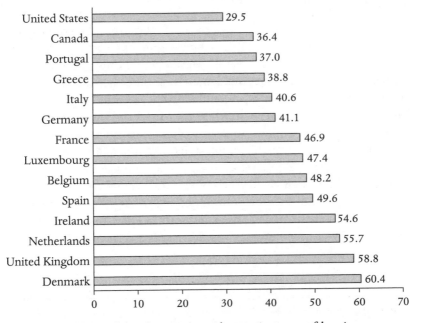

Figure 1.8: Income mobility, late-1980s–mid-1990s (per cent of low-income families leaving low-income status each year)
Source: OECD in Schmitt and Zipperer (2006)

from one year to the next (29.5 per cent). The corresponding rates in several European countries are greater than 50 per cent. Interestingly, the UK does well in this study, suggesting that the Thatcher years combined greater income inequality with greater income mobility.

One of the authors of the EPI study, Jared Bernstein, has published a book on what he calls the 'You're On Your Own' or YOYO economics. American conservatives preach the virtues of freer markets, less government and more individualism; they argue that by giving the taxpayers back their money, Americans can find their way back to the good life. As Bernstein says, the presidents and bankers who share this perspective have been setting the agenda for thirty years. The disturbing outcome is that over that same period, while the US economy has grown by 150 per cent and labour productivity has increased by 80 per cent, the typical earnings of male workers have hardly increased in real terms – while the minimum wage has actually fallen. At the same time, between 1980 and 2000, the real income of America's richest 1 per cent of households rose by 184 per cent.[45]

As for US workers, once the most productive and prosperous in the world, their incomes have remained static for a generation, and they have been overtaken by their European and Japanese counterparts. A German worker in the tenth percentile – i.e., the tenth slice from the bottom in the national income sliced into 100 household segments – earns twice as much as his American equivalent; this is even before taking into account the German worker's health, unemployment and other benefits. Even taking the EU-15, the average tenth percentile European earns 30 per cent more than his American counterpart when measured on a purchasing power parity basis. Little wonder that US capitalism, once seen by many Europeans as the best and the brightest, has lost much of its shine.

It is hardly surprising therefore that, while America may have a larger percentage of very rich people than other OECD countries, it also has the largest proportion of income-poor, functionally illiterate people who are more at risk of illness, incarceration and early death than anywhere else in the industrial world. Moreover, it would appear that the middle class too is being squeezed:

> After 2000, most people lost ground, but, by many measures, those in the middle of the skills and education ladder have been hit relatively harder than those at the bottom. People who had some college experience, but no degree, fared worse than high school drop-outs. Some statistics suggest that the annual income of Americans with a college degree has fallen relative to that of a high-school graduate for the first time in decades. So, whereas the 1980s were hardest on the low-skilled, the 1990s and this decade have squeezed people in the middle.[46]

While hard statistical evidence for the hollowing out of the 'middle class' is thinner than that for the concentration of wealth at the top, it is not altogether without foundation. As the American journalist Barbara Ehrenreich has observed:

> Stories of white-collar downward mobility cannot be brushed off as easily as accounts of blue-collar economic woes, which the hard-hearted traditionally blame on 'bad choices': failing to get a college degree . . . [or] failing to postpone child-bearing until acquiring a nest-egg. But distressed white-collar people cannot be accused of fecklessness of any kind; they are the ones who 'did everything right.' . . . In some cases, they were the high achievers who ran into trouble precisely because they had risen far enough in the company for their salaries to look like a tempting cost cut. . . . [W]hite collar unemployment – and the poverty that often results – remains a rude finger in the face of the American dream.[47]

An understandable reaction for those on the bottom of the pile is to look for scapegoats.[48] Thus, populist currents at both ends of the US political spectrum have turned increasingly to blaming foreign competition arising from 'globalization' for low wages and growing job insecurity. The solutions they advocate range from greater protection from foreign goods, particularly from China, and barring overseas purchase of 'strategic' US companies to halting the inflow of migrants and the 'whoosh' of jobs being sucked abroad towards cheap-labour countries.

In truth, 'globalization' explains everything and nothing. For example, the number of American service jobs that have migrated offshore is small: perhaps 1 million.[49] We know all too well from the 1930s where economic nationalism can lead economically and politically. It should be added that member-states of the EU may be more equal, but they appear no less prone to populist rhetoric. Speaking of the role of the term 'globalization' in New Labour rhetoric in Britain, the sociologist Michael Rustin has written:

> Globalisation is seen as a system of expanded economic competition, to which all national economies including Britain's are increasingly exposed. It is also seen as a system of communications which is transforming life-worlds, dissolving old collective identities (such as those of class or community) and engendering new and more individualised identities of subjects, as consumers, 'active citizens' and the like. New Labour's programme has been substantially one of adaptation to these proclaimed new realities, with the necessity to compete in global markets, and to respond to the demands of new individual subjects for choice in as many spheres of life as possible, as its major guidelines. Traditional 'socialism', whether social democratic or state-socialist, was deemed anachronistic, since it was held to depend on class collectivities which have largely disappeared . . . Because Marxist social analysis had always been closely tied to political perspectives of various kinds, and because the latter were deemed either wrong or unfeasible, it was assumed that the analysis could be thrown out of the window together with the politics.[50]

New Labour and the R-word

Redistribution has become the unmentionable 'R-word'. A basic reason why New Labour has not attempted to restore progressiveness to the tax system can be gleaned from the following passage by the current Cabinet Office Minister, Ed Miliband, son of the late Ralph Miliband and an early advisor to Gordon Brown at the UK Treasury:

> the economic crisis of the 1970s laid the groundwork for the . . . argument that too much equality could undermine incentives at the top and bottom and destroy the prospects for economic growth. How much one

can attribute the failure of the British economy at the time is evidently contestable, but *what is not in question is that the high tax rates of the time have become an emblem of the problem of overzealous egalitarianism* [my emphasis].[51]

The thrust of New Labour's politics was to distance itself from what its leaders have contemptuously dismissed as 'old Labour' philosophy. An essay in 2005 by Anthony Giddens and Patrick Diamond, both of whom were influential at the highest ranks of government during Tony Blair's tenure, contrasts the 'new and old' egalitarian views as follows:

1 Old egalitarianism treated economic dynamism as incidental to its basic concern with economic security and redistribution. New egalitarianism holds that expanding the productive efficiency of the economy is necessary for governments to have a long-term impact on the distribution of income and wealth. . . . The Thatcherites – quite rightly – placed competitiveness and wealth at the forefront of their philosophy.
2 Old egalitarianism was concerned with removing class distinctions and the pursuit of equality of status. New egalitarianism is about equalising life chances across the generations by levelling up more than levelling down . . .
3 Old egalitarianism held that social justice could be achieved within the boundaries of the nation-state, and that support for its reforms would come from forging a national coalition based on class solidarity. The new egalitarianism recognises the impact of globalising influences . . .
4 Old egalitarianism was inclined to treat rights as unconditional claims. New egalitarianism ties rights to corresponding responsibilities.
5 The new egalitarianism focuses primarily on widening opportunities rather than on traditional income distribution – equality of outcome – *per se*. . . . The new egalitarianism embraces the 'new Labour approach', but seeks to extend, entrench and deepen it . . . Work and employment will continue to be central. . . . The emphasis on labour market flexibility, far from betraying the ideal of social justice, has directly contributed to furthering it. (Giddens and Diamond, 'The New Egalitarianism', in Giddens and Diamond (eds), 2005: 106–8)

Whether any of these claims can be held to be 'new' is questionable, other than in the sense of confirming New Labour's determination to dilute egalitarian principles so as to make them compatible with the embrace of free-market ideology. The notion that growth must take precedence over redistribution suggests that the two are incompatible, or at best that redistribution is only feasible where it is financed from the extra income that growth brings. It is hardly surprising to be told that Thatcherites valued growth above equality. But many would argue that higher growth and greater equality complement each other, as clearly is the case in the Nordic countries. As for financing redistribution out of growth, New Labour has conspicuously failed to do so; Britain's tax structure continues to be regressive, so that the lion's share goes to the rich while the cost of poverty reduction measures is borne disproportionately by the lower half of the distribution.

Similarly, what does 'equality of life chances' mean? Giddens and Diamond appear to view the notion of meritocracy as unproblematic; later in these pages it is argued that for 'equality of life chances' to be meaningful, radical changes are needed in Britain, starting with the hugely different environments facing children well before they are of school age; as to 'more by levelling up than levelling down', the very phrase has deeply conservative political overtones. What precisely is 'old' about effecting redistribution within the boundaries of the nation-state since it is here that most of the necessary fiscal muscle is concentrated? The implied answer is that the proclaimed new reality of globalization makes redistribution fiscally nearly impossible, and further cripples Britain's competitiveness and potential for wealth generation. In any event, the authors claim, 'old' Labour was excessively preoccupied with rights, in contrast to a new 'responsibility agenda' in which individuals must carefully weigh up the opportunities conferred by market choice. And individuals who lose life opportunities because they fail to make the right choices about education, training, marriages, children and so forth must pay the price.

The giveaway is that income inequality is largely about being employed, and that the conditions for permanent full employment are created by adopting a 'flexible' labour market, i.e., a labour market unhindered by a high minimum wage, employment protection legislation, national wage bargaining, militant trade unions and the like. In subsequent chapters, these matters are revisited in detail; suffice it to say that the 'new egalitarianism' lacks conceptual coherence, and the empirical evidence in its favour is wanting.

Why Do We Care So Little?

An intriguing question for those who worry about growing inequality is why the general public seems to care so little. 'The rich are richer but, oddly, nobody seems to mind' is how a subhead in *The Economist* put it.[52] It could be that the public is simply misinformed – but that seems unlikely since we are bombarded on a daily basis with pictures and stories about the out-landishly expensive indulgences of the super rich. It could be, too, that ordinary folk have very mixed feelings about others being rich. After all, people are more afraid of mad cow disease and spiders than they are of cars; since we are much more likely to be killed in a car accident during a single month than by eating contaminated beef in an entire lifetime, our feelings of fear, pleasure, or whatever can sometimes be quite irrational.[53] We may hold entirely mistaken views about our income position relative to others: according to one survey, 25 per cent of Americans believe themselves to be in the top 10 per cent of income earners (just as 80 per cent of drivers illog-ically believe themselves to be 'above average'; psychologists call this the 'Lake Wobegone' effect).

Numerous studies have addressed social attitudes towards inequality. One study by the Institute for Social and Economic Research at the University of Essex argues that most people are content to be better off than their parents were. If they make comparisons, they tend to look down rather than up; their fear of downward mobility 'counts more' than their hope of moving upward. Paradoxically, the upper-middle class is more likely to resent the rise of the super rich than the lower-middle class. Such results are confirmed by studies showing that while a clear majority of Britain believe the gap between rich and poor to be 'too wide', only a minor-ity support redistributive tax policies. Broadly speaking, the middle 60 per cent of income earners fear that pulling up the underclass might undermine this own relative status.[54]

In general, the strength of feeling about the fairness of our perceived income position seems to depend mainly on what is happening immedi-ately around us; the world of the super rich is simply too remote for most people to relate to. The following story is instructive, as are the reactions to it. When a recent piece revealed that a local authority employee was earning an estimated '£91,000 to fix the lights' as the headline in London's *Daily Mail* put it, there was outrage.[55] A certain Ian Smith, employed by Birmingham Council as an engineer to fix street lights, had earned £70,000 last year plus an estimated £21,000 in bonuses. The article went on to reveal that road workers in Birmingham could earn up to £53,000 a year for paint-ing lines and cleaning bollards. Although their trade union, Amicus (now Unite), argued that the figures were misleading, typical reactions from *Daily Mail* readers were: 'There's no expense spared when it comes out of the public purse. Politicians, councillors and the BBC are society's bloodsuck-ers', and 'No wonder council tax keeps going up relentlessly. But if we refuse to pay we get sent to jail while these parasites . . . defraud the tax-payer and don't even lose the money, let alone go to jail. No wonder so many have sold up and left the UK.'

What is striking of course is that to the average punter, the fact that the council worker next door earns a large and apparently overgenerous sum produces outrage, but the earnings of investment bankers and top CEOs does not. As Gary Runciman (1966) remarked, envy is a difficult emotion to sustain across a broad social distance. In general, people judge their income, status and the legitimacy of their social position relative to that of their immediate peers. If some member of their reference group is per-ceived to gain greatly at their expense, they react with anger. By contrast, if the same person gains by winning the pools, perceived to be at nobody's expense, the windfall is legitimate. One observer, speaking about the United States, puts the point succinctly:

> When it comes to income, sociological studies repeatedly conclude that 'relative income is more important than absolute income in determining the happiness of individuals in the United States'. People feel pain and resentment about inequality when they see, firsthand, what they don't have and don't think they can get no matter how hard they work . . .
>
> For example, Americans are much more discouraged when they learn that, according to a Pew Foundation Report, the median annual income of American men in their thirties a generation ago was about $40,000, while today men of the same age make about $35,000 a year, adjusted for inflation (an average 12 percent drop between 1974 and 2004), than when they learn that the average CEO makes '531 times what the typical hourly employee took home.'[56]

The proliferation of what Robert H. Frank[57] has called 'winner-take-all' markets – markets such as in the entertainment business where small differences in talent plus a lucky break can result in jackpot-size earnings – has reinforced such perceptions. When traders on Wall Street and in the City earn millions and billions in fees, bonuses, stock options, self-awarded salaries and so on, such outcomes don't register to the man in the street as being at anybody's expense in particular. They are the 'rewards' paid out by that mysterious lottery called the financial market, a market remote and largely inaccessible to all but the lucky few. In effect, for the majority of people, the world of great wealth – much like that of great poverty – is largely invisible.

True, the super rich are beginning to become more visible. In the past year, the cumulative effect of stories of mega-buck bonuses, corporate greed and tax dodging may be gradually shifting public opinion. While the

US Congress held hearings in the autumn of 2007 on raising tax rates on private equity and hedge funds, in Britain, the annual gathering of the TUC Congress in Brighton made it clear to Prime Minister Brown that capping wages of low-paid public-sector workers did not go down well at a time when top CEOs are paying themselves seven- and eight-figure bonuses. Nevertheless, such changes hardly add up to a sea-change in public opinion – and even if a clear consensus were to emerge in favour of higher direct taxes on high income and wealth, the increases required to reverse the adverse distributional trend of the past three decades would need to be far more radical than any suggested so far. I return to this matter in chapter 9 below.

2

Do We Need Fat Cats?

Financialisation now runs the gamut from corporate strategy to personal finance . . . The individual is encouraged to think of himself or herself as a two-legged cost and profit centre, with financial concerns anxious to help them manage their income and outgoings, their debt and credit, by supplying their services and selling them their products.

Robin Blackburn (2006: 39)

Christmas at Farepak

Just before Christmas of 2006, a news item in the British press announced the collapse of a small savings-club company, Farepak, owned by European Home Retail (EHR) and funded by the Scottish banking group, Halifax Bank of Scotland (HBOS). Farepak, which is based south-west of London in Swindon, had taken in £40 million from small savers – the sort of people who are typically too poor to have bank accounts and who instead put away a few pounds a week in savings towards purchasing a hamper of treats from Farepak's bumper Christmas catalogue. The problem is that savers' money was used to stem the parent company's losses in other activities. When HBOS refused to bail out EHR, Farepak went broke, leaving its customers with about 15p of each pound saved and facing a bleak Christmas.

If this sounds Dickensian, there's worse to come. Because Farepak paid no interest to its customers, it was not classified as a savings bank and thus not subject to regulation by the Financial Services Authority. The head of Farepak is Sir Clive Thompson, who runs various other businesses. Sir Clive is reckoned to earn £1 million a year, and he is known for his right-wing views by his colleagues at the Confederation of British Industry where, as Chairman, he lobbied strongly against Britain's adoption of minimum wage legislation. At Rentokil, where he was previously Chairman, Thompson was nicknamed 'Mister 20 per cent' in honour of their impressive earnings growth. In the days following the collapse of Farepak, Sir Clive claimed that HBOS was responsible for the mess. This may be true, but it begs the question of why small savers are without adequate protection. In any event, a few days after the scandal broke, Sir Clive boarded a flight for Buenos Aires to escape adverse publicity.

The UK Treasury is working on a scheme for universal access to fair credit, as is the Association of Credit Unions. Such a scheme would need to be Post Office based since the poorest fifth of the population typically don't have access to, or don't use, banks. On a basic bank account, you don't have overdraft facilities and you pay a £30 penalty if you are a penny overdrawn. In most of continental Europe, the Post Office is the alternative for the poor. But here is the rub: Britain's semi-privatized Post Office is closing its 'unprofitable' branches and its banking system is a shambles. If you bank with the Post Office, they won't accept your pay cheque, they don't offer credit facilities or debit cards and they only allow you one withdrawal a week, and then only if you queue.[1]

Compare this with the Netherlands (where I lived for some years) where Post Office facilities are ubiquitous, their debit card is far more widely used than credit cards and there is even a full-service online banking facility. But what makes this story truly astonishing is the fact that the $40 million owed to Farepak's 150,000 customers has been diverted to the financial services sector, the same sector that paid out over 2,000 times that amount in bonuses to 4,000 City employees in 2006.

The Re-emergence of the Super Rich

There is little doubt that the re-emergence of the super rich is a sensitive subject. On the one hand, many people feel that there is something inherently distasteful in the idea of a CEO earning five hundred times the average wage or of City bosses walking off with nearly £9 billion in bonuses at the end of 2006, a sum large enough to modernize London's creaking transport system and much else besides. On the other hand, there appears to be little political support for capping salaries and/or raising personal taxation to the levels last seen in the 1970s.[2] In Britain, the Labour Party under Blair and Brown has favoured qualified poverty reduction; i.e., providing a life vest for the very poorest in the form of working tax-credits and other benefits, mainly means-tested. But Labour has been famously relaxed about the rise of fat-cat salaries and perks, preferring to treat these as a tide of 'wealth creation' that raises all boats. The Tories have largely ignored the issue while the Liberal Democrats, until 2005 favourable to introducing a top marginal tax rate of 50 per cent for salaries above £100,000, have since dropped the idea.

In the United States, there appears to be more of a debate than in Britain about unjustifiably high earnings at the top of industrial and financial companies. In the past two decades, the number of American billionaires has risen twenty-fivefold. The US House of Representatives recently passed a bill seeking to force companies to hold a non-binding vote on top pay at their annual shareholders' meetings (in Britain this is already Company Law).[3] There is a serious academic debate on inequality, too, in the United States. While household poverty is less of a political issue in the USA than in Britain, or more generally than in Europe, the rise of inequality as a political issue appears to be linked to the relative loss in status of the middle class, their 'hollowing out', to use the current phrase. Equally, the widespread publicity attracted by the reckless and illegal practices of companies such an Enron and WorldCom has helped fuel the flames of public resentment.

The arguments in support of growing inequality are generally of four types.[4] The traditional case for great wealth rests on the notion of the rich as 'benefactors'; were it not for the Rothschilds and Rockefellers – the old saw goes – who would donate to good works or finance great undertakings? Second, it is said that growing inequality is merely a reflection of growing meritocracy. Indeed, in Britain, New Labour rhetoric seeks to blur the distinction between a more 'just' society and one that is meritocratic. Third, it is argued that wealth creation is more important than wealth distribution; i.e., that rather than arguing about how to share out the pie, we should focus on making it bigger. The fourth argument is that wealth at the top harms no one. More specifically, it is said that while in the distant past the rich often gained their fortunes by exploiting the poor, today 'exploitation' is a thing of the past.

The Rich as Benefactors

Apologists for inequality argue that we owe many of the good things in life to the very wealthy. This is a particularly popular argument in America where museums, art galleries, educational institutions and all manner of other amenities bear the names of those nineteenth-century moguls such as Ford, Carnegie and Vanderbilt, who amassed great fortunes in industry, transport and commerce. To this list one could add the new philanthropists of the late twentieth century: Turner, Soros and Gates are some of the most obvious.

As many commentators have pointed out, the great philanthropists often earned their fortunes using great ruthlessness. Andrew Carnegie may have given away a large part of his fortune before his death, but in the late nineteenth century, the success of his steel empire in Pittsburgh depended on violently resisting union attempts to organize the steel workers. The famous Homestead steel strike of 1892, called to resist large-scale layoffs and longer shifts, was ultimately broken by hiring 300 men from a local detective agency who were ordered to fire on unarmed workers if necessary. Rockefeller was equally hated by workers, as was the pioneering twentieth-century industrialist, Henry Ford, whose battles with the Roosevelt administration were legion. And while one would not describe Bill Gates as having gained his wealth though the ruthless exploitation of labour, legal rulings in both the USA and Europe suggest Gates's methods of dealing with Microsoft's competitors were less than perfectly fair. George Soros may be admirably progressive, but as a major player in Britain's 'Black Wednesday' in 1992, he is regarded as having cost the Bank of England – and ultimately the taxpayer – billions of pounds.

What is perfectly clear is that the great philanthropists did not build their empires with a view to doing good works; they did so in order to make money, and to use their fortunes, power and privilege to make even more money. The reasons for philanthropy are varied. In some cases, charity serves to salve the donor's conscience, in others to ensure positive public recognition. Avoiding inheritance tax doubtless plays a role; the very rich are almost universally hostile to financing the state. And, of course, philanthropy pays; as Ted Turner is reported to have commented, 'I have learned that the more good I do, the more money has come in.'[5]

The British philanthropic tradition has other roots. For one thing, many of the great Victorian figures – the Cadburys and Rowntrees, William Lever or even the Earl of Shaftesbury – were ethical crusaders, often in the Nonconformist tradition, who believed that with privilege came responsibility and who sought to improve the physical and moral condition of their employees. They represented a small minority amongst the very wealthy and typically had gained their wealth in industry and trade, spheres generally shunned by the landed aristocracy who often had little direct knowledge of, or contact with, the labouring poor. In today's Britain, this tradition of Victorian philanthropy seems to be dying out. In the words of one observer:

> Wealthy Britons are less active philanthropists than their early predecessors and mostly much less generous. Giving in Britain accounts for less that 1 percent of gross domestic product, compared with 2 per cent in America.[6]

The same observer notes that the richest 20 per cent of British households give only 0.7 per cent of their income to charity in contrast to the poorest 10 per cent who give 3 per cent . Little wonder, therefore, that the very rich in Britain are less prone than their American cousins to ascribing the good things in life as flowing from philanthropy.

Meritocracy?

Nor is there anything particularly meritocratic about today's very rich. In Britain, the 'rich list' compiled annually by the *Sunday Times* still includes a good number of landowners amongst the wealthiest. The recent increase in their fortunes has resulted almost wholly from rising land values, while their right to collect the rent from such property was bestowed centuries ago. Kevin Cahill's seminal work on UK land ownership reveals that the top 40,000 millionaires amongst Britain's agricultural landowners (including the Queen's Crown Estates, the royal Duchies of Lancaster and Cornwall and the Dukes of Buccleuch, Atholl, Westminster, Northumberland and so forth) own some 28 million acres while Britain's nearly 17 million home-owners own only one-tenth of this figure, or 2.8 million acres.[7] It should be noted that the boom in Britain's land market is in no small measure due to this inequity in land distribution which leaves the average homeowner with just 0.16 of an acre.

Besides landowners, the rich list includes the descendants of many of the barons of the Victorian era, such as the Guinnesses, Rothermeres and Rothschilds, as well as those of the 'Mayfair set' who pioneered the art of asset-stripping in the 1960s. 'Becoming a business leader in Britain is still largely determined by the interconnected characteristics of a wealthy family and a prestige education . . . there has been no democratisation of British business over the last century and a half.'[8] And although the United States lacks a hereditary landowning aristocracy, the importance of 'a wealthy family and a prestige education' in securing the economic and social status of one's descendants seems no less important in the USA than in the UK. Social mobility studies show that the probability of moving from low to high socio-economic status in the USA is actually lower than in continental Europe and appears to have stagnated and even declined in recent years.[9]

The argument that growing income and wealth inequality reflects the growth of meritocracy is deeply flawed – as indeed is the very notion of meritocracy, a subject addressed in chapter 9. For the moment, consider the further proposition that huge City bonuses are all about wealth creation, another fanciful tune in the New Labour songbook. As Lansley (2007) rightly acknowledges, there are plenty of examples of successful entrepreneurs who

Top Landowners in the UK	Acres
The top 40,000 millionaire agricultural landowners in the UK	28,180,212
The 16.8 million private home owners in the UK	2,800,000
Forestry Commission	2,400,000
Ministry of Defence	750,000
Lands owned and controlled by Royal Family	677,000

Figure 2.1: UK distribution of land, 2001
Source: Cahill (2001, 19) Table 17/B

have brought us new products and services that are part of the wealth creation process – from James Dyson to Stelios Haji-Ioannou. Innovation through industrial investment is what Adam Smith had in mind in accepting that inequality helps oil the wheels of capitalist growth. Nevertheless, that is not the way today's huge fortunes are generally made.

The City of London sees itself as rewarded for offering a host of highly specialized financial services to the world, as indeed it does. Yet skimming off the top of the huge sums of money that circulate and re-circulate through the City is not wealth 'creation'; it is merely part of the complex business of financial services in which the name of the game is to use money to make more money, or, in traditional Marxist terms, to redistribute surplus value from one set of rentiers to another. When Tesco's share price overtakes that of Sainsbury's, what takes place is a redistribution of wealth and income between different portfolio holders; this is not the same as 'wealth creation' in the sense of adding to the total output of goods and services. In brief:

> The evidence is that today's escalating personal fortunes are not closely related to levels of wealth creation. Rather, the ranks of the rich contain tycoons, bankers and business executives who, far from creating wealth, have taken advantage of today's much more pro-rich culture to grab a larger slice of the cake for themselves, swelling their own bank accounts at the expense of others. (Lansley (2007: 153)

Finally, consider the argument that 'wealth creation' today is a positive sum game in which there are no losers. The logic of this argument is based on the misleading premise that the exploitation of labour in the early days of the industrial revolution has disappeared.

The eighteenth-century artisan who worked in the pin-factory[10], imagined by Adam Smith in *The Wealth of Nations*, was paid a pittance compared to the highly educated computer programmer who works for Bill Gates. The child labourer in Thomas Carlisle's satanic mills was ruthlessly exploited in a manner hardly comparable to the assembly line worker at Ford who today commands an assembly line of industrial robots and takes home a decent pay packet. But the latter is no less 'exploited' in the sense that his (or her) labour, aided by a huge stock of capital per worker, produces far more value than goes into that pay packet. The difference, allowing for further deductions made for raw materials and so on, is realized as 'surplus' by the capitalist – or as 'profit' by the company if one prefers. Without 'profit', there would be no capitalist production. Wealth creation in the twenty-first century involves extracting profit as much as it did in the nineteenth century, whether such extraction takes place on an assembly line in Detroit making automobiles or a sweatshop in Shenzhen making the cheap clothes that we now buy at the local Wal-Mart or Asda. In turn, cheap Chinese consumer goods – like imports of grain into Britain after the repeal of the Corn Laws in 1846 – help stabilize real wages in the industrialized countries.

Winner-take-all Markets

Doubtless 'growing filthy rich' in the modern market economy has changed in some respects. For one thing, there is good evidence that a higher proportion of the earnings of the super rich come from earned rather than unearned income. The 'earned/unearned' distinction used to be standard economics terminology; it refers to income earned from one's labour on the one hand and 'unearned' rental income (including that from land, shares, stocks and bonds) on the other. Whereas a century ago, the super rich depended almost entirely on unearned income, today a higher proportion of that income appears as remuneration, typically in the form of the very high salaries paid to the CEOs of big corporations. For another, today it is possible for all manner of celebrities to earn sums which were undreamt of a century ago – mainly because technology has revolutionized audiences for film, sport and entertainment in general.

Take David Beckham, the former Manchester United and Real Madrid star whose six-figure weekly earnings and astronomical transfer fees set the standard for European sports stars in the new century. Or, for that matter, take any number of celebrities whose names are universally known for a few days or months, only to disappear into obscurity again next week or next year. These are the winners in Robert H. Frank's 'winner-take-all' markets, i.e., markets in which thousands of talented (if poor and obscure) players vie for that moment of good fortune that brings recognition, fame and fortune to the lucky few.[11] Today there are more winners and a larger jackpot. In contrast to fifty years ago when Hollywood was the road to stardom and only a very few talented people got there, the communications revolution and its associated advertising revenues have greatly increased the numbers of people who can strike it rich. Equally, there are far more well-qualified people whose moment never comes despite their talent.

Nevertheless, neither the persistence of a landowning aristocracy nor the rise of winner-take-all markets provides an adequate explanation for the huge redistribution of wealth documented above. Nor is it explained by the growth and deregulation of the financial services sector, although doubtless this is an important piece of the puzzle, particularly in Britain. To understand the broad picture fully, it is necessary to consider in detail what happened in the 1970s.

Boosting Shareholder Value

The conservative revolution in the USA and the UK changed not just the popular perception of unemployment and inflation, but it ushered in a whole new school of thinking about corporate management. In the 1960s, as corporations grew fat during the post-war boom, so too did middle management; sociologists like Vance Packard once wrote books about the inexorable rise of men in grey flannel suits as if they would soon take over the world. Then, in the 1970s, as the profit squeeze set in, managers began to be seen as part of the problem.

If the family-owned corner shop runs at a loss, the owner tightens his belt. But if a corporation makes a loss, the manager's salary stays unchanged. Publicly incorporated corporations – what Americans today call 'public companies' somewhat confusingly to the European ear – are owned by their shareholders while managers are mere salaried employees who continue cashing their monthly pay-cheque in good times and in bad. The solution, proclaimed in business schools and on company boards alike, was to link management rewards more closely to corporate performance. Share options were the key.

Economists now began to teach the 'principal-agent' theory of corporate governance, according to which the principal (or corporate shareholder) relies on the market to discipline the agent (or manager); in everyday language, if managers are underperforming it must be that they are too sheltered from market discipline. One way of tying management rewards more closely to the market would be to issue executives with share options, i.e., packages of the company's shares negotiable only at some date in the future. If managers did well, the company's share price would rise and the share options would be worth a fortune when they matured. If the share price fell, managers would forego the reward. Moreover, this particular form of reward had the advantage of being tax-deductible; when share options were cashed in they could be written off as a charge against profits, becoming in effect 'free money'. And while share options were not particularly popular in the 1970s when a bear market prevailed, they became all the rage in the 1980s and 1990s as the bulls gathered pace and seemed ready to gallop on forever.

Perhaps the most important factor explaining the rise of options was that executives in the 1980s began to realize that the way to earn real wealth was not through salaries and bonuses but by gaining an equity stake in a company, and options were just such an instrument. While it took the CEO of Warner Communications nearly seventeen years to amass a fortune of $275 million, the junk bond king, Michael Milken, cleared twice that sum in a single year. In 1980, options represented about 20 per cent of annual CEO rewards; by 2000, for America's top 200 firms, the figure had risen to 75 per cent. In 1999, AOL's Steve Case earned a meagre annual salary of $575,000, but more than made up for it by exercising more than $110 million in options.[12] That tidy sum translates into making just over $300,000 a day, every day of the year. Yet it is only a fifth of the $565 million profit Disney's Michael Eisner is reported to have made by cashing in his options in 1997. For that matter, at the end of 2000, Oracle's Larry Ellison was said to have amassed options worth $3.4 billion.

The tax-deductible nature of share options did not go entirely unchallenged. In 1993, when the US Financial Accounting Standard Board proposed that they be treated as a compensation expense, corporate leaders protested loudly as did the *Wall Street Journal* until the Board backed down. It is estimated that companies like Microsoft, Cisco and PepsiCo saved nearly a billion dollars a year in taxes because of this. Warren Buffet, that most eccentrically frugal of investors, is said to have remarked caustically, 'If compensation isn't an expense, what is it? And if expenses shouldn't go into the calculation of earnings, where should they go?'[13]

CA: A Cautionary Tale

The case of Computer Associates (CA) is instructive. CA is an American company, based on Long Island, which back in the 1970s was a small high-tech start-up. The company went from rags to riches (and back again) in only a few years during the 1990s, and the case was prominent at the time in the financial press. Its growth illustrates the logic of options-based 'shareholder value' taken to its extreme limit; in effect, the company traded on its growing success until its collapse brought huge losses for shareholders.[14]

In 1995, CA was well-established and running smoothly under its CEO Charles Wang, when the executive board approved a new remuneration package offering Wang and his two top colleagues more than 20 million shares. The catch was that Wang and his colleagues could only exercise the option to sell their shares if the price rose by 20 per cent (to $53.33 or more) for at least sixty consecutive days within the next five years. In 1998 CA's shares did just that, bringing the three managers a windfall of well over $1 billion, of which Wang pocketed two-thirds. Subsequently, the share price fell back to well below its initial level, mainly because the payout to the three triggered a $675 million charge against the company's earnings, plunging it deep into the red. Shareholders sued the three executives, accusing them of having artificially inflated the company's share price. How?

The company's prime customers at the time were several large mainframe computer operators. Wang and his colleagues devised a clever accounting ruse to show as current income the value of multi-year contracts with their clients, a ruse which apparently fooled their auditors. The problem was that in the 1990s, big mainframe operators were doing badly and long-term contracts were increasingly hard to get. So CA did two things; first, it convinced some of its customers to extend their contracts, typically from five years to ten years, enabling them to turn longer future income streams into fatter 'current' earnings. Second, CA bought up its small rivals – companies that had long-term contracts with mainframe operators – and turned even more long-term contracts into 'fresh cash'. The increase in CA's share price enabled Wang to swing even bigger deals, buying up at first its medium-sized rivals and eventually some very large software companies in deals worth many billions of dollars.

This was in essence a high-tech pyramid scheme, and CA would eventually run out of companies to buy. Wang resigned as CEO in 2000, and subsequently became known for his philanthropic donations, including building the *Charles B Wang Memorial Center* at the State University of New York (Stony Brook). According to *Business Week*, at the time he left CA his personal earnings were nearly $700 million – amongst the highest of any American CEO – while the return to CA's shareholders had dropped by over 60 per cent. In short, here is a case where a profit-tied incentive plan designed to boost shareholder value did precisely the opposite.

Nor is the above example exceptional. By 2001–2, the business pages of the press were full of stories of corporate malfeasance; these included Enron, WorldCom, Tyco, AOL Time Warner, Bristol Myers, General

Electric, Lucent, Merck, Merrill Lynch and Halliburton, some of America's best-known corporations.[15] And Europe soon followed suit with its own scandals: Parmalat, Siemens, Daimler-Chrysler and BAE Systems, to name but a few. At issue were not merely standards of auditing and corporate disclosure, but the growingly opaque nature of huge conglomerates which combined manufacturing, communications and financial services. Congress passed the Sarbanes-Oxley Act in 2002, attempting to tighten standards of corporate governance. But some argued that not much had changed. In the words of Wendell Rawls, head of the Washington-based Center for Public Integrity:

> This has been going on for 150 years . . . The Rockefellers, the JP Morgans, the Vanderbilts of the world – they were all doing the same thing in the late 1800s, in the early 20th century. They made huge profits. That's the reason they [were called] . . . robber barons.[16]

But of course, a lot had changed, as the Enron affair showed. What made Enron so interesting is not just the fact that their top managers paid themselves huge salaries, but that after five years of investigation by the US Internal Revenue Service (IRS), such was the complexity of the company's dealings that it is still not entirely clear today what was legal and what was not. Another brief digression seems useful.

Enron: A Bird's Eye View

In 1990, Enron made about 80 per cent of its revenue from gas pipelines; delivering energy to companies across the USA was then profitable, but regulated. Enron then began to sell off its pipelines and to move into a variety of different fields. By 2000, it reported 90 per cent of its revenue and 80 per cent of its operating profits to come from 'wholesale energy operations and services'.[17] In reality, Enron had moved from delivering gas to buying and selling energy, using very sophisticated financial instruments; indeed, it had moved far beyond energy into telecommunications, and one of its subsidiaries even traded excess broadband capacity. It was Jeff Skilling, Enron's Chief Operating Officer (COO) in 1999, who coined the phrase 'logistics company', a company tying together current and future supply and demand for a variety of commodities by using derivatives like swaps, options and forward contracts to hedge against interest-rate and foreign exchange risks. Enron famously boasted that, each year, the 10 per cent of staff who failed to reach their targets would be sacked; its goal was to minimize its workforce and to outsource as much as possible. It was Skilling who had helped the company create a forward market in natural gas, and Kenneth Lay, the company CEO, had first made Skilling head of the newly formed Enron Finance Corporation in 1990, and in 1997 of Enron Capital and Trade Resources. In 1999, Enron launched EnronOnline, an Internet-based trading operation whose services were used by almost all the major US energy companies.

Skilling's big idea was that Enron should pay less attention to its real asset position and concentrate on turnover and share price; by 2001, it had become the largest US wholesaler of gas and electricity. But there were problems. For one, although Enron had reported a $2.3 billion profit to its shareholders for the period 1996–99, it had also managed to report a $3 billion loss to the IRS using a variety of ruses – including ghost transactions with its bankers (Citigroup and J.P. Morgan Chase were later cited) – to shift profits off the books. For another, Skilling introduced new accounting practices under which losses were airbrushed and anticipated future profits were treated as current revenue. In reality, like any company involved in risky ventures, some of Enron's deals had gone badly wrong and by the late 1990s the company had incurred large debts. To keep the venture going, continuous injections of new capital were needed. Cooking the books was thus essential to keep the company's share price rising and attract new investors. In 2000, Enron reported earnings of more than $100 billion and its share price rose by nearly 90 per cent. By early 2001, its share price was fifty-five times that of earnings, a P/E ratio more than twice that of its nearest competitor and far above the S&P500 average, making it one of Wall Street's 'hottest' buys. In 1991, Enron hid $3.9 billion in expenses, allowing it to post a net income of nearly $1.4 billion for the year.

Smart financial analysts were now beginning to question how long the party could go on. Jeff Skilling bailed out in August 2001, selling a large block of shares and leaving Kenneth Lay as CEO. Market sentiment now swung and Enron quickly went to the wall – it declared itself bankrupt in December 2001. Enron's employees lost their jobs and pensions, while thousands of investors lost their savings in what was the biggest bankruptcy in US corporate history. One of their big institutional investors was the State of New York, whose pension fund lost more than $300 million. The once respected firm of Arthur Andersen, Enron's auditors, went down too as it became clear how far Andersen had been complicit in the cover-up.

The US government investigation that followed revealed not merely the extent and complexity of Enron's dubious practices but showed just how much management had benefited at the expense of the company's employees and the public at large. In 1998 and 1999, the top 200 executives had paid themselves a total of nearly $700 million in salaries, bonuses and share options; in the year 2000 alone, the figure had risen to $1.4 billion, or an average of $7 million each. The bulk of the increase took the form of share options, one of the reasons management had sought to keep share prices rising by any means possible. For the period 1998–2000, Ken Lay's annual salary had risen from $16 million to $168 million, while that of Jeff Skilling had gone from $12 million to $139 million.[18]

The Rise and Rise of the Private Equity Buyout

The other novelty of corporate culture in the 1980s and 1990s was the rise of the 'corporate raider', the entrepreneur that specialized in buying out and turning around underperformers. In America, and to a lesser degree in Britain, institutional investors (including banks and pensions funds who were often their main shareholders) were coming to believe that corporations were atrociously managed. If 'shareholder value' was to be maximized, the laggards would need to be bought out and new, more dynamic (and more ruthless) managers placed at the helm. A new breed of entrepreneur appeared who specialized in the art of targeting suitable companies, perhaps at first buying a part of its equity and then, with the help of other managers or even of pension funds, bankers and bond-traders, putting together enough capital to seize control of the corporation by purchasing a controlling interest in its equity. The pain of the underperforming outgoing managers could be eased by giving them severance bonuses, what came to be known as a 'golden parachute'.

Crucially, these 'raiders' needed to convince annual shareholder meetings. The carrot was the purchase price offered for shares, and once the deal was done the stick was turning the corporation back into a private equity venture, in effect shielded from strict corporate disclosure rules, where the new management could do what it liked. Typically, once the company was 'privatized', its cash flow could be used to pay off loans (instead of shareholders), 'non-performing' assets like land and buildings could be sold off and rented instead, or whole divisions scrapped or merged, rendering the company apparently meaner and leaner with the aim of selling back to the market at a higher price. The new managers reaped handsome rewards both in terms of high salaries and new perks, and equally at the time of resale.

Such was the success of 'private equity' ventures that the 'raiders' were soon overtaken in zeal by company executives who themselves arranged leveraged corporate buyouts of their own companies in order to reap the tempting rewards. It is estimated that in the USA alone, by 2000, merger and acquisition (M&A) deals by private equity firms totalled $1.7 trillion. According to the same source, the value of M&A deals in Europe (including the UK) has also shown strong growth. In 2006, European deals increased 39 per cent to $1.4 trillion, compared to the 36 per cent growth that the USA experienced. Of this sum, about $150 billion was spent on private equity takeovers, up 41 per cent on 2005.[19]

Gordon Gekko, the fictional character in the film *Wall Street*, declared, 'I am not a destroyer of companies. I am a liberator of them', and that his brand of financial wizardry might be necessary to save the 'malfunctioning corporation called the United States'.[20] In the intervening twenty years, private equity buyouts have become common. In Britain, the names of once-famous publicly quoted companies such as Birds Eye, British Home Stores, Boots, Debenhams, NCP Car Parks and even the Automobile Association come to mind. Today, an estimated one in five employees in the private sector in Britain work for firms that have been 'privatized'. The groups behind the buyouts, such as Permira, Apax, Minerva and CVC Capital partners, are highly secretive about their operations, or indeed about the complex manner in which their deals are financed. But their deals are lucrative. Sir Ronald Cohen, the founder of Apax and adviser to Gordon Brown, is said to be worth £250 million, while Damon Buffini, a partner at Permira, is worth £100 million.[21]

Private equity can generate huge rewards for its investors in a short period of time; the degree of enrichment involved is on a par with (and linked to) the end-of-year bonuses paid out by City firms such as Goldman Sachs while, at the other end of the spectrum, the losers are often the firms' workers. A large firm may number fifteen to twenty partners, and supposing the firm to have an investment pool of £5 billion, some 20 per cent of this (£100 million) may be taken out each year in management fees alone, which comes to £5 million per partner. Not only do private equity firms charge enormous fees, but they benefit from tax relief on monies borrowed and pay little income tax. 'Private equity executives are "paying less tax than a cleaning lady." This is not some trade union malcontent talking, but Nicholas Ferguson, chairman of SGV capital which built Permira, Europe's biggest equity fund. Private equity owners pay only 10%, sometimes much less.'[22]

A much-publicized takeover several years ago was that of the Rover Group by Phoenix. BMW had acquired the ailing Rover Group in 1994 hoping to restore its fortunes, but by 1999 it had become a major financial liability. In 2000, the Phoenix consortium, a private equity group, presented an offer to BMW promising to retain high-volume car production and full employment at the Rover plant in Longbridge, near Birmingham. With the

Completed	Acquirer	Target	Value* (in billions)
April 28, 1989	Kohlberg Kravis Roberts	RJR Nabisco	$25.1
Dec. 21, 2005	Investor Group	Hertz	$15.0
Aug. 12, 2005	Investor Group	SunGard Data Systems	$11.3
July 21, 2005	Global Toys Acquisition	Toys Я Us	$6.6
Jan. 28, 2005	Zeus Holdings (IBO)	Intelsat	$5.1
Oct. 6, 2005	Investor Group	Neiman Marcus Group	$4.9
March 3, 2003	Blackstone Group	TRW Automotive (80%)	$4.7

Figure 2.2: Selected private equity deals in the USA
* excluding debt
Source: Matt Krantz, 'Private equity firms spin off cash', *USA Today*, 16 March 2006

support of the Transport and General Workers' Union, and following a last-minute injection of finance from the First Union Bank of North Carolina, a deal with Phoenix was agreed. Phoenix had clinched the deal by proposing a short-term plan to expand the MG range with sporting versions of existing Rovers, to introduce new versions of the Rover, to re-engineer and redesign the MG and eventually to replace the entire model range with new cars. Sadly, the new models would never reach showrooms. It is estimated that, by April 2005, the four Phoenix executives had made around £40 million from MG Rover, a good return on the £60,000 they had each invested. MG Rover and related companies were placed under the administrator in April 2005 and subsequently its workforce was made redundant.[23]

A more recent case is that of the respected and apparently well-managed British retailer, Debenhams, PLC. In 2003, a private equity group comprising of CVC, Texas Pacific and Merrill Lynch teamed up to buy the business for £600 million. They increased Debenhams' debt from £100 million to £1.9 billion. The freehold of the stores was sold for £500 million and the property leased back. Subsequently Debenhams was refloated on the stock exchange; the investment group took £600 million from the new shareholders, while paying itself a dividend of £1.2 billion. Debenhams now faces large interest payments and rental fees on the stores it once owned, while the corporate raiders made over three times their original investment in just over two years. Similarly, the department store group Allders was taken over by Minerva in 2003; unlike Debenhams, though, it collapsed in 2005, with the loss of 7,000 jobs and £60 million in pension liabilities.

In 2006, the amount spent in Britain on buying publicly quoted companies reached a record of £26 billion. Other well-known firms bought by private equity in that year included Associated British Ports, John Laing, Phones4U, Travelodge and United Biscuits. But takeover bids can fail too – increasingly because of adverse publicity and shareholder resistance to asset-stripping. In February 2007, CVC Capital Partners, Kohlberg Kravis Roberts (KKR) and the Blackstone Group announced that they were considering taking Sainsbury's private. The consortium grew to include Goldman Sachs and Texas Pacific Group, but in April the £10 billion bid was eventually declined.[24] And, as all football devotees will know, in early 2007 the majority owners of the north London side, Arsenal, turned down a takeover bid of $1.3 billion by the American entrepreneur Stan Kroenke (although currently it appears that the Uzbek billionaire Alisher Usmanov may attempt a takeover).

In America, in 2005, the household names taken over by private equity included Neiman Marcus, purchased for $4.9 billion, Toys Я Us, bought for $6.6 billion, and computer services firm SunGard Data Systems, bought for $11.3 billion. The biggest private equity deal in years came in December of that year when a group of firms bought the Hertz rental car company for $15 billion. According to the same source, if the trend persists, it could be just a matter of time before the biggest private equity deal of them all – the $25 billion takeover of RJR Nabisco by Kohlberg Kravis Roberts in 1988 – is surpassed.[25]

In short, beneath the rhetoric of corporate rescue and improved market efficiency, the reality is that private equity takeover is a lucrative vehicle for redistributing assets and income streams to the new management at the cost of wages, jobs and often workers' accrued pension rights. In 2007 the General Municipal and Boilermakers' Union – more familiar in Britain as the GMB – issued a report saying that a total of ninety-six insolvent pension funds which have been forced into government-funded rescue schemes have direct links to private equity owners; of the ninety-six, the GMB has been able to trace twenty-one pension funds with unfunded liabilities totalling nearly £2 billion.[26] Much the same is true of pension funds in the USA, as discussed in section 4.8 of chapter 4. In the words of Karel Williams at the Manchester Business School, the private equity deal 'is about extracting as much as you can, as quickly as you can . . . It is part of a broader series of changes in capitalism. These intermediary groups, like private equity and hedge fund managers, are able to enrich themselves in ways thought unimaginable a few years ago.'[27]

Wall Street Perils

The private equity buyout phenomenon was made possible by the financial wizardry of people on Wall Street like Michael Milken, the 'junk bond' king. Milken worked for Drexel Burnham Lambert, where junk bonds (high-risk, high-yield securities) were used to underpin leveraged buyouts, in effect a means of refinancing America's 'underperforming' corporations. In the 1980s, as deregulation spread and the creation of shareholder value became the watchword of corporate America, CEOs increasingly turned to the investment banks for advice on financial engineering, i.e., novel ways of making money. The bull market of the 1980s provided a huge flow of funds into the financial sector where leading 'full service' investment banks – Merrill Lynch, Goldman Sachs, Morgan Stanley and Lehman Brothers – acquired an awesome reputation in the market. Not only did such firms have enormous financial muscle, but their global reach and access to round-the-clock information gave the edge in trading, supervising initial public offerings (IPOs), arranging mergers or hedging risk though the use of new and complex products like derivatives. But 'gaining the edge' often meant sailing very close to the wind, and as the machinery of financial regulation that had initially been established in the 1930s was dismantled under Reagan, opportunities for illegal transactions became more tempting and more frequent.

The Boesky scandal of 1986 was just one example of the Wild West atmosphere prevailing on Wall Street at the time. Ivan Boesky – who is said to have inspired the Gordon Gekko character in *Wall Street* – was a trader who made a great deal of money by betting on corporate takeovers; his winning record was facilitated by using his corporate contacts to gain privileged access to information. Often, when a possible takeover is in the air, a firm's share price will rise in anticipation of a generous takeover offer. Anybody with access to the details of highly confidential takeover negotiations will have a huge advantage in betting on the firm's share price. In principle, this sort of 'insider dealing' is illegal and can be prosecuted, *inter alia*, under the 1970 RICO law (Racketeer Influenced Corrupt Organizations Law), carrying jail sentences of up to twenty years. Wall Street is regulated by the Securities and Exchange Commission (SEC) and illegal activities are investigated *inter alia* by the New York Attorney General's office. (Attorney General Elliot Spitzer would become well known in the late 1990s for his zealous investigation of securities fraud on Wall Street.) Boesky's crime was not merely breaking the law, but doing so openly and brazenly; he would make massive purchases only days before a takeover was announced.

Boesky cooperated with the SEC by naming others involved in illegal deals and, in consequence, received a large fine but a small prison sentence. One of the people he named was Michael Milken. The US Attorney who had prosecuted Boesky invoked the RICO Law and brought a case against both Milken and his parent firm, and this in turn set the stage for further investigations which uncovered a great many irregularities amongst some of the biggest fish in the pond. What is remarkable is not so much the extent of the rot, but the way in which the major players paid large sums to buy their way out of trouble.

Thus, in 1988, Drexel Burnham Lampert agreed to plead guilty to securities fraud and was fined $650 million while, later, Milken paid close to $1 billion in fines. In 1990, the head of arbitrage trading at Goldman Sachs was convicted of insider trading and fined $1.1 million; soon after, Prudential-Bache Securities, a smaller brokerage house found to have defrauded its investors, paid them $1.4 billion in compensation. In 1991, even the firm of Salomon Brothers was found guilty of rigging the US Government Treasury bond market, and fined.

The rot even spread to Britain, where it was discovered that the CEO of Guinness had mounted an operation during the takeover of Distillers to keep the share price from falling. The 'Guinness scandal' was not the only example to make the headlines. Trustees of the Maxwell Pension Fund took Goldman Sachs to court for having helped Robert Maxwell to defraud pensioners of £400 million. As trading in hugely profitable (but extremely risky) derivatives became fashionable, one trader, Nick Leeson, brought down Barings, one of the City's oldest and most respectable merchant banks, by losing $1.4 billion. Losses in derivatives trading in the USA were equally spectacular; in 1994, eighteen Ohio municipalities lost $14 million, City Colleges of Chicago lost nearly $100 million and the Municipality of Orange County in California lost $1.7 billion.[28]

Significantly, when the US government was faced with questionable dealings which threatened the institutional stability of the market, it played lender-of-the-last-resort. Some of the largest losses in the financial sector were underwritten by the government, the best-known example being the huge $125 billion bailout of the Savings and Loan Associations (or 'thrifts') in the mid-1980s. In essence, the thrifts came to grief partly because of an ill-conceived cap on what they could charge, but mainly because they had provided too many fixed-rate mortgages to clients at a time when rising interest rates eroded the value of their assets. Although the roots of the Savings and Loan (S&L) collapse are complex, one of the factors leading to their bankruptcy, as revealed during the Milken trial, was the extent to

Suppose you grow soybeans for sale next year and wish to hedge against the risk of a fall in soybeans prices when you're ready to sell. You can arrange a 'future' contract for the sale of your soybeans at (say) today's price, in effect shifting 'price risk' to somebody else. Let's assume the total value of the crop today is $1000. The future contract can be bought or sold in the secondary market for much less than the value of the soybeans, say $100 in this case. If the price of soybeans next year goes up, whoever holds the contract can buy your soybeans at today's price and resell them at next year's price (say $1500), thus making an enormous profit ($500) on an initial investment of $100. Note, though, that if the price of soybeans falls to $500 next year, the loss on the investment would be equally large. Dealing in 'futures' requires a thorough knowledge of the market plus the willingness to assume risk.

Figure 2.3: How to 'hedge' using a 'future' contract

which they bought junk bonds as their asset position weakened. Ironically, many S&Ls had got into trouble as a result of selling their mortgage loans to Wall Street banks which, by cleverly 'securitizing' and repackaging them as government-backed bonds, resold them at a considerable profit to the S&Ls. In effect, investment bankers were the winners and American home-owners and taxpayers were the losers in this curious story. (British readers will see the parallel with the current Northern Rock fiasco.)

Probably the best-known US example of government bailing out the financial market occurred in 1998 when the Federal Reserve put together a $3.6 billion rescue capital for Long Term Capital Management (LTCM), a hugely profitable hedge fund which came to grief in the wake of 1997–98 Asian debt crisis and the Russian financial default. Hedge funds are a special type of investment fund dealing in 'derivatives'. Hedge fund fees are typically 2 per cent of the money invested with them plus 20 per cent of the annual rise in capital value. By mid-2006, it is estimated that some 8,000 such funds existed, with assets totalling $1.5 trillion.[29]

Derivatives are financial products which help the holder to hedge against risk, e.g, futures, swaps options and so on (see figure 2.3). As financial markets grew in the 1990s, derivatives became increasingly complex, typically containing 'bets' on multiple financial indices, and were designed and evaluated using sophisticated computer modelling techniques. Indeed, such derivatives typically were sold 'over-the-counter' by offshore-based branches of large banks or companies known as special purpose entities (SPEs), well beyond the reach of regulation. Because of the growing importance of hedging against risk in an increasingly complex market, derivatives became an essential component of financial portfolios held by pension funds, corporations, banks and even government agencies. At the beginning of the new century, nine out of ten of the world's top 500 companies held them, and the value of all derivatives was estimated to be a whopping $12 trillion. Allan Greenspan, Chairman of the US Federal Reserve, thought derivatives crucial to the functioning of the world economy; Warren Buffet, by contrast, described them as 'financial weapons of mass destruction'.[30]

In the early months of 1998, Long Term Capital Management (LTCM) had achieved a return of 40 per cent for four years running, making the firm appear to be truly one of the 'masters of the universe'. Because LCTM specialized in betting on government short- and long-term bond trades which had quite small profit margins, its profits depended on the firm being highly leveraged (i.e., having a high ratio of debt to equity). LTCM – using $5 billion of its own equity and having borrowed nearly $130 billion more – amassed a derivatives portfolio valued at $1.25 trillion. In mid-1998, the Russian government defaulted on its own bonds, creating turbulence in the financial markets and causing large numbers of bond holders to switch out of European and Japanese bonds into US bonds. Such an occurrence had not figured in LTCM's sophisticated models; in consequence, the firm lost massively on its bond positions. At the end of August 1998, the firm is estimated to have lost $1.8 billion in capital; by the first weeks of September 1998, its equity value had fallen precipitously to $600 million. The fear was that as LTCM liquidated its securities, this would lead to losses on Wall Street and set off a wave of panic selling. The US government, using the New York Federal Reserve, organized a bailout to avert a possible meltdown. (Much the same is true today where hedge funds hold mortgage-backed instruments; a rise in mortgage defaults could trigger a sell-off of such instruments, bringing down some of the major financial market players.)

What is most remarkable of all, however, is that, despite the scandals and the greed, the power of Wall Street grew enormously in these years. Not only were American television networks pumping out financial reports to the millions of new small fish dabbling in the market, but the Street's free-market ideologues wielded ever growing influence over government in every area of policy – ranging from Clinton's failed attempt to make health care universal, to the US Treasury's strong support of IMF 'stabilization' polices during the crises in Latin America, Asia and Russia. Joseph Stiglitz put it succinctly: 'Among our heroes in the Roaring Nineties were the leaders of finance, who themselves became the most ardent missionaries for market economics and the invisible hand.'[31]

Ever-changing Capitalism

If the story told here seems to be all about greed and corruption, that is not the intention. Yes, capitalism is often about greed and the market's obsession with 'shareholder value' has for some firms – though certainly not for all – resulted in illusory gains followed by painful loss. If Joseph Schumpeter is remembered as one of the great economists of the twentieth century, it is because his description of capitalism – much like Marx's – recognizes the uneven, conflictive and often contradictory nature of capitalist development, or what he termed its cycles of 'creative destruction'.

Capitalism has changed fundamentally since the 1980s. Centrally, the welfare gains and growing egalitarianism of the post-war years, by the late 1960s and 1970s began to squeeze profits. Oil shocks helped fuel inflation, leading to slower growth and rising unemployment. State spending increased in order to counter unemployment. The new middle class, which this great surge in prosperity had greatly boosted, baulked at the prospect of higher taxes. As the struggle over distribution intensified, trade union militancy increased throughout the industrialized West, and particularly in the USA and the UK which, unlike Germany and the Scandinavian countries, lacked a tradition of national wage bargaining between 'social partners'. The stage was thus set for the Reagan-Thatcher revolution, the purpose of which was to break trade union resistance, roll back government regulation and spending and establish the conditions for renewed capitalist prosperity.

The years which followed were marked by three key features. The first was the technological revolution, a revolution which helped automate the factory floor and greatly increased the productivity of the industrial workforce while at the same time creating a unified twenty-four-hour world financial market with a turnover of $1 trillion a day. The second was the globalization of competition; in a world of cheap, high-speed transport and instant communications, it became possible for corporations to consign their labour-intensive operations to a cheap labour country, their marketing to their main customer base and their currency dealings to a financial hub. Equally, as financial markets became more sophisticated, mergers and acquisitions spread; the old world in which a few large national firms dominated the domestic market was transformed into one in which megafirms, whose ownership became increasingly transnational, competed ruthlessly in the world market. Innovation became ever more important; in the space of a few years, a giant like IBM could be overtaken by a start-up like Microsoft.

A third crucial feature of these years was the collapse of the Soviet bloc, and the transition of most of the remaining 'socialist countries' (e.g., China, Vietnam) to a competitive market economy, increasingly integrated into globalized capitalism. If the collapse of the USSR and the subsequent absorption of much of Eastern Europe into the European Union was of less economic significance than initially imagined (the much-heralded 'peace bonus' turned out to be negligible), its political consequences were enormous. No longer did capitalism seem to be under threat from an alternative system. The term 'socialism' appeared discredited, not only in much of the developing world but, crucially, in Western Europe where even the social-democratic left found its ideology weakened and its popular support eroded. Free-market capitalism, for a time at least, appeared triumphant. Its imperial aspirations could now be pursued without apparent hindrance, particularly in the economically crucial oil-exporting countries of the Middle East, albeit dressed up in the new ideological garb of exporting democracy and fighting terror.

All of this helped lay the conditions for renewed profitability. The great stock- market boom of the 1980s and 1990s, which ran for many years with brief interruptions, did not create new wealth. Rather, as I have argued, it helped distribute prosperity, albeit towards the top 10 per cent of income earners. But the boom served a twofold function. First, it enabled huge wagers to be placed upon technological innovation in particular sectors of the economy. Although a vast number of new technology start-ups would ultimately fail, some succeeded; companies like Microsoft, Cisco, Amazon and so on might not have innovated quite so rapidly or successfully had not the stock market continued to pour vast sums into buying their shares. Second, and at least equally importantly, the stock-market boom helped foster the illusion that in this new, dynamic environment of capitalist prosperity, everybody could be a winner.

In March 1999 I happened to be catching a connecting flight in Detroit when CNN Newscast showed the Dow-Jones about to climb through 10,000. Detroit Metro is par excellence a commuters' airport and its travellers come from all walks of life. Everywhere in this huge airport, crowds seem to gather around television monitors; when the moment came, there was spontaneous applause and whoops of joy. Some of these ordinary Americans would have held mutual funds,[32] but very few would have held private portfolios and gained directly as a result of what had just happened; nevertheless, they cheered what was perceived to be an event symbolic of America's new and continued prosperity. On that day, the material gains of the very few translated into a psychological boost for all.

True, two years later there were tears when the party stopped, but the end of the stock-market bubble in the USA did not trigger a major recession, in part because the Fed loosened monetary policy quickly and decisively, and the cheap money would in turn help set off a rise in house prices which could be re-mortgaged and turned into ready cash. The American housing boom kept the economy going for another five years while, today, some believe that the stock market will soon surge ahead once more.

Nevertheless, there is absolutely no economic justification for the huge disparities in earnings and assets which accompanied the neo-liberal revolution and the restoration of capitalist fortunes in the UK and the USA. City bonuses and US-style share giveaways cannot be treated as wealth-creation nor justified by recourse to the neo-classical 'theory of factor rewards' (i.e., the conventional theory of income distribution) any more than can the British aristocracy's monopoly ownership of land. And while the concept of winner-take-all markets is a useful one, it accounts for only a small part of the story. To understand the new inequality, one must understand that the egalitarian post-war boom itself was deeply contradictory.

Post-war prosperity, on the one hand, was based on building a more just social order with the promise of opportunity for all, made good by higher real wages and near-universal welfare provision. In much of Europe, the discrediting of the pre-war right because of its association with fascism opened new political space for the centre-left, and this opening shifted the political centre of gravity decisively leftward, even amongst conservatives. In the United States, where this new political consensus had already been anticipated by Roosevelt and where war had neither destroyed productive capacity nor fundamentally changed the social order, the post-war rewards were more limited; instead of a universal welfare state, there was a generous GI Bill of Rights. Everywhere, rapid economic growth, high productivity and full employment confirmed and sustained the new order. The growth of real wages as well as of entitlements – to health care, education, pensions and so forth – appeared to go on forever.

There is a fundamental principal of economics which says that wages can grow as long as labour productivity (output per worker-hour) grows, but if productivity growth slows below that of wages, the surplus (profits) will be squeezed, investment and innovation will slow, and growth must ultimately cease. Under these conditions, any attempt to maintain wage growth and full employment results in inflation. Thirty years after the Second World War, three broad factors contributed to a slowdown in growth and a rise in inflation. First, after 1960, productivity growth slowed and less time was spent working, so real output grew more slowly. The productivity slowdown was particularly important in the UK and the USA which, having emerged with their factories reasonably undamaged from the war, had not renewed their capital stock as extensively as elsewhere; the average age of machinery in Britain and the USA was more than twice that of machinery in Germany and Japan, or even in France and Italy. But real wage growth everywhere remained high – and, what is more, workers came to expect that their standard of living would continue to rise steadily.

Second, improved social provision meant that the government needed to spend more on transfers (e.g., pensions and other forms of social insurance), as well as on consumption and investment (e.g., teachers' salaries, nurses' wages, new schools, new hospitals and complementary infrastructure). Such spending is a claim on the private sector surplus, which was already under pressure from wage growth. Third, the internationalization of competition – which became visible to all after 1970 in the form of Japanese cars and ships and which today we call 'globalization' – further squeezed industrial profits. Jobs were being lost both as a result of the decline of traditional industries (coal, steel, textiles) and the competitive modernization of others. For a time, unemployment was avoided because of the rapid expansion of services, particularly in the public sector. But productivity growth in services – at least until the advent of computers and the revolution in retail distribution a generation later – was far lower than in industry; hence wage rises in services must in part be financed by squeezing private capital. By the 1970s, the convergence of these factors was squeezing profits heavily, particularly in the USA and the UK. The oil crisis loomed and the collapse of the fixed exchange-rate system only served to intensify the magnitude of the crisis; they did not cause the crisis.

If the neo-liberal counter-revolution laid the basis for renewed capitalist growth, the effects of that revolution have been felt unevenly. America's industrial decline has in part been offset by the rise of the so-called new economy of which three elements can be distinguished: a revolution first in the production of hardware and software, then in its application on a massive scale to industry and services, and more recently the spread of information technology. Britain's industrial decline has been counterbalanced by the revolution in financial services; it has become one of the great offshore financial centres of the world, offering a myriad of new financial products to the world, and is home to banks, insurers and traders from everywhere. Whether in Silicon Valley or in the City, the felicitous combination of luck and timely innovation can pay huge rewards as we have seen. It can also produce an 'hourglass society', one where the initial imbalance in class and educational rewards turns into an ever sharper division between the haves and have-nots until the pinch in the hourglass becomes so tight that the flow is only from top to bottom; the underclass must forever remain at the bottom, providing petty labour services but excluded from the gains of growth.

In much of continental Europe, while neo-liberal excesses have been avoided, it cannot be said that there has been no pain. France, which unlike Britain retains a highly productive industrial sector and excellent social and economic infrastructure, has suffered from over two decades of high unemployment which is concentrated amongst youth and ethnic minorities. In consequence, many of its citizens perceive the country to be in terminal decline and in need of a dose of authoritarian discipline: a Gallic version of Thatcherism, if somewhat muted under Nicolas Sarkozy. Germany swung to the right in the early 1980s under Kohl (a change largely accepted by subsequent governments); with wage increases and consumer demand constrained, in part to pay for reunification, and with the Bundesbank firmly in control of economic policy, its export-led model has thrived. Even in the EU's smaller and traditionally progressive countries – the Netherlands, Denmark and Sweden – political life has more recently lurched to the right. It would appear that the reactionary mood of the UK and the USA in the 1980s may have caught up with continental Europe a generation later. In the next chapter, I examine the neo-liberal revolution more closely.

3

The Rise of Neo-liberalism

Inequality of wealth and incomes is the cause of the masses' well-being, not the cause of anybody's distress . . . Where there is a lower degree of inequality, there is necessarily a lower standard of living of the masses.

Ludwig von Mises[1]

What Does 'Neo-liberal' Mean?

The term 'neo-liberal' first gained currency in the 1980s. It refers to the Austrian school of economic thought associated with the writings of Friedrich Hayek, Ludwig von Mises and others, particularly its strongly anti-Marxist founders, Eugen Böhm-Bawerk and Carl Menger. Friedrich Hayek, who regained influence during the Thatcher-Reagan years, first rose to prominence in the 1930s at the London School of Economics and is best known for his book *The Road to Serfdom* in which he defends free-market capitalism against its socialist and social-democratic critics. Today, neo-liberalism refers to that current of neo-classical economic thought which is anti-Keynesian and strongly pro-market.

Traditional or 'classical' liberal doctrine is generally considered to be the product of writers from the eighteenth and nineteenth centuries, such as Adam Smith, David Ricardo and John Stuart Mill, who were concerned to explain the workings of the 'invisible hand' of the market in securing greater wealth through individual choice. These classical economists opposed state intervention in the regulation of trade (mercantilism), and their views were systematically formalized, often mathematically, by their neo-classical successors, starting with Jevons, Walras and Menger in the late nineteenth century. Their pro-market views differ from the ones held by that other great classical economist, Marx, which is one of the reasons why 'Liberal' political parties in Europe are generally associated with the centre-right rather than the centre-left as in America where Marxist thought and socialist movements had negligible popular impact.

However, not all classical and neo-classical economists were as fervently pro-market as is sometimes thought. Smith recognized clearly that the rights of employers were far better protected in law than those of workers, while Alfred Marshall recognized that monopolies could easily form, that market failure could occur, and even suggested that the principle of diminishing marginal utility,[2] when applied to income, strongly justified progressive taxation. And, of course, Keynes himself, writing at a time when industrial capitalism was buffeted by the Great Depression, defended robust state intervention to supplement the workings of the capitalist market but strongly opposed socialist economists like Lange and Kalecki who called for central planning as the cure for the cycle of boom and bust.

In the 1930s, both Hayek and his patron at the LSE, Lionel Robbins, were involved in fierce debates with Keynes and the 'Cambridge School'. Hayek in particular argued that the Depression could best be cured by curbing all forms of political intervention in the market, starting with that of trade unions. And although the voices of the pure free-marketeers were eclipsed by those of Keynes's supporters, particularly in the golden years of the post-war boom when America prospered and Europe was rebuilt, the anti-Keynesian right gained influence once again in the 1970s. This was particularly true in the United States at a time when the fixed exchange rate regime was breaking down, inflation was accelerating, growth slowing and financial markets becoming increasingly unstable.

In the 1970s the best-known economist of the anti-Keynesian school was Milton Friedman, and the influence of 'monetarism' (initially identified with the University of Chicago where Hayek had moved in 1971) spread first in the USA and Latin America, and then in the UK and much of continental Europe. Monetarism's core notion is that inflation is caused by too fast an increase in the money supply, typically arising from excessive government expenditure; consequently, its cure must involve a reduction in the size of government. Friedman was more than just an academic economist; he was a brilliant polemicist and publicist who understood the importance of capturing economics departments, politicians and even television audiences. By the 1980s, 'shrinking the state' had become the rallying cry of conservatives of every persuasion, including Latin American generals, IMF managing directors, central bankers and, most famously, Margaret Thatcher and Ronald Reagan. In economics, it gave rise *inter alia* to a theory of 'public choice' pioneered in the USA by James Buchanan[3] and premised on the universal validity of free-market principles; the need for government regulation of the market was conjured out of existence. The 'neo-liberal' project had come of age.

The 1970s Profit Squeeze

It is useful to distinguish between two views of the neo-liberal project. One holds that neo-liberalism is a utopian political design for organizing international capitalism in an age of globalization. Alternatively, neo-liberalism can be viewed as a '*political* project to re-establish the conditions for capital accumulation and to restore the power of economic elites'.[4] The latter is in keeping with the influential recent contributions by academic authors such as Duménil and Lévy (2004), Harvey (2005) and Glyn (2006). Broadly speaking, it is a view which I share, although the danger of such a view is always that, unless carefully qualified, it can easily collapse into no more than conspiracy theory. To avoid this danger, a brief detour is required into the history of the post-war years.

The story of the USA and Western Europe in the two decades following the end of the Second World War is one of economic growth, buoyant private and public investment and steady productivity and wage growth against a background of low unemployment, low inflation and stable exchange rates under the Bretton Woods arrangements. But post-war prosperity, driven by the twin motors of European reconstruction and an apparently permanent US capital outflow, the latter providing the pool of dollars with which to finance the growth in international trade, contained within it the seeds of its own downfall.

In retrospect, three factors stand out in explaining the end of the post-war boom. First, a tight labour market and higher real wages squeezed profits. Second, the early 1970s saw the collapse of the fixed exchange-rate system which had promoted a relatively stable post-war trading environment. Third, the internationalization of manufacturing production greatly stiffened the competitive environment for previously secure domestic manufacturing industries, reducing their profits and their ability to invest, and thus slowing their productivity growth.

The growth in the real wage share, reflecting the growing power of labour, squeezed profits. By the end of the 1960s, organized labour's bargaining position had increased throughout the OECD. The post-war compromise in Europe had provided that the working class would share the benefits of growth in the form of higher money wages and the social benefits of a welfare state. If America had less of a welfare state, even there the benefits of productivity growth were shared out with greater equity. Growth tightened labour markets everywhere and unemployment fell and remained low. Throughout the OECD countries, trade union membership grew. By the mid-1970s, the average number of hours worked per year had fallen by the equivalent of half a day per week compared to 1950; employment protection legislation (EPL) was stronger, and workers' rights (both at work and when unemployed) were greater. The stronger labour grew, moreover, the greater was the push for enlarging labour's share of the pie.

As Glyn[5] points out, although the most spectacular example of growing working-class militancy was the 1968 wave of strikes in France, costing 150 million working days, this was by no means its only manifestation. In 1969, Italy recorded 60 million strike days, culminating in substantial wage and benefit gains for workers, while in the UK the figure was 25 million in 1970–1. Workers' militancy also increased in West Germany. In 1970, the country with the most strike days per worker was the United States; throughout the OECD, strike days increased, eventually peaking in the mid-1970s. At the same time, money wages increased dramatically and the real wages in the OECD rose on average by 4 per cent annually in the early 1970s.

But as the share of wages in OECD National Income rose, the share of profits fell and investment – particularly in manufacturing – slowed, in turn slowing productivity growth.[6] A sharp decline in labour productivity is apparent after 1973 throughout the OECD. In the USA in the 1970s, labour productivity growth fell by half and remained low until the mid-1990s. As productivity slowed, the struggle over distributional shares intensified between the economic elite and ordinary working people. Rising inflation, ostensibly triggered by the oil price rises in the 1970s, was in good part a reflection of this struggle.

A second factor was the growing cost of the cold war. America, self-appointed guardian of the 'free world', was particularly affected by the difficulties of financing high defence expenditure at home and war overseas. If Lyndon Johnson was driven from office because of an unpopular war, his legacy was one of rising inflation resulting from the attempt to finance two things without raising taxes: the Vietnam war – which involved over a quarter of a million troops after 1965 and huge aid injections to South Vietnam – and the Great Society program at home. As inflation began to bite in the early 1970s, the external current deficit swelled, US gold reserves dwindled and, in 1971, dollar parity with gold was abandoned, precipitating the collapse of the Bretton Woods system of fixed exchange rates[7] and the emergence in 1973 of a regime of flexible exchange rates. Within the OECD group of countries, which accounted for the bulk of 'free world' trade, both nominal and real exchange rates became more variable. Not only did this bring new uncertainty to trade, but with the emergence of huge dollar holdings in Europe and the oil-rich Arab states, currencies became vulnerable to speculative attack. The shaky nature of world financial institutions was amply demonstrated by the secondary banking crisis of 1973–5.[8]

A third factor was the growing internationalization of competition. This aspect of globalization meant that, as manufacturing spread further afield, corporations that had previously benefited from considerable flexibility in setting domestic prices and 'passing on' cost increases found themselves constrained by cheap imports. An example was US automobile manufacturing in the 1970s, which for the first time faced significant competition in its domestic market from Japanese and European car-makers. Glyn (2006) admirably summarizes the combined effects of wage pressure, slowing productivity, trade uncertainty and globalization on the rate of profit:

> the net rate of profit on capital employed in manufacturing (in the OECD) had fallen by nearly one half by the end of the 1970s (relative to 1970). It was apparent that the profit squeeze was reflecting a combination of militant wage pressure pushing up . . . [costs] and international competition restraining price increases. The rise in imported material costs and the weakening of productivity growth . . . further exacerbated the distributional struggle. (Glyn, 2006: 7)

Other factors were doubtless important in the crisis of the 1970s. One manifestation of workers' real wage gains was the rising share of state spending on transfers for welfare, i.e., unemployment benefit, pensions and the like. For the OECD as a whole, state spending in the early 1970s was about one-third of GDP, but by the late 1970s and early 1980s it had risen to 40 per cent on average, and it was considerably higher in the main European countries and in Scandinavia. Just as with wages and inflation, the debate about state spending was part of a struggle over distributional share. Indeed, it became fashionable in the 1980s for opponents of the labour movement to attribute inflation almost entirely to 'excessive' state spending.

Equally, as Glyn (2006) and others have pointed out, on top of rising state spending came a series of initiatives from the labour movement to curb the power of capital. In Germany, workers achieved equal representation with directors on company boards, or 'co-determination' as it became known. In Sweden in the mid-1970s, under a scheme proposed by Rudolf Meidner and supported by the LO (Swedish Trade Union Congress), firms above a certain size would be required to issue new shares corresponding to 20 per cent of their annual profits; the shares would be owned by the workers'

(Average annual % growth rates of GDP)					
	1960–73	1973–9	1979–90	1979–82	1982–90
USA	4.0	2.4	2.6	−0.1	3.6
Europe	4.8	2.6	2.3	0.9	2.8
Japan	9.6	3.6	4.1	3.5	4.3
OECD	4.9	2.7	2.7	0.9	3.4

Figure 3.1: The growth slowdown, 1960–1990

Source: Glyn (1992: 72)

movement and used to finance pensions and other social provision. Ultimately, such a scheme would have implied workers becoming the owners of their companies. In the early 1970s in Britain, the Labour Party for a time backed the Alternative Economic Strategy (AES), aiming to take many of Britain's largest firms and banks into public ownership and to force many others to enter into planning agreements with government. A similar approach was adopted by the French Socialist Party, though the economic crisis that ensued in 1981 when the Mitterand government came to power forced it to back down. In short, by the late 1970s and early 1980s, capital saw itself fundamentally threatened by the growth in strength and militancy of the labour movement, made possible by the long period of postwar prosperity.

Many economists have come to accept this interpretation of the root causes of the 1970s crisis, even if there is less agreement over how the wage share subsequently came to be restored. For example, Roberto Torrini (of the Bank of Italy and the London School of Economics) writes:

> A widely accepted explanation for the fall in the profit share during the 1970s is the unprecedented wage-push episode which occurred in many European economies in the first half of the decade, together with the first oil shock and the slowdown in total factor productivity growth. There is much less consensus on the interpretation of the recovery of the 80s and of the sharp rise in profit share observed during the 1990s. (Torrini, 2005: 1)

Just as the institutions of organized labour had grown in power in the 1970s, employers' organizations did the same. Nowhere was this backlash more evident than in America and Britain. In the United States, the US Chamber of Commerce – perhaps the most influential of grass-roots organizations representing small and medium enterprises – expanded its base from 50,000 firms in 1970 to 250,000 in just over a decade, joining forces

Year	US	France	Germany	Italy	UK
1968	4.2	4.5	1.6	1.2	4.9
1969	5.5	6.6	1.8	2.5	5.2
1970	5.7	4.7	3.7	1.2	6.9
1971	4.4	5.6	5.1	4.8	9.2
1972	3.2	6.3	5.6	6.2	7.1
1973	6.2	7.1	7.0	10.2	9.4
1974	11.0	13.9	7.0	19.4	15.8
1975	9.1	11.7	6.0	17.1	24.5
1976	5.8	9.6	4.2	16.7	16.4
1977	6.5	9.6	3.6	19.3	15.8
1978	7.6	9.1	2.7	12.5	8.3
1979	11.3	0.6	4.2	15.5	13.5
1980	13.5	13.7	5.5	21.3	17.9
1981	10.3	13.4	6.2	19.3	12.0
1982	6.2	11.7	5.2	16.3	8.5
1983	3.2	9.7	3.4	14.9	4.6
1984	4.3	7.4	2.4	10.6	5.0
1985	3.6	5.8	2.1	8.6	6.0
1986	1.9	2.6	-0.2	6.1	3.4
1987	3.6	3.2	0.2	4.6	4.2
1988	4.1	2.7	1.3	5.0	4.9
1989	4.8	3.5	2.7	6.6	7.8
1990	5.4	3.4	2.7	6.1	9.5

Figure 3.2: Inflation in selected industrial countries, 1968–1990
Source: Edward Renshaw, Table 16.3 (emphasis added)
<http://www.albany.edu/~renshaw/leading/ess16.html>

with the National Association of Manufacturers to become a powerful lobby group. The year 1972 saw the founding of the Business Roundtable, a powerful group of CEOs representing America's largest corporations whose combined political spending at that time was nearly $900 million.[9] It was money on this scale which helped found conservative think tanks such as the Heritage Foundation, the American Enterprise Institute and even the relatively liberal National Bureau for Economic Research (NBER). As David Harvey has noted:

> With abundant finance furnished by wealthy individuals (such as brewer Joseph Croors who later became a member of Reagan's 'kitchen cabinet') and their foundations . . . , a flood of tracts and books . . . emerged espousing neo-liberal values. A TV version of Milton Friedman's *Free to Choose* was founded with a grant [from one of these] in 1977. (Harvey, 2005: 44)

Restoring Labour Discipline

If one accepts that the post-war growth in working-class power was a major factor in precipitating the crisis, one must accept that curbing this power was the main aim of capitalists as they sought to emerge from crisis. At the same time, it must be borne in mind that creating a 'reserve army' of unemployed was not a universal response in rich countries of the OECD. At one end of the spectrum were the UK and the USA, both of which relied on 'liberalizing the market'; at the other extreme were the Nordic social democracies. In the words of Andrew Glyn:

> At one extreme is the 'market' solution of low real-wage increases and expanded job opportunities in the market sector. At the other, more interventionist end, subsidies to preserve jobs in the market sector are combined with heavy taxation accepted by workers to finance expansion of public-sector jobs. The former, to which the USA approximates, represents a rough and ready egalitarianism, or spreading of the misery, which is the rougher the more pronounced are earnings differentials. The latter is the conscious, social-democratic egalitarianism exemplified by Sweden in the 1970s and early 1980s, but generally somewhat reined in during the later 1980s as limits to the compression of take-home pay were reached. (Glyn, 1992: 82)

There can be little doubt about the figures for the largest OECD countries. Inflation rose in the 1970s, while in the 1980s unemployment in several countries rose to heights not experienced since the 1930s (see figures 3.2 and 3.3). At the same time, union membership declined and the influence of the trade union movement ebbed away – nowhere more so than in the UK, where Mrs Thatcher's defeat of the miners in 1984–85 was emblematic.

Inflation coupled with mass unemployment not only neutralized workers' power, but destroyed whole industries and impoverished a substantial number of workers. In the UK, where inflation had been high in the mid-1970s but had fallen below 10 per cent by 1978, it rose again, reaching nearly 18 per cent in 1980. By 1984, the headline unemployment figure rose above 10 per cent (to over 3 million workers), where it remained until the end of 1986. Unemployment led to massive poverty and inequality: over the decade, the Gini coefficient rose by ten points, the fastest rise in inequality experienced anywhere in the OECD.

The Rise of the Monetarists

The right-wing explanation for this state of affairs was that workers had no one to blame but themselves, a view which I have argued contains a kernel

Year	US	France	Germany	Italy	UK
1968	3.6	2.7	1.1	3.5	3.2
1969	3.5	2.3	0.6	3.5	3.1
1970	4.9	2.5	0.5	3.2	3.1
1971	5.9	2.8	0.6	3.3	3.9
1972	5.6	2.9	0.7	3.8	4.2
1973	4.9	2.8	0.7	3.7	3.2
1974	5.6	2.9	1.6	3.1	3.1
1975	8.5	4.1	3.4	3.4	4.6
1976	7.7	4.5	3.4	3.9	5.9
1977	7.1	5.1	3.4	4.1	6.4
1978	6.1	5.3	3.3	4.1	6.3
1979	5.8	6.0	2.9	4.4	5.4
1980	7.1	6.4	2.8	4.4	7.0
1981	7.6	7.6	4.0	4.9	10.5
1982	9.7	8.3	5.6	5.4	11.3
1983	9.6	8.5	6.9	5.9	11.8
1984	7.5	10.0	7.1	5.9	11.8
1985	7.2	10.4	7.2	6.0	11.2
1986	7.0	10.6	6.6	7.5	11.2
1987	6.2	10.7	6.3	7.9	10.3
1988	5.5	10.2	6.3	7.9	8.6
1989	5.3	9.6	5.7	7.8	7.3
1990	5.5	9.1	5.0	7.0	7.0

Figure 3.3: Unemployment rates in selected industrial countries, 1968–1990
Source: Edward Renshaw, Table 16.4 (emphasis added) <http://www.albany.edu/
~renshaw/leading/ess16.html>

of truth. Nevertheless, the manner in which the story was told by economists, financial journalists and eventually most politicians bears closer
examination.

The conventional Keynesian response to the oil price shocks of the
1970s had been to treat them as eroding real wages, amounting in effect to
a cut in demand. Maintaining aggregate demand therefore required an
increase in government spending, and this indeed was what many OECD
states attempted. But given the continuing struggle over income shares,
boosting aggregate demand in an already inflationary climate did not lead
– as some economists expected – to faster growth and renewed private
sector investment. Because wages had been rising faster than productivity,
pump-priming simply led to higher inflation and continued stagnation. In
fact, Keynes had argued that fiscal pump-priming was important in a
deflationary climate, not an inflationary one, but this point was largely

lost. 'Monetarists' now argued that inflation was the result of an irresponsible increase in government spending and that the culprit was 'big' government.

In somewhat more sophisticated terms, the monetarist argument was that the root cause of the dilemma lay in the fact that workers, anticipating inflation, put in higher and higher wage claims in a mistaken attempt to secure a real wage increase; what economists call 'money illusion'. In a seminal piece in 1968, Milton Friedman had argued that the apparent trade-off between lower unemployment and higher inflation is not stable for this very reason. Monetarists argued that the only way to cure money illusion was for unemployment to rise to its 'natural' rate, and indeed beyond it for a time in order to effect a lasting cure. The term NAIRU – the *Non-Accelerating Inflation Rate of Unemployment* – passed into the economics lexicon, although monetarists were generally reluctant to assign a value to this rate. By the late-1970s, even Jim Callaghan, Britain's Labour Prime Minister, had joined the anti-Keynesian chorus by proclaiming that government could not spend its way out of recession.[10] Indeed, following the interest rate shock administered to the US economy by Paul Volcker at the Fed in 1979, followed by the start of the Reagan-Thatcher era in 1980, recession set in and the US unemployment rate climbed. Nowhere did it climb more precipitously than in the UK. It was only a matter of time – a decade as it turned out – before the new 'reserve army' of the unemployed would serve to halt the advance of real wages and restore profits.

The restoration of the share of profits in national income in the 1980s is illustrated by figure 3.4. Broadly speaking, real wage growth in the OECD, which in the 1970s had been over 3 per cent per annum – slightly more than productivity growth – now fell to just over 1 per cent annually, while productivity growth rose as new investment came on stream.

The evidence shown in figure 3.4 is consistent with the observation that trade union militancy – as measured by the number of annual strike days lost – fell dramatically over the same period. Looking at the OECD countries as a group, in 1974–79 the figure had been forty days per 100 workers; for the period 1980–89 this fell to twenty-five days, while by 1989–90 it was only sixteen. The fall is particularly notable in Italy and the UK, the two most strike-prone countries in Europe, where, at the end of the 1980s, the strike rates were around one quarter of those of 1973–79. Indeed, the most dramatic fall occurred in the USA which went from forty-seven days at the beginning of the period to ten at the end.

Change in share of profits in net value added (% points over period)		
	1973–79	1979–87
OECD	−4.2	4.7
Europe*	−5.4	5.3
USA	−3.0	1.8

Figure 3.4: Change in GDP share of manufacturing profits
* 'Europe' is taken above as comprising of Belgium, France, Germany, Italy, the Netherlands, Switzerland and the UK.
Source: Glyn (1992), Table III

Shrinking the State and Increased Inequality

If the 1970s had seen government spending increase sharply as a share of GDP, in the 1980s and 1990s, the share at first increased (largely because of the growing burden of unemployment benefit payments) then stabilized and eventually fell. The 1980s also saw significant reductions in the top rate of tax throughout the OECD, as shown by figure 3.5. For the OECD group of countries, government's share of GDP in the 1970s had gone up by 8.5 percentage points, and although the rate of increase slowed noticeably, it rose by a further 1.2 points in the 1980s. The same is true of Europe (and also of the Nordic countries, not shown in figure 3.5). Changes were much smaller in the USA, reflecting the far smaller share of social transfers in government spending. Equally, top rates of tax fell everywhere, though most dramatically in the USA under Reagan and in the UK under Thatcher.

In sum, the struggle to increase labour's share of the pie which had characterized the 1970s was reversed in the decade that followed. Labour unrest fell, government budgetary discipline was re-imposed, inflation receded, the stock market recovered and the share of profits in GDP rose again. It was particularly in the USA and the UK, where labour's bargaining power was most weakened, that inequality rose sharply. But there is an important caveat: not all of labour's gains were reversed, particularly in continental Europe where the political assault on labour was more muted. The point is made succinctly by Glyn:

> Cuts in expenditure on social welfare, reductions in the progressiveness of the tax system, the increased weight of unearned income and capital gains during the 1980s, represented a reversal of the egalitarian trend, even in those countries where commitment to full employment was consciously preserved. Obviously such reversals were from a range of starting points, so that, for example, the cut in government spending in

Government expenditure Change in top rate % of GDP of income tax (%) changes		
	1970–79	**1979–89**	**c.1980–c.1989**
OECD	8.5	1.2	−17
Europe	7.9	−0.1	−14
USA	2.4	2.1	−37

Figure 3.5: Changes in government expenditure and top tax rates
* 'Europe' is taken above as comprising of Belgium, France, Germany, Italy, the
Netherlands, Switzerland and the UK.
Source: Glyn (1992), table VII

> Sweden still left it amongst the largest spenders on social welfare.
> Moreover, many of the gains made during the 'golden age' were only
> nibbled at rather than comprehensively reversed. Thus expenditure on
> social welfare at the end of the 1980s was frequently double the share of
> GDP it had been at the beginning of the 1960s, and in no country much
> under 150 per cent of that starting point. (Glyn, 1992: 82)

Building a Conservative Consensus

The politics of the time has been captured well by Harvey (2005) whose
phrase – 'the construction of consent' – underscores the manner in which
the ruling classes both in the United States and Britain consciously organized themselves to reverse the post-war gains of the labour movement . In
the words of one American writer:

> During the 1970s, business refined its ability to act as a class, submerging
> competitive instincts in favour of joint, cooperative action in the legisla-
> tive arena. Rather than individual companies seeking only special
> favours . . . The dominant theme of the political strategy of business
> became a shared interest in the defeat of bills such as consumer protec-
> tion and labour law reform, and in the enactment of favourable tax, reg-
> ulatory and antitrust legislation.[11]

The main expression of this new mission was the zeal with which corporate America set out to capture the Republican Party. The 'Grand Old Party'
(GOP) had of course always been the more pro-business of the two parties
for which US voting arrangements ensured a duopoly of power. However,
during the Eisenhower years of the 1950s, it had remained under the clear
hegemony of the East Coast establishment, although the waning of that
base was first signalled in 1964 when Barry Goldwater won the Republican
presidential candidacy.

Under the Federal Election Campaign Act, passed in 1971 and affirmed by the US Supreme Court in 1976, Political Action Committees (PACs) – the US term for any group set up to support a particular cause or campaign – were allowed to make unlimited contributions to particular causes (though limited contributions to particular candidates) subject to loose rules about disclosure. Corporate PACs grew precipitously, and, under the influence of politicians like Ronald Reagan in the 1970s, the Republicans urged PACs to support explicitly right-wing candidates. It was in this period too that explicit ties were formed with early Christian conservative groups. Jerry Falwell's Moral Majority emerged in the late 1970s as did Christian Voice (whose initial headquarters in Washington was at the Heritage Foundation), and there followed such organizations as the Christian Coalition for America, the American Coalition for Traditional Values, the Family Research Council and the Council for National Policy.

The ideological battle to broaden the political base of right-wing politics in the USA assumed a variety of forms. White working-class anxiety increased in the 1970s as jobs in steel, automobiles and other traditional industries gradually disappeared and a once prosperous blue-collar class suffered real hardship. Patriotic sentiments were cleverly turned into political slogans as bumper stickers with American flags proliferated during the Vietnam war; more darkly, 'liberals' were blamed for the increased social provision and protection afforded to minorities, whether in the form of housing benefits and food-stamp programs or in upholding the rights of women, blacks, homosexuals and other special interest groups. The 'culture wars' which began in the 1970s laid the foundation for recruiting new constituencies in support of an agenda of reaction. The cloak of intellectual respectability was provided by a coterie of strongly right-wing intellectuals such as Irving Kristol, Norman Podhoretz, Richard Pipes and Robert Conquest.

By the 1980s, the right was firmly in control of the Republican Party machine which was now under explicit corporate tutelage. Reagan was in many ways symbolic of the deep shift which had taken place. He was an experienced media celebrity with little experience of (or interest in) complex political issues, and was firmly wedded to traditional American values, religion and anti-Communism (as shown by his role during the McCarthy period). The Democratic Party by contrast was caught in the contradictory position of delivering on its promises to the traditional labour constituency – complicated by the need to weld its increasingly diverse new constituents into a broad coalition – while attempting to remain sufficiently pro-business to retain some measure of corporate funding. The result is aptly summarized by Harvey:

The political structure that emerged was quite simple. The Republican Party could mobilize massive financial resources and mobilize its popular base to vote against its material interests on cultural/religious grounds while the Democratic Party could not afford to tend to the material needs (for example for a national health-care system) of its traditional base for fear of offending capitalist class interests. Given the asymmetry, the political hegemony of the Republican Party became more sure.[12]

Under Reagan, there ensued a veritable offensive of measures designed to bring about a fundamental rightward shift in US politics. Carter's appointment of Paul Volker to run the Fed (America's Central Bank) presaged a decisive shift away from Keynesian-style stabilization towards monetary policy; a massive hike in interest rates brought the US economy to a halt, raised unemployment and 'squeezed' inflation. Reagan was firmly committed to economic deregulation, tax and budget cuts, and a package of ancillary measures which favoured big business. His sacking of all US air-traffic controllers following the PATCO[13] strike in 1981 sent a clear message to the trade union movement. The Office of Management and Budget, part of the Executive Office, was required to carry out cost-benefit analyses of all government regulations and scrap those which could not be justified, thus resulting in striking from the books some 40 per cent of 1970s decision considered too favourable to labour or to consumers.[14]

The tax code was revised to introduce 'free depreciation', an accounting concept that allowed corporations to write off investment against tax in a manner that lowered their tax burden substantially. The top rate of income tax for individuals was reduced in a series of steps from 78 per cent to 28 per cent, a measure based on the dubious logic of Arthur Laffer, then an obscure professor in California, who had worked with Dick Cheney and Donald Rumsfeld during the Gerald Ford presidency and whose views were famously characterized by Vice-President George H. W. Bush as 'voodoo economics'. Reagan's giveaways to the private sector are legion: perhaps most infamous was the decision to give the patent rights for HIV-AIDS related drugs – the precursors of anti-retroviral therapy – originating at the National Institute of Health to the private pharmaceutical companies.

Neo-liberalism in Britain

In Britain, the struggle between capital and labour had always had far more overt institutional and ideological expression in the trade union movement, the Labour Party and popular extra-Parliamentary groups on the left. In the post-war period, however, the Beveridge reforms had laid the basis of a compromise under which capital, in return for conceding significant benefits to the working class (the NHS, state pensions, greater job security in the nationalized industries, universal educational provision and so on), was never fundamentally challenged by labour. In the 1960s, although the Labour Party might continue to include Clause IV in its Constitution, it was generally accepted by the political class that a Labour government would not significantly extend public ownership and that, in return, Conservative governments would adhere to Keynesian policies designed to deliver nearly full employment. [15]

This 'Butskellite' compromise, so called after Hugh Gaitskell and Rab Butler who had been Chancellors under successive Labour and Conservative governments, began to unravel in the 1970s. Industrial militancy increased greatly, and Britain's major unions – the National Union of Mineworkers (NUM), the Amalgamated Engineering Workers (AEW) and the Transport and General Workers' Union (TGWU), the most powerful in the Trades Union Congress (TUC) – gained a place at the bargaining table with government that they had not previously held. Ted Heath's misjudgement of the public mood led to the miners' strike, the four-day week and industrial turbulence in 1974, and subsequently to a general election which returned a Labour government under Harold Wilson.

Inflation reached 26 per cent in 1975 and public unease was considerable. It is conventional to ascribe the inflationary surge to the 1973 oil-price hike, but at the time economists agreed that the direct impact of oil on the price level was relatively minor. Crucially, dearer oil meant higher costs, and it was the anticipation of higher costs that fed expectations of rising inflation leading in turn to a wage-price spiral. Strikes multiplied as organized workers, their shop stewards often in the lead, fought to maintain their real wages. First under Wilson and then under James Callaghan, who became Prime Minister following Wilson's departure in 1976, the Labour Party attempted the difficult task of reconciling its trade union constituency with what it saw as its role to govern in the interests of the country as a whole. Moreover, lacking an overall majority in the Commons, Labour was forced into temporary coalitions with the Ulster Unionists and the Liberals. To make matters worse, Britain's growing budget deficit was accompanied by a balance of payments crisis forcing the country into the hands of the IMF which imposed conditions of fiscal austerity and urged wage restraint.

With Denis Healey as Chancellor, the government capped wage increases in successive phases and attempted to implement a new national wage-bargaining policy. With the cooperation of the TUC, the policy was at first successful, but broke down in late 1976 when trade unions insisted on a return to free collective bargaining. Healey reluctantly accepted this position when introducing Phase II of the Incomes Policy in mid-1977, but in 1988 he announced a Phase IV cap on pay rises of 5 per cent. There followed the infamous 'Winter of Discontent' of 1978–79, so named by the editor of *The Sun*. Government's attempt to impose the 5 per cent limit, despite the TUC's opposition and the much higher settlements agreed only weeks before for car workers at Ford and Vauxhall, simply fuelled the flames. There followed strikes by hospital workers, grave diggers and – memorably – rubbish collectors which left bin bags piling up in streets throughout the country. A popular view of the Labour government now took hold – with a little help from Fleet Street – that it was too weak to stand up to the unions. A vote of no confidence on a minor issue in 1979 brought down the government and the subsequent general election saw the Tories back in power under Margaret Thatcher.

Thatcher & Co.

Heath had been Chief Whip under Macmillan, and was by temperament a technocratic corporatist, not an ideologue. Thatcher was a very different political animal. For one thing, she had a big majority; for another, she surrounded herself with new ministers, including hardline conservatives like Sir Keith Joseph, a follower of Hayek whose pathological anti-union views soon served to divide true believers from the 'wets', or old-style one-nation Tories. While most Tory MPs had been relatively ineffective in opposition, a handful of diehards had been laying the intellectual foundations for a new anti-union crusade. In 1974 Keith Joseph (together with Margaret Thatcher and Alfred Sherman) had founded the Centre for Policy Studies, a think tank to promote the monetarist economic orthodoxy of Hayek and Friedman. Equally important was the Adam Smith Institute, set up in 1977 by Eamonn Butler and Madsen Pirie (previously of the US Heritage Foundation), and responsible for working out policy prescriptions on privatization, the outsourcing of public services, the introduction of the poll tax and the introduction of an internal market for the NHS.

Sir Keith had been given overall responsibility for policy and research in Thatcher's Shadow Cabinet. His views and those of like-minded Cabinet colleagues such as Norman Tebbit ultimately prevailed, setting the scene for a dramatic shift towards monetarist doctrine in macro-economic management, in drastic limitations on trade union power (including amending the right to strike, outlawing secondary picketing and abolishing the closed shop) and, ultimately, the wide-reaching privatization of public enterprise in the 1980s and 1990s.

Most importantly, Thatcher presided over a period which saw a rapid decline in British industry and the growth of Britain as a financial centre. In the pre-war and post-war period there had been continuous tension between these two poles of the economy, as reflected crucially in exchange-rate policy. The City of London had always favoured a strong pound, believing that the alternative might weaken sterling's role as a trading cur-rency. *Per contra*, a low pound favoured British industrial manufacturers. Thatcher's arrival on the scene signalled clear favour for finance capital, with industry supported only to the extent of lowering the real wage. Although inflation rose for two years after Thatcher's victory in 1979, the implementation of tight monetary policy and 'spending targets' triggered a recession in 1981 and unemployment skyrocketed. Alan Budd, one of Thatcher's advisers, was later quoted as saying 'the 1980s policies of attack-ing inflation by squeezing the economy and public spending were a cover to bash the workers.'[16] For a time, Thatcher's poll ratings fell, but the Falklands War in 1982 restored her fortunes and she went on to win general elections in 1983 and 1987, becoming Britain's longest-serving Prime Minister since Lord Salisbury.

Thatcher's main goals were to reform economic policy and to reduce union power. The miners' strike of 1984 lasted for nearly a year and was pivotal in this respect; their defeat in part was due to the disastrous tactics adopted by their leader, Arthur Scargill. By the time Thatcher left office in 1990, many of Britain's traditional industries had either disappeared or were in terminal decline: coal, steel, shipbuilding, civil aircraft and motor cars are the more obvious examples, and with them went their unionized work-force. National wage bargaining, the practice of holding industry-wide 'wage rounds' (usually) in consultation with government, became a thing of the past. Privatization was the order of the day, and having first scrapped subsidies and appointed new managers to make public enterprise more efficient, it was then sold off – often at bargain basement prices – to the private sector. Under Thatcher and her successor, the list included British Aerospace, British Airways, the British Airports Authority, British Telecom, British Steel, British Gas, Britoil, the Central Electricity Generating Board, the Coal Board, the Water Board, British Rail, the National Bus Company and various smaller state-owned groups.

But her reforms had secondary effects too. Her sell-off of council housing to tenants proved highly popular, and helped legitimize her priva-tization of state enterprise. When faced with opposition from local coun-cils and municipal governments such as in London and Sheffield, she reduced their power (e.g., abolishing the Greater London Council) and undermined their financial independence by capping rates. In the areas of health, social services and education, Thatcher limited herself to laying the groundwork for privatization, i.e., in setting out the principles of an 'internal market' for the NHS, in squeezing local authority house-building programmes and in sounding out the public on the use of 'vouchers' for education. Neo-liberal reform in these areas had to await the coming of Blair's New Labour project.[17]

In terms of success in achieving her political goals, there can be little doubt that Margaret Thatcher was one of Britain's most effective politicians of the twentieth century; her legacy was one of breaking the trade unions, promoting free markets through deregulation, cutting government spending and cutting personal taxation. Britain prospered while the share of profits in national income rose rapidly at the expense of labour, as reflected in a far less equitable distribution of household income, prolonged high unemployment and a steep rise in poverty, particularly amongst the very young and the old. Perhaps the most telling feature of the Thatcher revolution is that it led to a long-term rightward shift in the centre-ground of British politics. Under both Major and Blair, the public sphere became subordinate to the market and Britain became less 'European' and more like the USA.

An important similarity between Thatcher and Reagan was the manner in which both were able to incorporate new constituencies to politics. The decline of industrial employment and in institutionalized working-class solidarity, together with the rise of a new lower middle class, the 'white-collar worker', either employed in the new service industries or (often precariously) self-employed, helped undermine the post-war 'welfare' consensus built on the twin pillars of state-sponsored social provision and Keynesian full employment. While a few prescient voices on the left recognized the importance of these changes,[18] it was the right which seized the initiative in organizing this constituency around a new individualistic ideological consensus stressing market-based freedom.

The 'new' Labour Party that assumed power in 1997, while retaining some elements of traditional social democracy such as a commitment to refinance the health service, in effect consolidated many aspects of Thatcher's neo-liberal revolution by adapting to the new political landscape.[19] Things might have been otherwise: re-nationalizing the railways, raising top-rate taxes to rebuild Britain's economic and social infrastructure; a genuinely radical reorganization of secondary education aimed at providing universal education until the age of eighteen; abolishing the NHS 'internal market'; these and similar measures would have found widespread support while signalling Labour's intention to challenge the Thatcherite legacy. But there was no attempt to signal a radical new direction. Instead, Labour's domestic agenda accepted conservative spending priorities by firmly rejecting 'tax and spend' in favour of public–private partnership and Public Finance Initiatives (PFIs); redistribution was demonized as 'the politics of envy'; public services were to be 'modernized' through the introduction of competition and widespread outsourcing to the private sector; local wage bargaining and flexible labour markets were thought preferable to an industrial and national wage bargaining structure and trade unions remained marginalized.[20] In foreign affairs, after a brief flirtation with an 'ethical' foreign policy, the old imperial ambitions reasserted themselves as Britain became junior partner to the remaining superpower. As the sociologist and historian, Stuart Hall, has written:

> The Labour election victory in 1997 took place at a moment of great political opportunity . . . There was therefore a fundamental choice of directions for the incoming government. . . . One was to offer an alternative radical strategy to Thatcherism, attuned to the shifts which had occurred in the 1970s and 1980s; with equal social and political depth, but based on radically different principles. . . . The other choice was, of course, to adapt to Thatcherite/neo-liberal terrain. There were plenty of indications that this would be New Labour's preferred direction. [21]

Why the USA and the UK?

While the spread of neo-liberalism in the United States and Britain of the 1980s cannot be put down to a single cause, it was doubtless a response to a crisis precipitated in part by the huge gains which labour had made in the golden age of the post-war years, gains that had squeezed capital in the USA and the UK and in much of continental Europe. If the crisis was particularly acute in America and Britain, it was in part because industrial capital was more vulnerable. Japan and most continental European countries, particularly Germany, had rebuilt their economies after the war and benefited from a capital stock which was relatively new compared to the industrial capital in the USA and the UK.

The crisis may have produced a similar ideological response in the UK and the USA, as we have seen, but the two countries were in fundamental respects quite different. Post-war Britain combined a strong trade union movement and an important public sector with a relatively uncompetitive industrial structure which left the country exposed to repeated balance of payments crises; this state of affairs was further complicated by the conflicting interests of the financial and industrial sectors. While the governments of Thatcher, Major (and even Blair) played a key role in imposing industrial discipline, reforming public finance and selling off public enterprise, this tidying up of the British economy took place against a background of an interlinked technical and financial revolution on a global scale from which London was a major beneficiary. The share of manufacturing industry in Britain's GDP is today one-third of what it was in the 1970s; the financial services sector today is far stronger than manufacturing, both in terms of employment and as a contributor to GDP. If Gordon Brown was the most successful Chancellor of the Exchequer in living memory, it is very largely because the British economy has been driven by a flow of repatriated profits, capital and highly skilled labour from abroad. This is less true of the United States. Certainly the US financial services sector has grown; in 1981 it accounted for only 18 per cent of corporate profits while, in 2001, the figure was 39 per cent.[22] Although the Reagan years laid the ground for a finance and high-tech boom in the 1990s, it is far from clear that the new 'knowledge-based' economy can (or should) permanently replace traditional manufacturing as the country's locomotive force. US growth at the beginning of the twenty-first century appears to be based more on a debt-fuelled surge in consumer spending financed by overseas savings (see chapter 8).

If continental Europe avoided a crisis on a similar scale, it is largely because the rapid growth of labour productivity took place within a more 'corporatist' political culture, enabling the gains of growth to be shared out in a manner which did not threaten profitability to the same degree. That is not to say that continental Europe was immune from crisis, as shown by the 'events' of the late 1960s in France, presaging the rise of permanently high unemployment in the 1980s and a weakening of trade unions, the eclipse in Germany of the SPD and Helmut Kohl's rise to power in 1982, and growing militancy and violence in Italy, culminating in the collapse of its post-war ruling class in the early 1990s, or even the quite serious recessions which gripped the Nordic countries in the early 1990s and nearly broke the social democratic hegemony underlying 'social partnership'.

Continental Europe's 'answer' to crisis, too, was the promise of a strong, unified Europe with its own currency and new levels of economic and political governance. If these disappointed some, it was not so much the influence of neo-liberal ideology that counted as that of core Europe's tradition of sound money overseen by strong central banks, led of course by the Bundesbank. Germany had no mainstream tradition of Keynesian fiscal policy, and it had a strong folk memory of hyper-inflation. At the same time, the 'European model' appears to have maintained social cohesiveness, underpinned by variants of the welfare state, more successfully than in the USA and the UK. Doubtless, this difference is due to the peculiarly central-ized character of the British state, which gave Thatcher much greater power than was indicated by her share of the vote.[23] In Germany, and to a degree in Italy, a federal structure and more proportional voting system made it much more difficult for central governments to impose radical changes. The strengths and weaknesses of the alternative European model are addressed in the chapter which follows.

4

America, Europe and the Welfare State

By the 1990s, the European generation who had been attracted by the 'American dream' were being replaced by those who saw no special attraction, and no special virtue, in the American way of life. For this generation of Europeans, the USA became a less positive force – no longer an exotic and successful cousin, more an old, powerful and sometimes arrogant uncle.

Stephen Haseler (2004:60)

The Challenge of Europe

In recent years a spate of new books have been published examining the rise of Europe, mainly focusing on whether the European Union is strong enough to challenge US political hegemony and whether European 'soft power' is ultimately more decisive than America's formidable military might.[1] While there is much new material, too, on the economics of the EU, this literature tends to be relatively conventional and technical, devoted to trade flows, customs union, monetary union and the like.

As one might expect, the Anglo-Saxon camp is sharply divided on the issue of the European Union, as much on the left of the political spectrum as on the right. American liberals tend to support it, while neo-conservatives are hostile, seeing Europe as a long-term threat to global US political and economic interests. For many on the left in Britain, the Treaty of Rome was no more than a document designed to ensure the co-hegemony of France and Germany in post-war capitalist expansion, a step ultimately leading to the Treaty of Maastricht that set out the rules of a monetary union as conceived and approved by a committee of bankers and technocrats. It is a political project of which many on the British left want no part, preferring instead to rally the masses to a strictly home-grown version of British socialism.[2] Equally, much of the British right is anti-European, though their objections are quite different. Europe is seen alternatively as impinging on age-old British sovereignty, a sentiment informed by a strong current of imperial nostalgia, or as driving a wedge in the transatlantic 'special rela-tionship'.

Nor are the British Treasury and the Bank of England keen to embrace Europe more tightly, as Gordon Brown made clear during his years as Chancellor. Joining the euro would diminish the power of both these insti-tutions. Hostility towards Europe on both sides of the political spectrum is reinforced by a daily diet of chauvinist nonsense appearing in the British press whose main owners, Lord Rothermere and Rupert Murdoch, are rabid Euro-sceptics whose political views are closely aligned with those of American neo-conservatives.

What, if anything, can one make of these divergences? Is the USA indis-putably richer, its labour markets more flexible and its productivity higher? Is the welfare state an unaffordable luxury in the twenty-first century, or on the contrary should Europeans be proud of their 'social model' and con-tinue to aspire to a different balance between equity and growth than that currently on offer in the United States? Much contemporary economic commentary extols US-style dynamism and flexibility while implying that US-style inequalities are largely avoidable. In this chapter, I consider the economics of the EU and the USA in more detail. At the same time, one must recognize that 'Europe' is a convenient abstraction; in reality, whether we consider the EU-13 (Eurozone), the EU-15, or the EU-25 and 27, this col-lection of national economies is still far more varied in incomes, economic institutions and its polity than the 50 US states.

Income Distribution versus Prosperity

Per capita gross domestic product (GDP) in the USA is about 40 per cent higher than average GDP of the EU-15 when measured at purchasing power parity (PPP). The gap is slightly greater if we consider either the twelve Eurozone members (EU-13) or add the accession states (EU-25). Although GDP per person is a poor indicator of measure of welfare or hap-piness, let's agree to use it with qualification for the sake of simplicity. The main reason the USA is richer is, first of all, because Americans work about 20 per cent more hours per year than Europeans and, second, because a higher proportion of Americans are in employment. When we adjust for both these factors and look at GDP in 2005 per person per hour worked, there is virtually no difference between Germany, France and the USA.

Economists often speak of this as revealing different American and European social preferences for work and leisure. In truth, both the employment rate and how long the average person works are explained

Non-economists are sometimes baffled by the difference between using 'median income' and 'average income' to compare countries. Consider two countries, A and B, each with a population of only three persons. In country A, income is equally distributed and each person gets 100 units a year. Total income is 300, and average income (or income per head) in A is 300/3=100, as is the median (or middle person's) income. In country B, the first two people get 100 a year but the third gets 400, so the total is 600, the average is 600/3=200 but the median is still 100.

Inter-country comparisons using median income are thus less influenced by differences in income distribution. Take the USA and Canada: 2006 per capita income in USA was about $44,000 but only $35,700 in Canada measured at Purchasing Power Parity. The two countries are much closer when looking at median household income measured on a similar basis: $46,000 vs $43,000 respectively.

Figure 4.1: Median and average GDP comparisons
Source: Based on IMF, *World Economic Outlook* (2006)

mainly by differences in political history. Until the late 1970s total hours worked were falling both in Europe and in the USA; since then, total hours worked have continued to fall in the EU-15 but have risen again in the USA. Equally, if we look at employment data by age group, Americans join the work force earlier and leave it far later than Europeans. The key to understanding why this has happened is the change in US income distribution. Since 1979, the bottom 40 per cent of income earners in the USA has been treading water while the bottom 20 per cent has become poorer. US workers have needed to put in more years and longer hours simply to maintain their real income position. Greater poverty and inequality in turn are associated with greater criminality, although the difference in incarceration rates between the EU and the USA cannot be explained by this factor alone. The prison population in the USA is now just over 2 million, very much higher proportionately than the EU; economists have estimated that this fact alone may reduce US unemployment by up to a full percentage point.

Does the USA grow faster than the EU? Again, the answer depends on what we measure. When we compare the growth rate of GDP of the USA and the EU-15, the USA rate averaged over the past decade is about 1.2 percentage points higher than that of the EU-15 (oddly, the difference is slightly smaller if we use the EU-25). But the usual measure of growing prosperity is GDP per head. (Note that if, hypothetically, GDP grows at 2 per cent but population grows at 3 per cent, then *per capita* GDP must be falling!) US population growth is a full percentage point higher that that of the EU-15, mainly because US immigration in the past decade has been higher.

Expressed on a per capita basis, GDP growth rates in the USA and the EU are virtually the same over the past decade. The same is true of per capita labour productivity growth.

What is also true is that, after the 2001 recession, the USA bounced back faster than the EU. For the period 2001–6, both GDP growth per head and labour productivity grew faster in the USA. But recent US productivity gains[3] are concentrated in distribution rather than in manufacturing, and US growth continues to pull in more imports than it produces exports, resulting in a growing external deficit – funded in part by the EU current account surplus. Also, job creation has been much slower in the USA in the 2000s than it was in the 1990s; in 2006, employment rates were still over 1 percentage point below their peak levels in 2000–1.

On the EU-15 side, lower growth is reflected in a high and prolonged average rate of unemployment, which has remained about three points above that of the USA for some time. Equally, looking at the disaggregated data, some EU-15 countries have done better than others over the past decade in terms of prosperity and unemployment, e.g., the UK, Ireland and the Nordic countries. But these differences exist for quite different reasons; if we disaggregated US data to compare growth in (say) North Dakota and California, many of the same differences would emerge – although the latter could not be attributed to differences in labour market regulation or fiscal policy.

Flexible Labour Markets

Perhaps the most common argument is that which contrasts the job-creating virtues of the US 'flexible' labour market with the sclerotic state of the EU where unemployment is persistently high. Economics students attending US universities (and increasingly those in the EU as well) learn that because EU labour is supplied at an 'artificially' high wage rate, employment in the EU is lower and unemployment higher.

While it is true that the USA has a better employment and unemployment record than the EU-15 as a whole, the key to understanding the difference between the EU and the USA lies in disaggregating employment by age group. If we compare employment rates in 2005 of the 25–54 age group, there is virtually no difference; e.g., the employment rates are 86 and 88 per cent for the EU-15 and the USA respectively (ignoring differences in how the data are recorded). The US data show a higher employment rate for youth (15–24) and a much higher rate for pre-retirement (55–64) and post-retirement (65 and over) groups. What the average employment and unemployment figures hide is the age-specific nature of the 'European

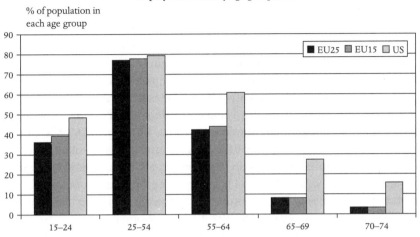

Figure 4.2: US and EU employment rates by age group, 2005
Source: Terry Ward, Alphametrics, Cambridge and Brussels, 2006

problem'. The picture remains much the same when comparing the USA and the EU-25.

Once again, the crucial element in understanding these differences is income distribution. At the youth end of the scale, young workers in the USA get less education and those who go to university are more likely to work part-time while at university than their European counterparts. At the older end of the scale, pension provision in the USA is neither as broad nor as generous as in the EU, so people carry on working – particularly the poor who cannot afford to save for retirement.

Making labour markets 'more flexible' (i.e., cutting wages) does not cure these problems; if anything it makes things worse. By contrast, putting resources into active labour market policies such as improved education, retraining and high benefit provision contingent on job searching helps workers to find and retain high-productivity jobs. This is the strategy pursued by the Nordic countries, one which has paid and will continue to pay handsome rewards in terms of prosperity and job security. As Dixon and Pearce write of the UK:

> Although [employment in Britain] is at a similar level to the social-demo-
> cratic welfare states such as Sweden and Denmark . . . there are marked
> differences in the way these levels have been achieved. Britain has an
> extensive low-wage, low-skill private (service) sector and low levels of
> unionisation which contribute to the much greater income inequality

generated by the labour market in the UK, whereas wages in the low-skill service sector tend to be kept high in the social democracies as these jobs are often unionised and in the public sector.[4]

Nor does comparing the economic performance of the European Union with that of the USA lead one to conclude that America has the more dynamic economy, or that it has performed better in the past or will do so in future. The most important feature of the comparison is neither the growth nor the unemployment record of the USA and the EU. It is, rather, that US growth – unlike that in the EU with the exception of the UK – is funded by a perilous mountain of foreign debt. US external indebtedness has in turn been driven by the US house-price bubble, enabling US consumers to spend more than they earn. Ironically, it is the EU which – together with China, Japan and the oil-exporting countries – continues to lend the money to the USA, keeping their households spending and their economy growing.

The truth is that neither side 'wins' in this beauty contest. Europe merely does less badly than the USA in some crucial respects. Yet, while it is true that the core Eurozone countries could perform far better, Germany, France and Italy have quite different problems – in comparison both to the USA and to each other – which require different solutions. The USA does not provide a one-size-fits-all model of dynamic capitalist growth which the EU should copy.

Is the EU More Egalitarian than the USA?

In comparison with the United States, the EU is more egalitarian; it does better than the USA on most major quality-of-life indicators, whether literacy, life expectancy or crime and incarceration. The EU has higher standards of welfare provision that are funded from a more progressive tax system. The above holds true for the core Eurozone member-states, if not necessarily for the full EU-25 since recent entrants are considerably poorer than the core states. Most people – or at least Europeans – would agree that a level of inequality comparable to that in the USA is undesirable, but neoliberals argue that too much welfare and bureaucracy blunts individual initiative and chokes off the entrepreneurial spirit.

The view that Europeans are over-coddled by a welfare state has been most succinctly put by Francis Fukuyama, until recently one of the academic pillars of the US neo-conservative establishment. According to Fukuyama, Europe is a collection of 'flabby, self-satisfied, inward-looking,

Sweden 1995	.221
Finland 1995	.226
Luxembourg 1994	.235
Netherlands 1994	.253
Belgium 1997	.255
Denmark 1997	.257
Germany 1994	.261
Austria 1995	.277
France 1994	.288
Spain 1990	.303
Ireland 1987	.328
Italy 1995	.342
UK 1995	.344
Greece (CHER, 1999)	.362
Portugal (CHER, 1999)	.375
EU-15 average	0.288
USA 1995	.372

Figure 4.3: Gini coefficients by country
Source: Smeeding (2002); Atkinson (2003)

weak-willed states whose grandest project was nothing more than the creation of a Common Market'.[5]

Per contra, supporters of the welfare state hold quite different views about its future. Some argue that globalization, particularly the pressure of ever-greater international competition, means that the 'EU welfare model' must inevitably be undermined.[6] Others point to the diversity of 'models' within the EU itself while noting that a number of northern European countries outperform the USA in terms of welfare, employment and growth. Still others point to a universal tendency for tax revenues and public provision to fall, and income distribution to worsen in recent years. Below I consider the merits of such arguments, but for the moment let us simply look at equality.

In general, income is more evenly distributed in the EU than in the USA when measured both before and after taxes and transfers.[7] Figure 4.3 shows post-transfer Gini coefficients measured on a comparable basis for the USA and the EU-15.[8] The most egalitarian countries (those with the lowest Gini values) are the Nordic group; at the other end of the scale one finds the USA and the UK where inequality has grown significantly since 1980.[9] The highest EU values are for Portugal and Greece; given that the latter are the least developed member-states of the EU-15, this is hardly surprising. (See Figure 6.1 for how the US Gini coefficient has changed over time.)

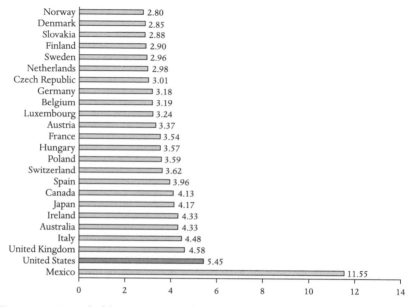

Figure 4.4: Household income inequality (ratio of 90th to 10th percentile)
Source: Schmitt and Zipperer (2006)

A different way of measuring inequality is to compare the household income of different percentiles (1 per cent slices) of the population. The greater the ratio of the 90th percentile (rich) – i.e., those who occupy the 90th slice from the bottom – to that of the 10th percentile (i.e., the poor who are only ten slices from the bottom), the greater the degree of income inequality. Figure 4.4 shows these ratios for selected countries, and the ranking corresponds roughly to that found above where Gini coefficients are compared. The most egalitarian countries are the Nordic group where the ratio in all cases is below 3.0. In the list of countries covered, Britain and the United States come close to last: the UK's ratio is 4.58 while that of the USA is 5.45. Mexico's score of 11.55 makes it highly unequal even amongst developing countries and is included solely for comparative purposes.

What is also important, but is not illustrated here, is the dispersion of household income at the top of the distribution. Suppose we confined ourselves to the top 10 per cent of the distribution; the top decile or 'the rich', and sliced this into ten levels from (relatively) less affluent to the very, very rich. Surprisingly, we would find that the degree of inequality amongst the rich is no less striking than for the population as a whole. Indeed, it is at the top end of the distribution that inequality has been growing fastest in the past twenty-five years. As the saying goes, you are rich if you can live comfortably on the interest from your capital but you are *truly* rich if you can live comfortably on the interest from the interest on your capital. The gap between the 'rich' and the 'super rich' has become as great as that between the rich and the poor.

A particularly interesting theme of recent study is the question of whether the European welfare states are becoming more unequal. Regardless of whether one accepts the 'knowledge economy' hypothesis or even the general argument that globalization has undermined the foundations of the EU welfare state, the intuitive hypothesis would be that inequality in the EU is growing. The fact that top rates of tax have fallen in the past twenty years not just in the USA and the UK, but throughout the EU (see figure 1.4 in chapter 1) would appear to lend weight to such a hypothesis.

Several studies therefore have looked at the change in Gini coefficients over time for countries and country groups.[10] While there is some evidence that Gini coefficients have increased in Europe, and even in the Nordic countries, the rises are far smaller than in the USA and the UK. Other than in the case of the USA and the UK, a study by Smeeding finds no conclusive evidence of a long-term trend towards income inequality in the OECD countries.[11] Esping-Andersen has found some evidence for growing inequality in the EU (and even in Sweden), namely, in comparing younger households to older households, which he attributes largely to the fact that the elderly have become more equal.[12]

Echoing an earlier reference to Krugman's view, it would appear that growing inequality is above all a political phenomenon, attributable to the policies followed by specific right-wing governments rather than an inevitable attribute of globalization. This point emerges clearly when looking at the UK under Thatcher in the 1980s. In the period 1984–90, the inequality (as measured by the Gini coefficient) for the UK rose by ten points. This change was larger than that in any other OECD country, and it happened more quickly. In 1990, the UK Gini value was nearly seven points higher than the highest value recorded in the 1960s.[13] Not only did inequality increase more rapidly in the UK than in the USA in this period, but there were differences in its root causes. In both countries the rich grew richer; in the UK, however, a combination of deindustrialization, a steep rise in unemployment and the assault against trade unions and welfare means that the poor grew poorer more quickly in Britain than in the USA.

Poverty amongst Children and the Aged

It is generally recognized that the incidence of child and old-age poverty has been historically high in the USA when compared to the EU-15 or to other

OECD countries. Even though the poverty threshold in the USA stands at about 43 per cent of median income – the USA convention is somewhat more relaxed than that in the EU – US poverty outcomes are worrying. In 2000, for example, after transfers, about 17 per cent of US children and 10 per cent of the elderly (aged sixty-five and over) were in poverty, with poverty for the population as a whole standing at 11.3 per cent – the 2005 figure was 12.6 per cent. Moreover, it should be noted that if a poverty threshold measure of 50 per cent of median household income were used in the USA, the figure would rise from 11.3 per cent to 17 per cent; (for 60 per cent of median income, the figure would be would be 24 per cent).[14] A 50 per cent poverty threshold in the USA would result in a rate of child poverty of 21.9 per cent and an elderly poverty rate of 24.7 per cent. The equivalent UK results (for 2000 based on a poverty threshold of 50 per cent of median income) are respectively 15.3 per cent (children), 20.5 per cent (elderly) and 12.4 per cent overall. The USA and UK results contrast sharply with France and Germany where the respective figures are all 10 per cent or less, and even more sharply with the Nordic countries. For example, taking the incidence of post-transfer childhood poverty, the figures are: Denmark (2.4 per cent), Finland (2.8 per cent), Norway (3.4 per cent) and Sweden (4.2 per cent). The figures for *overall* poverty are: Finland (5.4 per cent), Norway (6.4 per cent) and Sweden (6.5 per cent).[15]

It is popular in right-wing circles to argue that the 'welfare state' in general and social expenditure in particular are wasteful and unaffordable. It is alleged that not only does social expenditure turn people into 'welfare dependents' incapable of exercising rational choice, but it hampers wealth creation in that firms and entrepreneurial individuals face crippling levels of taxation. The logic of this argument is deeply muddled. Children can hardly be said to have much 'choice' about being born poor, and in most advanced countries the progressive incidence of personal taxation is largely offset by the regressive incidence of indirect taxation (particularly VAT); hence, the burden of taxation does not fall on firms and entrepreneurs.[16] Moreover, as shown in Figure 4.5, there appears to be a clear relationship between child poverty rates and the share of national income devoted to social expenditure. At one end of the diagram is the United States, where the child poverty incidence is high and social expenditure accounts for just over 2 per cent of GDP; at the other end are the Nordic countries with high social expenditure and low child poverty.

Consider differences between countries in child poverty incidence before and after taxes and transfers, i.e., tax credits, child allowances, social service provision and other benefits. In 2000, the child poverty rate in the United

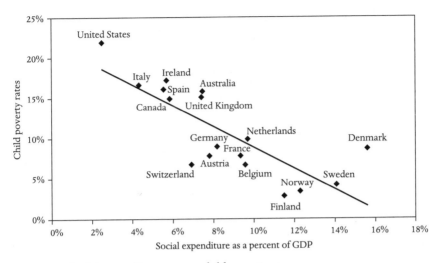

Figure 4.5: Social expenditure versus child poverty
Source: Figure 8H from: L. Mishel, J. Bernstein and S. Allegretto (2007)

States was 26.6 per cent; taxes and transfers reduced this to 21.9 per cent. The UK did somewhat better; before transfers the rate was 25.4 per cent but after transfers it fell to 15.4 per cent, an improvement of about 10 percentage points. Even more striking was the case of France which had a higher child poverty rate before transfers than the USA (27.7 per cent) but where transfers reduced it by nearly twenty points (7.5 per cent). At the top of the league tables were the Nordic countries as one would expect.

Much the same argument applies to health, although with an important difference. The United States and Britain differ radically from one another with respect to health-care provision. The former spends a higher proportion of its national income on health than any other advanced nation, yet health outcomes are relatively poor (as measured by life expectancy, for example) and coverage is far from universal. In Britain, the existence of a National Health Service provides universal free health coverage at the point of delivery, while in terms of health outcomes, although Britain is not the highest in the OECD rankings, it achieves results which lie near the middle of the pack.

Figure 4.6 plots health spending per capita against life expectancy at birth. Higher per capita health spending is generally associated with a higher life expectancy – as shown by the positive slope of the line, but the relationship is less pronounced at high levels of income. In this diagram, the USA is the exceptional case – it has the highest per capita level of spending (about twice the average for the OECD), yet life expectancy at birth is about

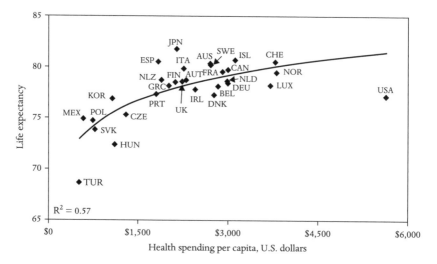

Figure 4.6: Life expectancy at birth and health spending per capita, 2003
Source: Figure 8J from: L. Mishel, J. Bernstein and S. Allegretto (2007)

the same as in Denmark (77.2 years) and well below the average for the OECD. Other indicators of health outcomes, such as infant mortality, confirm the above result. In 2003, infant mortality in the USA was 7.0 per 1,000 live births, the highest in the OECD. The US figure compares to 5.3 for the UK, and figures in the range of 3–5 for eleven of the fourteen other EU countries considered.[17]

Another interesting difference between the USA and the EU is the persistence of poverty in low-income families, i.e., the probability that once a family with children has fallen into poverty it will remain there for some years. An OECD study[18] shows that the Nordic countries display the lowest *persistence of poverty* and the United States the highest. In Denmark, for example, 60 per cent of families falling into poverty exit after two years and 70 per cent after three years. While a US-style 'flexible labour market' can keep people employed at very low wages, a Nordic-style 'active labour market' with strong safety nets achieves a far more desirable result. In general, the persistence of poverty appears to be strongly correlated with the level of inequality that obtains in any given country.

Inequality in Europe

Although it is sometimes convenient to treat EU welfare states as if they were all much the same, clearly, they are not – as the spread of Gini coefficients suggests. Several questions arise here. First, do inequalities across the EU-15 arise from differences between member-states, or are inter-state differences swamped by intra-state differences? Second, is there a discernible typology of EU welfare regimes and, if so, how might this illuminate trends in inequality – or, for that matter, trends in productivity and total employment which bear strongly on inequality?

The nature of inequality between different EU states and regions is important because the guiding principle of policy in Brussels has been to reduce the divide between richer and poorer member-states and their regions. The lion's share of the Union's 'own resources' is spent on the Common Agricultural Policy (CAP) and the Structural Funds. The CAP, whatever one thinks of it today, was set up on the principle that predominantly industrial member-states (e.g., Germany) should aid their poorer, predominantly agricultural neighbours. By the same logic, the Structural Funds targeted extra resources at the poorer regions of the EU.

Within EU member-states, the distribution of income after taxes and transfers is (as we have seen) more egalitarian that that in the USA. Hence we would expect the average Gini coefficient for the EU-15 to be lower (more egalitarian) than for the USA. By contrast, if one looks at income variance within the EU as a whole – say, as measured by the difference in regions accounting for the top 10 per cent of incomes and the lowest 10 per cent of incomes, the regional income disparities in the EU are very wide indeed – considerably greater than in the USA.

For example, Bavaria in Germany and Inner London in the UK are amongst the richest regions while Voreio Aigaio in Greece and the Portuguese Azores are the EU-15 poorest; the former have an average income more than twice as high as the latter.[19] Such regional differences reflect the fact that the accession countries have generally been much poorer than the EU 'core' – not just the Eastern and Central European states joining in 2004 but Portugal, Spain, Greece and Ireland which joined in previous rounds. Although some of the accession countries from earlier enlargements are amongst the fastest growing in the EU (e.g., Ireland), the catching-up process takes time. The United States has been an integrated economic unit far longer than has the EU.

Several studies have found that inequality is most marked within member- states, not between them. As one of these studies concludes:

> None of the indices show that more than 7.8% of overall inequality is attributable to the between-group component. In other words, more than 92% of overall EU inequality is attributed to income disparities within member states.[20]

The study in question refers to the EU-15 in 2003, not the EU-27 as it is today. Nevertheless, such a finding suggests that poverty reduction sponsored by Brussels could be better targeted. It is already self-evident that the provision of subsidies to crops rather than farmers is, from a redistributional perspective, spectacularly inefficient. It is perhaps less evident that member-states – rather than targeting specific sectors and regions – might do better by introducing incentives to modernize their welfare provision, expand education and health care, reduce poverty amongst children and pensioners, alleviate long-term unemployment and enforce progressive taxation regimes (starting with combating tax evasion by the very rich).

This is does not mean, obviously, that all regional policy is a bad thing. Clearly, there will be cases when large-scale investment is required in regional economic and social infrastructure. But such investment is best carried out in the name of regional growth rather than under the banner of poverty reduction. The current climate in Brussels of anti-Keynesian macro-policy and deregulatory micro-efficiency targets does not augur well in this respect. What the EU most needs is a set of common standards for social policy (with particular attention to 'best practice' provision in the Nordic countries), as well as comprehensive modernizing of its infrastructure, in order to speed the full economic integration of its newer and poorer member-states into the core economy.

Can Europe Afford a Welfare State?

It's amazing how many people seem to think the answer to this question is an unqualified 'no'. Globalization, one hears repeatedly, makes the world increasingly competitive, driving down prices and killing off manufacturing industry. If Europe is to survive – the argument goes – it must cut costs, particularly the tax burden shouldered by business. That means shedding our dependence on lengthy paid holidays, lavish unemployment benefit, generous pensions and other such luxuries we can ill afford. This argument is repeated by respectable economists and politicians in London, Paris, Berlin and Brussels. As we have seen, it is particularly popular in America where Europeans are seen as 'welfare addicts'. Nevertheless, it is highly misleading.

There are three main reasons why globalization doesn't mean abolishing high levels of welfare. First, it is simply untrue that we can no longer afford welfare. Second, the EU is not becoming 'less competitive' because of globalization. Finally, decent job protection, social insurance provision and universal health care correlate strongly with high levels of prosperity.

The EU is rich: the EU-25 has a combined GDP higher than the United States. Germany ranks consistently at the top of the world league in the value of total manufacturing exporters, while output per hour worked in the core EU states is as high as in North America. As Europeans become richer, it is a collective political choice whether to devote more of their extra income to private consumption or to public provision. In Britain under Mrs Thatcher, extra income went predominantly to private consumption while the rest of the EU, particularly the Nordic countries, spent more on social and economic infrastructure. Of course, higher public provision usually means higher taxation, but the bulk of such taxes are what economists call 'transfer payments', money put away during the good years to cover the years when we are unemployed, ill or retired. Ordinary working people may not like paying higher taxes, but we know that in the absence of collective provision, we might not save enough privately to cover our needs. Employers, too, cover part of these costs, but what they recoup is an educated, healthier and more productive workforce.

Meaner Pensions in Britain

Pension provision raises the question of inter-generational equity. Most EU countries rely on a relatively generous state-funded scheme, backed up by a mixture of private occupational pensions and Treasury top-ups. Here again, British 'exceptionalism' is evident. In 2002, when Lord Turner was first asked to investigate, Britain had one of the meanest schemes in the EU, comprising of a minimal state pension topped up by such private arrangements as the individual could find in the market. If you work in low-paid employment in the UK and particularly if you're a woman, the chances are that you'll have no occupational pension at all. So serious has the problem of 'pensioner poverty' become that the Chancellor has needed to devise ever more elaborate pension credits and other mean-tested benefits to deal with it. Without Turner-style reforms, it is estimated that by 2050 over 70 per cent of pensioners would require such benefits. Those wondering why so many ordinary Britons hate inheritance tax – which only affects 6 per cent of all estates – should consider the manner in which the rise in property values has cushioned the current generation of homeowners in their retirement.[21]

The Turner Commission rightly pushed for greater universality and generosity in basing occupational pension membership on an opt-out rather than an opt-in principle, and it insisted on indexing benefits to real growth rather than simply to inflation. Under Turner's proposals, occupational pensions would be government-supervised (the National Pension Savings Scheme) and contributions would come from employees, employers and from the Treasury out of general taxation. At the same time, the Commission saw that more generous and broader pension provision would be squeezed as the population aged and the dependency ratio increased, which is why it wanted both to push back the retirement age and to raise taxes.

But under pressure from Gordon Brown, Adair Turner quietly dropped the notion of increased fiscal funding, and he was also forced to make the NPSS a 'defined contribution' rather than a 'defined benefit' scheme. Not only will occupational pensions be less generous than initially envisaged, but Brown appears to have closed the door on 'hardworking Britons' retiring to a pension reflecting their final earnings. Moreover, under the new scheme, contributions are to be deposited entirely with fund managers in the City; the funds will contribute to boosting consumption and investment in the private sector. Part of these funds could of course be set aside for funding new public investment in much-needed economic and social infrastructure – everything from transport to affordable houses – but that opportunity has again been missed. It can be argued that if Brown, when Chancellor, had chosen this bolder course of action, he would have been accused by the press of diverting 'our' money to fund 'bigger government'.

As explained above, pension provision is not a 'real cost' in the same way as is government expenditure on new schools or private expenditure on a new car; it is a 'transfer'. We defer consumption today through saving in order to consume in the future. The state's role is crucial. Collective provision is required because individual market choice produces poor results, particularly if income is inequitably distributed. Exactly the same logic holds for regulating other forms of insurance; e.g., in much of the EU, the state provides universal health-care schemes; we are all required by law to insure our car against injury to another party and so on.

State pensions in most OECD countries (including the USA) were originally based on the pay-as-you-go (PAYG) principle, which means that when you retire your pension will be 'paid' by the contributions of new labour-force entrants. The twin pressures of pensioners' increased longevity and the babyboomer retirement bulge have put PAYG under growing pressure. Hence, most state pensions combine PAYG and 'funded' principles.[22]

In the UK, because occupational pensions are so important and are generally controlled by fund managers and largely invested in the private sector, ours is basically a privately 'funded' pension system. The great advantage of this arrangement from the point of view of the Treasury is that state pension liabilities remain low. This is why Brown was initially reluctant to accept Lord Turner's recommendation that state pensions be indexed to average earnings, or that a state-sponsored final salary-based pension scheme be made available to all.

But pure 'funded' schemes have their drawbacks. A market downturn can play havoc with a company pension scheme. According to *The Economist* in 2006, a small reduction in corporate bond yields raised the pension deficit for FTSE-100 companies by an estimated £30 billion. And if the company goes bust its workers may be left with nothing at all – as is the case for those not covered by the 2005 Pension Protection Act. Victims are justifiably angry when it was the government which encouraged them to go down the supposedly riskless private route in the first place.

Consider the following example from the United States. As Robin Blackburn notes, stripping workers of their pension rights has become a highly specialized field:

> American companies that enter Chapter 11 bankruptcy protection ask the courts to pass over their pension liabilities to the PBGC [Pension Benefit Guarantee Corporation, a government-run insurance scheme] which becomes responsible for the payment of benefits, albeit at a reduced rate – beneficiaries generally get 75 per cent of their pension and none of their retiree healthcare benefit. . . . 'Pension deficit disorder' has produced a new breed of financier . . . who specialises in extraction value from firms burdened with large pension liabilities, largely by stripping employees of their entitlements . . . At Chrysler in the 1980s, [Steve] Miller used threats from the company's creditors and bankers to extract concessions from the unions and the PBGC. As CEO of Bethlehem Steel in 2001, he closed down the company's pension plan, leaving $3.7 billion of unfunded liabilities to be inherited by the PBGC. . . . Miller went on to become chief executive of Federal Mogul, a car-parts maker with factories in the UK as well as the USA. In July 2004, the UK subsidiary of this company went into receivership and successfully shed pension obligations for over 20,000 employees with losses for a further 20,000. . . . By the late summer of 2005 Steve Miller was CEO at Delphi . . . with 180,000 [employees] worldwide. Miller's sign-on fee was $3 million and an annual salary of $1 million . . . while urging the great mass of employees to accept huge cuts – of 50 per cent or more – in their wages and healthcare and pension entitlements, saying that only this would save their jobs and help Delphi avoid bankruptcy. (Blackburn (2006: 48–9)).

As privately funded occupational pensions become riskier and their benefits unpredictable, so the young are turning increasingly to the property market where asset appreciation has enabled so many ageing babyboomers to retire in comfort. The new generation's eagerness to get a foot on the ladder before it's too late is one of the factors driving what has until recently been the apparently limitless upward trend in house prices.[23] And, if the trend continues, many other young people will never get a foot on that ladder; they will remain today's 'couch surfers' who pay £75 a week schlepping around London to sleep on somebody's sofa.

Decent pensions are not an unaffordable luxury, and the extra resource cost of providing them does not bankrupt the state. What is true is that, since the average worker under a PAYG scheme will be required to support more retirees, it is vital that PAYG be supplemented by own-generation savings if inter-generational equity is an objective of policy. In principle, it matters not a whit whether such savings are private and voluntary, or administered by the state. In practice, though, pension choices cannot be left entirely in the hands of private decision-makers since the poor and the young tend to under-save for their old age, while the rich may invest speculatively in tulips, property and other bubbles. This is a familiar case of 'market failure'. Pensions require collective provision. As citizens, we choose a system under which the state makes all citizens save during their working life in order to enjoy a decent retirement. We can if we so wish supplement state and occupational pensions with further savings of our own. We also have a say – or at least should have – in how those funds are used during the period in which they are in trust to the state; i.e., on whether they are fully returned to the private sector through the stock market, or whether they can in part be used to improve our environment and infrastructure.

Globalization and Competitiveness

A further fallacy is that globalization results in our countries becoming less competitive; i.e., we must 'cut costs' to keep up with China and other rapidly industrializing countries in our trade. Paul Krugman has rightly dismissed this view as 'globaloney'.[24] What goods and services a country trades depends not on absolute cost advantage but on its comparative advantage. China can produce both textiles and machine tools more cheaply than Germany, but China's comparative advantage at present lies in textile production (which is why Germany still exports so many machine tools). American or Italian workers who complain about the threat of cheap labour from China would do well to recall that in America, at the turn of the twentieth century, a flood of cheap labour from Europe helped make the USA the leading manufacturing nation; in Italy, cheap labour from the *Mezzogiorno* spurred the Italian 'economic miracle' of the 1960s and 1970s.

Of course, comparative advantage changes over time – as small textile producers in Italy have discovered. That is why the Multifibre Agreement was drawn up: to give advanced countries time to adjust by setting quota limits on production in the Third World. Thankfully, that Agreement is now history. It would be silly to continue protecting our less competitive industries since such protection prevents richer countries from developing new areas of comparative advantage while denying poorer ones the opportunity of moving up the industrial ladder. Two generations ago Sweden and Finland exported mainly timber and raw materials; today they excel at exporting mobile phones and other high-tech goodies.

Not only have leading industries in the rich countries changed, but these countries are becoming increasingly service-industry orientated. Despite the growth of call centres in India, service industries are far less globally mobile than manufacturing. Take the case of Britain, once Europe's industrial powerhouse. Today, a higher proportion of its GDP comes from financial services than manufacturing. Globalization may affect the sort of jobs we do, and doubtless has social costs. But it does not make us poorer, less competitive and less able to afford welfare. As Joseph Stiglitz has argued, it is not globalization per se that is the problem but rather an international order enabling globalization to be managed in favour of the rich and powerful.[25]

Although globalization is a problematic notion, there is an important sense in which it can weaken the welfare state. To the extent that traditional manufacturing relocates to low-wage countries and rich countries fail to adapt, labour's political institutions – notably, the trade union movement – are weakened. Globalization can weaken the welfare state *politically*, even in countries like Germany which continue to have a highly competitive and technologically innovative manufacturing sector. And when jobs are shed and costs cut, it benefits labour's detractors, at least as much as its supporters, who cite globalization as the culprit.

Prosperity Means Better Social Provision

The most telling argument of all is that social provision and prosperity go together – as statisticians say, they are positively rather than negatively correlated. There are a variety of reasons why prosperity implies good social provision (and vice versa). For one thing, as societies grow wealthier, the importance of public goods increases. Public goods are those things we consume collectively: economic infrastructure, education, health and protection from the unforeseen – including, incidentally, environmental catastrophe.

Put simply, when people are very poor they devote nearly all their energy to keeping food on the table and a roof over their heads. As they grow richer, they want not just more private consumption items like fridges and cars, but more things like affordable medical care and good public transport. Because public goods make everybody better off, their provision is part of what we mean by living in a civilized community, one characterized by social solidarity and cohesiveness. Societies which lack such goods – or where their provision is not universal but limited to the wealthy few – are more likely to suffer from anxiety, conflict and individual and social breakdown.

The causal relationship runs not just from higher prosperity to higher social provision, but the other way around. A higher level of provision leads to higher prosperity. This is because advanced countries need a healthy, well-educated and highly skilled workforce. Once again, the Nordic experience provides an excellent example: sustained levels of high social provision have helped strengthen the social fabric and minimize social exclusion under conditions of rapid economic transformation. Had it not been for strong social provision, countries like Finland and Sweden might have found it much more difficult to weather the economic shock of the early 1990s that resulted in part from the disintegration of their giant eastern neighbour.

Equally, there is an important point to be made to those who wish us to deregulate and privatize. To the extent that expanded trade or deregulation or privatization or similar policies make us on average wealthier, these same policies make the welfare state easier to maintain. Everything depends on how the new, higher, income is distributed. To the extent that workers disproportionately bear the brunt of expanded trade in manufacturing and increasingly in services, or of labour-market and product-market deregulation, the case for using the greater national riches to fund, in part, greater welfare-state expenditures becomes even stronger.

All this does not mean, of course, that European social provision is perfect in every respect. We don't know the ideal trade-off between employment protection and active labour market policies. We have only just begun to think about how to solve the long-term problem of pension provision and retirement. What we do know is that private sector market-based solutions cannot be the only answer. So the next time somebody tells you that we can no longer 'afford' the European social model, don't just nod your head in reluctant acquiescence. The argument is neither logically nor economically well-founded; i.e., it's wrong!

Why We Need a Welfare State

A high-tech industrial nation needs to devote more resources to education and R&D since a highly literate and skilled workforce is vital to maintaining the dynamism necessary to adapt in a globalized world. We are told repeatedly that the generation entering the workforce cannot expect the security and continuity of employment characteristic of an earlier industrial age. If this is true, then social inclusiveness and cohesion will depend increasingly on comprehensive social insurance against temporary job loss and illness. Basic research and development, too, must be funded, at least initially, by the state. Even in the USA where successive administrations have sought to 'shrink' the government's role, the state remains the main provider of education, and much R&D is financed either directly or indirectly from massive defence expenditure.

Equally, we know that the demographic profile of our societies is changing: in future, members of the active workforce will have to support a greater number of retired persons for longer, and the current generation will need to save more to fund its own retirement. As the economic cost of pensions grows, the principles of equity and universality can only be maintained by placing less emphasis on pay-as-you-go systems (which reduce inter-generational equity) and more on 'funded' pension systems. Privatizing pensions does not reduce their costs; it merely shifts it from the state to the private sector. Because individuals – particularly the young and the poor – tend to underestimate their family retirement needs, it is a matter of collective responsibility to ensure that adequate arrangements are in place. The alternative – the elderly forced into menial jobs and growing pensioner poverty, particularly amongst women – is increasingly deemed unacceptable in a rich society.

The arguments in favour of a welfare state are eloquently resumed by the Danish sociologist, Gøsta Esping-Andersen.[26] He argues that we cannot afford *not* to be egalitarian in the advanced industrial societies of the twenty-first century, not just out of idealism, but because securing a continuous improvement in human capital is vital to the knowledge economy. The minimization of poverty and income insecurity is seen as a precondition for an effective social investment strategy. A commitment to social citizenship – which many in the EU see as a basic right – means pooling social risks collectively. Broadly, the argument is that the 'three pillars' of the European welfare model – individual market choice, family solidarity and state welfare – are eroding asymmetrically. As the nuclear family becomes more fragile and the state faces a growing budget constraint, we become ever more dependent on the market. 'We can ill afford a future working population in which maybe 20 or 30 per cent are functionally illiterate and/or have failed to attain even secondary level education.'[27]

Europeans face a choice between adopting the 'Anglo-Saxon' (Esping-Andersen's term) or 'liberal' welfare model in which private welfare provision is the norm (or in the UK rapidly becoming so), supplemented by means-tested in-work state benefit to compensate for cases of extreme market failure. At the other end of the political spectrum lies the Nordic model, with its emphasis on universal income guarantees, active labour markets and social inclusion for marginalized groups. While the Nordic model is financially far 'more expensive' for the state, with individuals paying higher taxes rather than purchasing their care individually in the market, its success in promoting social solidarity – what Robert D. Putnam calls 'social capital' – cannot be doubted. Equally, in contrast to the UK, the Nordic model is far less financially centralized, as Jenkins (2007) observes. Somewhere in between is the 'continental European' model, strongly reliant on employment-linked social insurance. These three 'models' – liberal, Nordic and continental European – are of course convenient abstractions; one could imagine a finer, more nuanced gradation. But they serve to contrast important political choices.

In Esping-Andersen's view, the weakness of what he terms the 'Anglo-Saxon model' is that it provides little more than a thin cushion against the inequities of a deregulated labour market. Because benefits are increasingly job dependent and means-tested, welfare is minimal and there are likely to be severe gaps in coverage. Moreover, 'if the welfare state provides ever fewer benefits to the middle classes, their acquiescence to high taxes will gradually evaporate'.[28] This is an important insight, particularly in the case of Britain where social policy research in the 1960s revealed just how well the middle class did out of the welfare state and where, from the 1980s onwards, the middle class was told it could pay low taxes. In consequence the quality of welfare provision deteriorated sharply, and Britain's main political parties have done little to arrest the cycle of welfare on-the-cheap and inadequate provision.

In continental Europe – primarily Germany, France and Italy – the problem is somewhat different. Employment-linked social provision has worked well where the head of household remained in stable employment, and where employment came with strong guarantees making it, in effect, lifelong. These are features of traditional industrial culture which are rapidly disappearing. This model performs poorly for those whose connection to the labour market is tenuous. In Esping-Andersen's words:

> Passive income maintenance, combined with strong job guarantees for male breadwinners, becomes problematic with rising marital instability and non-conventional households. Strong protection for the stably employed combined with huge barriers to labour market entry has, in many countries, nurtured a deepening 'abyss' between privileged 'insiders' and precarious 'outsiders'.[29]

Moreover, because the traditional European model relies so heavily on transfers to combat social exclusion, it suffers increasingly from fiscal overstretch. By contrast, the Nordic model decouples social insurance from the head-of-household while discouraging social exclusion through high benefits to the unemployed, active training for job placement and services in kind for the elderly and the very young. And while remaining fiscally 'costly', it is far more efficient than either the Anglo-Saxon or the continental European model in combating social exclusion in the increasingly riskier context of post-industrial societies.

Finally, there is the question of risk-bearing. Like wealth and income, risks are inequitably distributed in the population and, as Beck (1992) has argued, advanced industrial societies tend to be riskier societies – a version of this same argument appears in Hacker's book *The Great Risk Shift*, discussed in chapter 6. The salient point in Beck's argument is that mitigating risk requires access not merely to financial resources but to knowledge. Technological development may be vital to economic growth, but it also creates new risks; e.g., from nuclear waste, environmental toxins and the like. While the wealthy may have the financial resources enabling them to mitigate the effects of risk, insuring against new forms of risk is not even an option for the person unaware that the risk even exists. Advanced societies provide safety nets both in the form of collective provision and by ensuring that all people benefit from a high level of education, so ensuring they are fully aware of risk.

A Very European Paradox

Throughout this chapter, I have given little space to the progressive critique of the EU, notably, that the Maastricht Treaty was designed by bankers and embodies a degree of monetarist orthodoxy that should warm the heart of neo-liberal economists. And, indeed, there is a strong element of truth in this argument which I have examined in detail in a recent book.[30] The macroeconomic architecture of the EU places excessive power in the hands of the European Central Bank (ECB) whose exclusive concern is inflation (unlike the USA Fed which has an obligation to balance inflation with growth and employment); fiscal policy, by contrast, is not centralized but remains with the member-states who are bound by the rules of a poorly conceived Stability and Growth Pact. The EU budget, much like the accounts of the corner grocer's shop, must balance annually and Brussels has no power to borrow abroad; Brussels cannot even use the profit (or *seignorage*) made by the ECB. In short, the EU is a monetary giant but a fiscal dwarf.

Such a situation is replete with danger as more than one specialist economist has observed; this lack of fiscal muscle leaves the Eurozone, whose members no longer have exchange-rate authority, entirely dependent on one-size-fits-all interest rate adjustments. Moreover, with the emergence of conservative political regimes in both Germany and France, and the growing detachment of the UK under Prime Minister Brown or any likely successor, there seems little chance that a coalition of reform-minded member-states will emerge to modernize the Union's economic governance.

At the same time, there is an apparent contradiction in the argument heard on the left, particularly in Britain, that the EU's corporatism and neo-liberalism must lead it to disaster. If one believes that neo-liberalism is a coherent capitalist response to the profit squeeze, then the dominance of neo-liberal orthodoxy in Brussels is perhaps unsurprising. Indeed, this would appear to be the position of some 'classical' Marxist economists, such as Meghnad Desai who argues that globalization is best understood as inherent in Marx's theory of capitalist expansion.[31] The significance of this Marxist form of explanation is that it identifies sites of contradiction and conflict which are obscured by globalization theory per se. While not unsympathetic to this view, I find it more satisfactory to argue that in an advanced capitalist economy, a strong state is necessary to maintain social cohesion through social spending, and capitalist profitability through modernized infrastructure. In effect, this is the thrust of my argument about Europe. Although the EU's neo-liberal defects are manifest, and the current political climate may seem increasingly reactionary and xenophobic, that is all the more reason for progressives to join forces in order to defend a more egalitarian and socially inclusive version of the market economy in which the public sector plays a key role.

In the following chapter, I turn to what, ostensibly, is something entirely different: the 'happiness' debate. I say 'ostensibly' because the notion that more money (and growth) can't make us happier is part of a broader critique of the consumption-driven social model associated with America and Britain. Although I think that socio-economic inequality is one of the many drivers of consumption, I do not think that the case for a more just society can be made on the grounds of 'maximizing happiness' as the next chapter makes clear.

5

Happiness and Pareto

> Annual income twenty pounds, annual expenditure nineteen pounds
> nineteen and six, result happiness. Annual income twenty pounds, annual
> expenditure twenty pounds nought and six, result misery.
>
> Mr Micawber in Dickens's *David Copperfield*

Happiness

Richard Layard's book in 2005 on the 'new science' of happiness was a best-seller.[1] In a nutshell, his argument is that as rich societies get richer, they don't become any happier – or, to use a fancier phrase, their 'subjective well-being' (SWB) doesn't improve. Of course, it can be argued that many economists (and other social scientists) have been saying this for years. When a very poor society gains extra income, it is likely that some people are raised out of poverty – and most would agree that this is a good thing. But when a very rich society gains an extra unit of income, that extra income is likely to produce a lesser benefit, or, in some cases, no benefit at all. Most economists agree that this principle of 'diminishing marginal utility of income' applies to national income as well as to individual income. Indeed, most economists – at least those who give introductory courses to first-year students – point out that national income measurement is a crude proxy of welfare, and that it needs to be supplemented by other indices, the best-known example being the UN's Human Development Index (HDI).[2] Saying that getting richer doesn't always make you much happier is a variant on this theme.

The philosophical basis of Layard's work is to be found in nineteenth-century utilitarianism, the principles of which strongly influenced the early development of neo-classical economics in general, and 'welfare economics' in particular. The nineteenth-century liberal Italian economist, Vilfredo Pareto,[3] is one of the founders of welfare economics, that branch of the discipline which analyses when and whether a change in public policy is a good thing. Pareto taught at the universities of Turin and Lausanne, and is credited with spelling out the conditions under which resources in a pure free-market are 'optimally' distributed; i.e., when, under given tastes and techniques, the market is producing maximum output with given resources and no one can be made better off unless someone is made worse off. (He also did research on income distribution and famously remarked that 80 per cent of Italy was owned by 20 per cent of the population.) Presently, I discuss whether 'Pareto optimality' is a helpful notion in a world where one's income and consumption status is judged relative to others, but for the moment it will be convenient to dwell on the story of 'economic happiness'.

For some years there has been a branch of social science called 'hedonics,' or the study of what makes us happy, and there is even a *Journal of Happiness Studies*. Daniel Kahneman, a psychologist who strongly influenced Layard, won a Nobel Prize for his work on what people 'maximize' when they make financial decisions. However, there are at least two problems with maximizing 'happiness'. First, classic utilitarianism is unhelpful about distributional issues. Unless one first *assumes* that extra units of happiness – call them 'utils' if you wish – are of diminishing marginal utility (which Jeremy Bentham did not), one cannot distinguish between a society in which each of 1,000 citizens possesses one util and a society in which one person alone has 1,000 utils and the rest have none. Even then, as Sen has argued, interpersonal comparisons of SWB between rich and poor may be highly misleading.[4] Second, the notion of happiness is notoriously slippery; like the proverbial hippopotamus sloshing about in glorious mud, it is far easier to sing about than to analyse.

Psychologists make quite a useful distinction between three levels of happiness.[5] Level one involves the emotion of pleasure or joy which we all know; the smile which accompanies meeting an old friend, the delight at playing with one's children or the simple pleasure of reading a good book or watching a beautiful sunset. One could multiply the examples, but the salient point is that happiness is a momentary emotion we all experience, recognize and can share. Level-two happiness is more cognitive and reflective. Looking back over today's efforts at writing or last night's dinner with friends at home, I am happy because, on balance, I feel it was successful and pleasurable. There may have been awkward moments. I found my brain particularly slow this morning, in part because of the wine drunk last night, but I finished the day having put to paper (or rather to computer) a number of thoughts which cohered reasonably well with the argument I am trying to make. And while by accident I may have spilled some wine on the tablecloth and the conversation occasionally may have at times seemed quite incoherent, on balance we all enjoyed each other's company and look forward to our next meeting. (I might have judged the event to have been far less happy had the entire bottle of wine accidentally been spilled over one of the guests!)

Level-three happiness is even more reflective. On balance, am I happy with my life, with the state of politics in the world, or with the trajectory of life, the universe and all that? Level-three happiness is not about an emotion, or even the result of a reflection on a limited number of events. It is more about life as a whole, about generally feeling 'good in one's skin' as the French say, or perhaps even about having attained a broad, mature emotional balance which according to some cultures is associated with tranquillity and wisdom.

The point to grasp here is that psychological studies of happiness based on survey data generally refer to the second level. When people say they are happy, they usually don't mean that they are experiencing a feeling of intense pleasure at the very moment the interviewer puts his or her question (still less, that they have lots of 'utils'). Nor do respondents generally interpret psychologists' questions as pertaining to the attainment of the Buddhist state of nirvana. The questions are usually phrased in such a way as to elicit clear, contextually relevant responses about level-two 'happiness'. Note that what Layard calls 'happiness', another well-known economist, Robert H. Frank, calls 'subjective well-being' (SWB), which is the more usual phrase used by psychologists to refer to level-two happiness. Nevertheless, hedonic measures are always problematic with respect to the type of questions asked, the way they are asked, the socio-economic status of the respondent and so forth. Social scientists involved in such studies doubtless do their best to control for the various types of bias that can affect survey results, but measurement in social science is notoriously trickier than in the physical sciences. With these qualifications in mind, let's proceed to the business at hand.

Money Can't Buy You Love

There may be an element of truth in the old chestnut that if money can't buy you what you want, you've been shopping in the wrong place. Nevertheless, there are numerous studies by psychologists, economists and others showing that becoming richer does not seem to make us happier, or at least not if we are already well above the poverty line. Broadly speaking, survey evidence reveals that as per capita income rises from the very low levels found in parts of the Third World to levels typical of semi-industrialized countries, people

Percentage Very Happy by Family Income

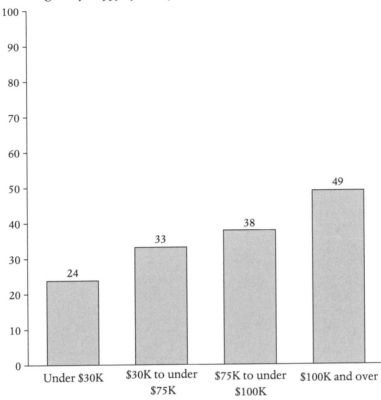

Figure 5.1: Household income and 'very happy' people
Source: Pew Research Center (2006: 3)

are generally 'happier', but once a country has become relatively prosperous, a further rise in the standard of living generates no corresponding increase in satisfaction.

On the other hand, as shown in Figure 5.1, in America the rich seem to be happier than the poor, which is perhaps not so surprising. The diagram, taken from a 2006 study by the Pew Research Center, shows the percentage of households reporting themselves to be 'very happy' rises with their income position. But the reader should be cautious: there are similar studies showing either no change in happiness as income rises, or suggesting that as income rises, people become *less* happy.

Figure 5.2 shows a 'happiness index' (as measured by the World Values Survey, 1990) plotted against levels of per capita income (measured in purchasing power parity US dollars). Clearly, people from poor countries feel

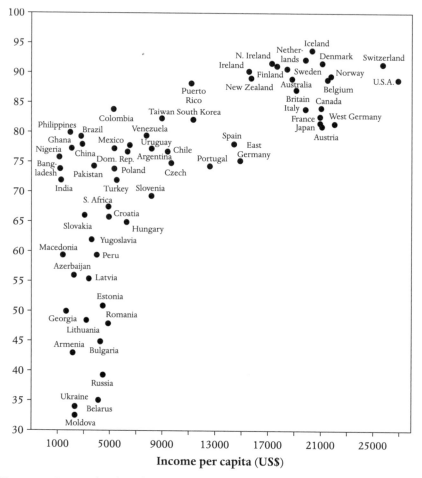

Figure 5.2: Income level per head and reported happiness for selected countries
Happiness Index
Source: Layard (2003a: 4)

themselves better off as they move up the income scale. But beyond some level of income – about $15,000 per head in the diagram – getting richer doesn't seem to affect happiness very much.

Crucially, this result – that as people in rich countries get richer, they don't gain in happiness (and sometimes actually lose) – holds for cross-sectional and time-series (longitudinal) data, and for both Britain and America. When 'happiness' is plotted against income for the past fifty years – a period over which real income both in Britain and the United States has risen more than four-fold – a similar result obtains. People consider themselves 'no happier', although their standard of living (including life expectancy, health, nutritional status, survival rate of children and so on) is vastly higher. Why is this so?

One answer might be that as income increases, so too does extra effort and work-related stress. While there is casual evidence for this hypothesis – e.g., traders and financial analysts in the City of London may earn a lot of money but suffer too from early 'burnout' – the weight of evidence points overwhelmingly in the opposite direction. The incidence of physical and mental illness is considerably higher amongst those in poorly paid, low-status jobs. Even today, in all the rich OECD countries, the poor are at greater risk of ill-health and die younger than the rich.

Another answer, an argument unpopular amongst many economists today but put by Alfred Marshall at the end of the nineteenth century, is that extra money income has 'diminishing marginal utility', i.e., an extra six-pence may mean nothing to a king, but to Mr Micawber it represents the difference between misery and bliss. The more money we already have, the less we value an extra pound, dollar or euro – if one already owns several Rolls Royces (the Sultan of Brunei is said to own 350) – what pleasure can there be from buying yet another? Indeed, this was the main justification for progressive taxation first proposed by Adam Smith and implemented throughout the developed world in the first half of the twentieth century. The few economists, like Lionel Robbins at the LSE in the 1930s, who resisted progressive taxation did so on the grounds that we could not prove scientifically that an extra unit of income was less valuable to a millionaire than to a pauper, an argument which is still kicking around today.

Happy Relative to What?

The most satisfactory answer to the question of 'why we are no happier' is generally given by psychologists. They point out that an individual's 'happiness' cannot be defined in a manner which leaves out his or her social context. We derive satisfaction from our situation because we make comparisons in at least two different ways; we compare our current situation with our past situation, and we compare our current (and past) situations with those of others. We tend to derive satisfaction if our status has improved within our peer group – and economic status is one of the dimensions of perceived social status. Equally, we derive satisfaction from being better off today than we were yesterday – although far less so from being better off today than we were a decade ago.

Take the point about time-comparison first. Why are we happier if we have recently been made better off, and less so the further in the past was our change in fortune? An important part of the answer lies in the fact that we adapt to a change in fortune. If we buy a new and bigger car, the novelty value will be strong at first but will wear off as time passes. A year from now we will have got used to our new car, and two years from now it will no longer be new. Our newfound satisfaction soon wears off, and to renew it we must trade in the old and keep purchasing, as indeed we are urged to do by ceaseless and ubiquitous advertising for every manner of new gadget.

When I see a picture of myself taken at my desk many years ago, I marvel at the fact that I once had to bash away on a portable typewriter and correct my mistakes with typing fluid. My experience of computers then was going to the university computer centre with a stack of punchcards and admiring the huge IBM 360/65 on which, with luck, the cards might be processed within a day or two. Today, both my laptop and my desktop computers are many times faster than was the old university mainframe, and infinitely more convenient to use – not just for solving mathematical problems but for wordprocessing, surfing the Internet and a myriad of other uses quite unimaginable at the time. In short, part of the reason we feel little extra satisfaction today from being far richer than a generation ago is that we have adapted to our new material goods and comforts and, in effect, take them for granted.

Comparisons made within our peer group are equally important. When I was a student, I did not need a new car or a new laptop – still less the latest pair of Reeboks, Levi jeans or mobile phone – because none of my friends owned those things. Of course, even in those days some people owned new cars and had a wardrobe full of jeans – but my friends were mainly other students living frugally on (now largely defunct) local authority grants. Then, just as now, we tended to judge our standard of living not in absolute terms but relative to that of our peers. But not only do our personal peer groups change over time, so do peer groups in general. Fashion industry advertisers make millions by convincing young people that it's cool to wear this or that brand, particularly when the accessories are advertised by superstar footballers, basketball players or other celebrities.

Perhaps what is most important to note about comparisons made with our peer group is that we derive our relative status from it. Put most simply, if Joe Bloggs's brother-in-law gets a hefty salary rise and Joe does not, he may feel that his relative status has fallen – or, equally important, Joe's partner may feel unhappy. Indeed, it is generally recognized amongst labour economists that trade unions are often more concerned with maintaining their members' income position relative to that of other skilled workers than with the absolute size of their increase in wages. The welfare economist's basic principle that a Pareto improvement is a desirable outcome – that as long as one person's income rises and everybody else's stays the same, society is better off – is not only deeply misleading, but flies in the face of today's evidence about how we perceive our well-being. Relative income matters!

Keeping Up with the Joneses

As long as our peer group is relatively modest in its perceived needs, the pressure to keep up with the Joneses is reasonably benign. But, as anybody who has raised children and/or observed their changed spending patterns over the past two decades knows, we (in Europe and America) live in a culture where the pressure to keep up has greatly increased – as has the potential social stigma associated with failing to do so. Our children's generation is probably the first to have been specifically targeted for its disposable income.

My generation was not entirely immune from such pressures; in the 1950s and 1960s, buying pop records, wearing the right clothes and going out to clubs formed a not unimportant part of one's personal image – and, of course, finding the right personal image is a universal concern for adolescents. The pinnacle of consumer achievement in such a world might be buying a second-hand Vespa (or, even better, a Lambretta); only in California did teenagers like James Dean own cars, and they lived in a world which could only be reached by cinema.

But for my own children things were different, just as for my future grandchildren the world of the consumer may have changed by another order of magnitude. I remember wondering why everything my kids wore had to have the right label, particularly when the label seemed to double the sticker price of the item. This subject became a delicate – and eventually dangerous – subject of family conversation, pitting the subjective well-being of youth against the budget constraint of their parents. In the context of a reasonably well-to-do middle-class home where both parents worked, the financial burden was tolerable enough. But doubtless, the adolescent consumerism caused genuine pain to less fortunate families than our own. The pain was occasioned not just by the children's spending; nor was it confined to the month or two in which the family bank account went into the red. How we parented our children through these times – whether we indulged them, or ourselves, or else adopted 'Victorian values' of dour frugality and penny-pinching thrift – will largely determine how our children deal with these matters, i.e., how successful they are as parents.

We have moved towards an 'aspirational' culture, one in which our aspirational consumption horizons are continuously being widened.[6] Moreover, this seems to be as true for the rich as it is for those who live on modest incomes. Take holidays: two generations ago, only the very well-to-do 'toured' continental Europe; today, average working-class families are looking beyond going to Ibiza, next year travelling to Disneyworld in Florida and the year after that perhaps Sydney or Phuket. Equally, the reasonably rich who last year perhaps were thinking of a cruise on the *QE2* observe the very rich hiring a NetJet to fly to some private and exclusive holiday island. With an aspirational culture comes the notion of an 'aspirational income' – the income we would need to feel that we can satisfy our desires.

The numerous surveys asking people what they feel they need to earn all reveal an interesting pattern. Aspirational income tends to rise in line with actual income. If you earn £20,000 per annum, you understandably may feel that £25,000 is what you really need to meet your needs, but if you earn £200,000 a year, survey evidence suggests that you will feel you can only survive on £250,000. Frank reports, for example, that for workers in New York City, their estimates of a 'minimum comfort' budget have approximated about half of the US per capita income level over the whole of the twentieth century.[7] As a country's income rises, our peers are better off and our view of the basic necessities we require, our 'minimum comfort' income, rises accordingly.

What all this means is that today, almost irrespective of our position in the income ladder, we are likely to feel we need more, and therefore to work even longer hours to get it. However, once we have more income, we soon adapt to our new living standard, take it for granted and feel we need to earn even more. Equally, the more you earn, the more I feel I must earn even more. Once on the 'hedonic treadmill',[8] not only do we need to run ever faster to stay in the same place, but there seems to be no getting off.

At the same time, one must be careful not to moralize about consumption, as though consumption were itself a bad thing and the solution to the anxiety and stress of status-seeking were simply to change one's lifestyle and to step off the hedonic treadmill. Doubtless modern techniques of marketing and advertising help internalize consumption norms, just as these same techniques play on the perception that maintaining one's socioeconomic status requires buying the latest Reeboks for the kids, an ever larger television, car, house or whatever. But we cannot therefore simply dismiss it as 'turbo-consumption' driven by the Moloch of capitalist greed. Neal Lawson, the founder of *Compass* and former adviser to Gordon Brown, appears to do just this when writing in the *Guardian*:

Welcome to the consumer society and the world of the turbo-consumer. It's a world driven by competition for consumer goods and paid-for experiences, of hi-tech and high-end shopping signals that have become the means by which we keep score with each other. . . . On these terms the new poor are falling far behind in an age when keeping up is everything. . . . So if you want the causes of crime then look no further than the impulse of the poor to belong and be normal. So strong is this urge that the failed consumer will lie, cheat and steal to 'earn' the trappings of success. In the world of the 'me generation', people become calculating rather than law-abiding in their overwhelming desire to be normal. This is crime driven by the rampant egoism of turbo-consumerism, where enough is never enough. And precisely because of its competitive nature, consumer-driven crime cannot be switched off through tougher laws.[9]

What's wrong here is not that the new poor are driven by rampant consumerism, but that they are poor; or, to paraphrase Bill Clinton, 'it's inequality, stupid!' Certainly, consumers may be short-sighted in their purchases, unduly influenced by advertising or subject to peer-group pressures to 'keep up'. But what is alarming is that the poor fall far behind (as Neal Lawson would also argue) because they have unequal access to education, decent housing, well-paid jobs and, in general, to the opportunities traditionally taken for granted by the middle classes.

Consumption is driven by many things, such that for most people most of the time the decision to purchase is entirely legitimate. We have access to a variety of goods – from washing machines to mobile phones – which are technologically far superior to those we could buy ten or even five years ago, assuming we could buy them at all. The migration of textile manufacturing to China and other parts of the Third World may mean that some workers in the West lose jobs, but Chinese peasants gain jobs in urban industry, Western workers find new employment and Western consumers benefit from the stable prices made possible by low wages in the periphery. Many of the components in my computer's motherboard are likely to have been assembled in Taiwan or the Philippines. But I could certainly not be writing this book without it, or for that matter without high-speed Internet access and a host of other goodies the modern world affords a family living in relatively prosperous circumstances in Europe or America. The reader will forgive this apparent digression, but it serves to make the point that attacking consumerism per se is hardly the point in rich societies where many people remain poor and opportunities for advancement are so unequally distributed.[10]

Addicted to Work?

The 'hedonic treadmill' provides a partial explanation of why we some-times feel ourselves to be addicted to work. In the UK and the USA, the term 'work–life balance' has gained wide currency recently. It seems to imply that we work too much and leave insufficient time for family, friends and leisure pursuits – that we must re-establish a more satisfactory balance between the apparent need for greater material comfort for which we work, and our emotional and spiritual needs as social beings.

Indeed, the evidence of the hours we work is worth considering. Americans work far more hours per year than Europeans, and, amongst European countries, the UK tops the list in hours worked per annum. This was not always true. In 1960, average hours worked were about the same in the USA as in Germany, France and the Benelux countries. Today, the data show clearly that while the average American worked about the same number of hours per year in 2001 (1,821 hours) as he or she did in 1979 – just over 1,800 hours per year – the average European worked fewer hours. For the Eurozone, the average number of hours worked per year has fallen from about 1,750 in 1979 to about 1,500 today.[11]

Some economists treat national differences in hours worked as reflecting 'social choice'.[12] But the high and growing number of hours worked in the USA and the UK are not in any sense a reflection of different countries' leisure preferences. Not only do Americans work longer hours per year, they work more years than their average EU counterpart. This in part reflects the fact that the average European has longer paid holidays and is more likely to have more generous retirement arrangements. It also tells us something about relative poverty on both sides of the Atlantic. A larger number of Americans fall below the poverty line than in Europe – reflecting far greater inequality in the USA – and many of the poor have no access to the social and/or health insurance generally taken for granted in continental Europe. Such people have little 'choice' about the optimal trade-off between work and leisure; they work long hours merely to survive.

Economists are addicted to abstracting sociological phenomena in the form of simple models. One such 'textbook' model is that minimum wage legislation severely limits the supply of relatively low-skilled and part-time jobs available in the service sector. In consequence, since industrial employ-ment is universally on the decline, the unskilled in America hold down some form of job while Europeans swell the ranks of the unemployed.[13] Since numerous studies show that the employed are always happier than the unemployed, it appears to follow that Americans benefit from their more 'flexible' labour market. On closer examination, however, this argument turns out to be nonsense. A number of European countries, particularly in northern Europe, have stronger employment protection laws, a higher minimum wage and an unemployment rate which is either comparable to, or lower than, that of the USA.

Another economist's abstraction which purports to explain this difference merits more careful attention. Psychologists regularly report that people are more 'rivalrous' about income than they are about leisure. In other words, if you and I are neighbours and your income goes up by 10 per cent while mine stays constant, I will feel unhappy. But if your holiday allowance goes up by 10 per cent, I am unlikely to lose much sleep over it. If this is true, then your extra income carries an 'external cost' (i.e., a cost not registered by the market) for me, but your extra leisure time does not. In effect, the market overvalues the social benefit of extra income relative to leisure, and so the market mechanism cannot be relied upon to strike a socially optimal balance between work and leisure. This argument provides a powerful – and often overlooked – justification for setting a legal limit to the working week and providing everyone with annual paid holiday leave.

A Weakening Social Fabric

There is a good deal of evidence that as job stress increases, as geographical mobility increases and traditional social bonds loosen, and as income inequality increases and the subjective perception of social status declines for those lower down the income ladder, social satisfaction falls; i.e., society becomes 'less happy'. The classic study of weakening social fabric is Robert Putnam's *Bowling Alone*. As Layard, Putnam and others have argued, if people live where they grew up, close to their parents and their old friends, they are more likely to be happy. On the other hand, if people are highly mobile, they feel less bonded to the people among whom they live; crime appears to be lower when people trust each other, and people trust each other more if fewer people are moving house and the community is more homogenous.

Consider the accompanying data. In Britain in the middle of the twentieth century, over half of people surveyed felt that 'most people can be trusted'; by the end of the century, this figure had fallen to less than one-third. Similarly, in the United States in 1951, when people were asked whether their lives were as 'as good, honest and moral as they used to be', about half of all respondents agreed; by 1998, only about one-quarter agreed. Naturally, such evidence is less 'hard' than, say, measuring

Year	per cent
1959	56
1981	43
1995	31

Figure 5.3: Per cent of population in Britain who think most people can be trusted
Source: Layard (2003c), table 3

the incidence of crime or mental illness. But it does tend to confirm the intuitively plausible hypothesis that, in the USA and the UK at least, a combination of factors – all-pervasive individualism, geographical mobility, lack of job satisfaction, and insecurity, along with social inequality – has left people less trustful of one another.

A somewhat more complex argument has to do with the relationship between social trust, cooperation and the cash nexus. An interesting Swiss experiment suggests that individuals assume collective responsibility when called upon to do so as citizens rather than as 'consumers'. In the early 1990s, citizens in Swiss cantons were asked to vote on whether they would be willing to have a waste dump in their community. Two social scientists did an attitude survey, revealing that, although such a dump might be toxic and would almost certainly lower property values, about half of respondents thought it their duty as citizens to approve the proposal.[14] Now for the interesting bit! The respondents were then asked whether they would accept the waste dump if they were given an annual payment equivalent to just over what the average Swiss would earn in a month. Although it was expected that this payment would provide an additional incentive, the proportion approving the dump fell from 50 per cent to 25 per cent.

The apparent paradox illuminates the manner in which we perceive our interests as citizens and as consumers. As responsible citizens, a considerable proportion of respondents would accept putting up with an annoying civic duty. But when offered a cash incentive, these good burghers in effect were being told to put aside their role as citizens and see themselves instead as consumers, the economist's utility-maximizing agent weighing up extra inconvenience against extra cash. In this role, for most respondents the cash reward on offer was insufficient. There is doubtless a moral here for those politicians who see collective services as commodities to be packaged and sold to 'customers' rather than citizens; to those who would 'modernize' the public realm of collective goods by introducing greater consumer choice in an artificially created market.

Psychologists' surveys yield all manner of interesting findings. A particularly well-known example (one of my favourites) involves a group of students at Harvard University who are asked to choose between the following two worlds:

- World A: You earn $50,000 and others get half that;
- World B: You get $100,000 but others get double that.

Most preferred world A. But then they were asked to choose between two further worlds:

- World C: You get 2 weeks' holiday and others get half that;
- World D: You get 4 weeks' holiday but others get twice that.

Most preferred D. In the first case, the choice of A in preference to B suggests that we are less concerned with the absolute level of income we earn, and more with our income status relative to others; one may be poorer in World A, but one is at the top of the ladder. In the second case, the absolute length of holiday outweighs the relative status of getting shorter holidays than others. This result may in part reflect the high value Americans place on leisure time because, unlike income, they have so little of it. But, mainly, it suggests that income status is a far stronger social marker than leisure status.

But think a bit more about the above. Although these students were not economists, they thought very much like 'textbook economic experts'. Their choices were clearly not made on altruistic grounds. In the example above, the utilitarian should prefer those outcomes where the collective benefits from both the highest income and longest holidays: i.e., choices B and D. But market-driven individual choice does not necessarily lead to 'the greatest good for the greatest number'; once again we are talking about the difference between choice in the individual and collective spheres. What people choose as consumers may differ from what they choose as citizens, and as the sphere of collective choice is narrowed or eliminated, social policy must suffer.

Happiness and Utilitarianism

In *Happiness: Lessons from a New Science*, Richard Layard wants to maximize happiness, and, although he recognizes that happiness is an elusive concept, he is unapologetically utilitarian. He argues that people, once they are well-off, get very little satisfaction from growing richer. Logically, this is a variant of Marshall's 'diminishing marginal utility of money income' discussed above, i.e., the richer you are, the smaller the satisfaction of receiving an extra unit of income. At the same time, Layard espouses strict utilitarian principles. 'The good society is the one where people are happiest,' he says, '[a]nd the right action is the one which produces the greatest happiness.'[15]

Various objections can be raised to the notion that maximizing happiness is either definable or useful, and there is a lengthy academic literature on this debate.[16] For one thing, happiness is not easily measured; indeed, if defined narrowly enough to be measurable, it may be trivial. The academic psychologist Daniel Nettle expresses the dilemma clearly:

> The problem with the concept of happiness is trying to make it do enough without making it do too much. If we define it narrowly as a certain type of feeling or physiological state, then we can, in principle, measure it objectively, but it is too trivial a thing to be the foundation of all public life and private decisions. On the other hand, if we define it broadly as something like 'the elements of the good life', then it is so broad as to beg the question, and certainly too broad to be measured in national statistics. Yet we intuitively feel there is something called happiness, something unitary but not trivial, concrete enough to strive for yet broad enough to be worth striving for. (Nettle, 2005: 5)

The utilitarian principle enjoining us to strive to attain 'the greatest good for the greatest number' is even more problematic since, unless carefully qualified, it can lead to impossible dilemmas: for example, torturing a prisoner may yield information that will save a hundred innocent lives, but does that justify the use of torture? A non-hypothetical and still-controversial example is the argument in favour of dropping the atomic bomb on Hiroshima and Nagasaki in 1945 – that it was justified because it led to an immediate Japanese surrender, thus saving millions of lives. For that matter, the same logic was used to support the 'liberal interventionist' principle applied by Bush and Blair in Iraq. Clearly there are a very large number of such examples, real and hypothetical, suggesting that Bentham's 'felicific calculus' (calculation of society's total happiness) is flawed. One is reminded of Bertrand Russell's remark to the effect that the Benthamites merely adapted Darwinism and imagined a world of global free competition in which victory went to the animals that most resembled successful capitalists.

The above are fundamental objections to Layard. At first, it seems odd that he adopts the utilitarian injunction because of his dissatisfaction with the selfish individualism of *homo economicus*, or textbook person. Look a bit more closely and you will see that Layard's 'happiness' appears suspiciously similar to neo-classical 'utility', and that maximizing total happiness (what welfare economists call a 'social welfare function') in the manner he proposes raises a number of well-known problems of rationality, transitivity and majority voting first explored by the Nobel Laureate, Kenneth Arrow.[17]

What are these problems? Put most simply, assume that there are three individuals (A, B and C) who maximize their own utility (or happiness) and four alternative ways of dividing $100. The alternatives are:

1. A gets nothing; B and C get $50 each;
2. B gets nothing; C and A get $50 each;
3. C gets nothing; A and B get $50 each;
4. divide the $100 equally amongst A, B and C who get $33 each.

It will be apparent that in our three-person world there must always be a majority against the egalitarian choice (i.e., choice 4). The above is a simplified example of what economists know as the 'Arrow Impossibility Theorem'. Although solutions to this paradox have been found by adding a variety of qualifiers (such as 'weak' and 'strong' preference orderings), the Impossibility Theorem is just as fatal to Layard's goal of maximizing happiness as it is to neo-classical welfare economics in general. As Joan Robinson once quipped, marginal utility is defined as an extra unit of happiness, while extra happiness is defined as marginal utility – an entirely circular state of affairs. To arrive at the egalitarian outcome which Layard wants, one must step outside of the world of utilitarian 'felicific calculus' altogether into one in which social solidarity and altruism are central values.

In fairness, Layard does briefly step out of the utilitarian world when discussing the work of Robert Axelrod, an American political scientist known for his work on the social evolution of cooperation. There is a famous game in the social sciences called the 'prisoner's dilemma' in which two isolated prisoners can either act on the basis of their self-interest alone, which results in each getting a prison term, or cooperate and go free. The prisoners are isolated, so each must 'guess' what the other will do. Economists usually assume that each prisoner 'guesses' that the other will act selfishly, so making an unfavourable outcome to the game inevitable. Axelrod[18] has shown that when subjects are allowed to play the game repeatedly, they will ultimately converge on cooperation as their optimal survival strategy, and that this convergence is actually helped by occasional instances of selfishness in which non-cooperation results in punishment. But having considered Axelrod, Layard eventually returns to utilitarianism, using the following argument. I leave it to the reader to judge its merits:

> In the West we already have a society that is probably as happy as any there has ever been. But there is a danger that Me-First may pollute our way of life, now that divine punishment no longer provides the sanction for morality. If that happened, we should all be less happy. So we do need a clear philosophy. The obvious aim is the greatest happiness of all – each person counting for one. If we all really pursued that, we should all be less selfish, and we should all be happier. (Layard, 2003c: 20)

Efficiency versus Equity

While Layard is rightly concerned that too narrow a focus on economic growth may obscure quality-of-life issues such as growing job insecurity, status anxiety and family breakdown, a crucial weakness is that he says almost nothing about redistribution. Having spent 250 pages arguing that: (a) more money does not buy prosperous people more happiness; and that (b) we should seek the greatest happiness for the greatest number; Layard conspicuously fails to close his syllogism by arguing that income and wealth need to be taxed at much higher rates if improved social provision (which he clearly favours) is to be financed. Instead, he posits that redistribution has an efficiency cost, i.e., taxing the rich will affect their incentive to work, and thus slow down growth. If redistribution involves a trade-off between a larger pie and a more fairly distributed pie, then the economist must therefore use cost-benefit analysis to determine the optimal trade-off for every public policy measure.

> The pie shrinks as it becomes more equally distributed. At some point this efficiency cost of further redistribution will outweigh the gain in fairness. At this point we should stop any further equalisation, even though the rich man's dollar is still less valuable that the poor man's dollar . . . It is against that background that cost-benefit analysis of other government policies has to be done . . . If we then analysed all the possible policy changes one by one, we would ultimately arrive at the best possible outcome, given our initial resources. (Layard, 2005: 136–7)

This is a disappointing conclusion to say the least. There is plenty of evidence to suggest that efficiency and equity may be positive, not negative, correlates (about which also see chapter 9). After all, in the twenty-five years following the Second World War, Britain and America achieved high growth and a more equal distribution. Moreover, it is quite impractical, if not absurd, to suggest that cost-benefit analysis using income weights could be applied to every public policy measure. Cost-benefit analysis is sometimes used for large public sector projects, but hardly ever with income

weights.[19] The use of such weights has been aptly described as 'redistribution by stealth' by various cost-benefit specialists.[20]

Put simply, economists posit an equity-efficiency trade-off when deriving
an upward sloping labour supply curve: the more you get paid, the more
'leisure' you are willing to give up in order to produce more output. There
are several problems here. One is that the slope of the curve is hypothetical; one can just as logically assume that more labour will be available at a
constant price (as, for example, does Arthur Lewis in his famous article on
economic development with an unlimited supply of labour). Another
problem is that very high CEO rewards, as I have already argued, can
neither be assumed to correspond to an equilibrium between supply and
demand, nor to reflect the CEO's 'marginal' contribution to output. The
market for CEO remuneration is quite simply inefficient. Under such conditions, even assuming labour supply generally to be upward sloping, redistributing income from overpaid CEOs in the USA and the UK to workers
would bring about an efficiency gain rather than an efficiency loss.

Equally, there is no evidence that redistribution – say, back to the equality levels last seen in 1970 – would have a significantly negative impact on
growth. No one currently arguing the case for redistribution would suggest
that we should move to a perfectly egalitarian utopia. The current debate is
about making income tax more progressive – so that total tax incidence
becomes progressive – and about changing the even-more-unequal distribution of assets. Post-war Britain from (say) 1950 to 1973 was both more
equal and grew just as fast. Several EU countries at present have a lower
Gini coefficient and are growing at least as fast as (and more sustainably
than) the UK and the USA. Frank (1999), amongst others, sets out a strong
case for a return to progressive taxation and sets out a proposed consumption tax scale with a top rate of 70 per cent (see Chapter 9, section 6).

Indeed, there are various studies suggesting that growth and inequality
are negatively correlated in developed countries. Corry and Glyn (1994),
surveying the post-war experience of OECD countries and dividing their
data into pre- and post-1970, showed that growth was higher and inequality lower in the former. Another study in Glyn and Miliband (1994), using a
dataset drawn from the World Bank and the OECD for industrialized countries and covering the period 1979–90, found that more egalitarian countries
generally have a higher rate of labour productivity. Alesina and Rodrick
(1992) studied sixty-five countries and found that where the top 5 per cent
and the top 20 per cent received a high share of income, growth was less
strong than where more went to low- and middle-income groups.[21] Frank
(1999) has argued that the evidence is now so strong as to be conclusive.

There are further weaknesses in Layard that deserve mention. For one thing, if the trade-off between equity and efficiency is accepted as self-evident, one can easily go on to accept a number of other related neo-liberal views: e.g., the Laffer-type argument that lowering taxes can be self-financing; that trade union attempts to bid up real wages are self-defeating and so on. For another, the view that money does not buy happiness is a two-edged sword. While it may appear to promote the case for greater equity, it can equally be used to enjoin the poor to accept their allotted circumstances and to hope for happiness in the afterlife.

What Layard does suggest is that in order to reduce unhappiness and the incidence of depression, our societies need particular forms of psychotherapeutic intervention.[22] I shall not consider the arguments for and against his proposals for tackling mental health difficulties by using Cognitive Behavioural Therapy (CBT), except to say that the mental health problem is undoubtedly serious and growing, and that it is clearly linked to growing job stress, status anxiety and poor social provision for those most at risk. Such problems cannot be tackled without facing up squarely to the re-emergence of vast inequality in Britain and America. The following passage from Glyn and Miliband makes the point succinctly:

> [W]elfare . . . depends on relative material circumstances as well as absolute levels of consumption. A sense of inferiority and social exclusion, which relative material deprivation engenders, clearly imposes huge social burdens on those affected. But their responses, which may include mental and physical illness and anti-social forms of behaviour, can in turn impose heavy costs on the rest of society in the form of health care costs, crime prevention and so forth . . . [R]edistribution can release society from some of these costs of exclusion, as well as liberating the economic potential of those excluded. (Glyn and Miliband,1994: 14)

Challenging the Economics of Affluence

Above, I refer briefly to cost-benefit analysis – weighing up the costs and benefits of proposed social policy. Orthodox micro-economic theory does not have much to say of interest about the social problems of affluence and inequality. Consider the epidemic rise of obesity in America (and Britain), something generally agreed to be socially undesirable because, quite apart from its psychological effects, obesity correlates with significantly higher rates of diabetes, heart disease, hypertension, i.e., with diseases which are life-threatening. Not only is dying younger generally accepted to be a bad thing, but it entails a diversion of economic resources to extra health care, a loss of economically active members of the work-force and so on.

One would imagine that, in general, economists would agree with every-body else about the perils of overeating, but they don't. Neo-liberal eco-nomics extols 'freedom of choice' above all else; since consumers are the best judges of their welfare, obesity can be seen as a rational outcome of informed choice. In his recent book, the economic historian, Avner Offer, cites an example taken from *The Journal of Economic Perspectives* in which the authors conclude that the net benefits of snacking and eating at the local fast food restaurant are positive.[23] The costs are measured strictly in terms of food pur-chase and preparation time, while the benefits are in essence the 'time saved' by eating junk food; since time equals money, the value of 'time saved' can be quantified by assuming that the subjects would have spend a percentage of the time saved in performing beneficial work and the rest in leisure, which can equally be valued. The reader might want to argue that such a study fails to take into account the short-sightedness of consumer choice or the asym-metry of information between the producer and the consumer: e.g., between the CEO of a fast-food chain who knows the health dangers of what's on offer and the typical low-income, poorly educated consumer. Not a bit of it, says the orthodox economist: consumers must be assumed ratio-nal, in possession of all relevant information and non-myopic. In an efficient market economy, *ex hypothesi*, consumers cannot make 'wrong' choices.

Offer dissects this sort of foolishness with the precision of a neurosur-geon. His book provides a trenchant and detailed critique of the neo-liberals' veneration of the 'market' in an affluent society. Much as with Layard, Offer's initial argument rests on the 'hedonic' premise that in a rich society, increased income and wealth has done little to improve the average citizen's sense of well-being. Crucially, however, he is concerned to qualify the conventional theory of rational choice. Modern consumption theory may tell us that individuals are rational, informed, far-sighted and prudent, but in reality we make poor choices every day. We smoke, get drunk, overeat, fail to save for retirement and so on.

Choice is most particularly fallible because individuals find it difficult to postpone gratification, to exercise what Offer calls 'self-control'. Normally, self-control is assured by a combination of 'commitment devices', ranging from personal rules about not eating too many chocolates to impersonal contracts (mortgages, pension plans etc.) which bind us to far-sightedness, to the social sanctions associated with everything from turning up late for meetings to being unfaithful to one's spouse. Because in affluent societies the flow of novelty and innovation may undermine the norms, conventions and institutions which ensure self-control, government regulation is required; for example, to ensure that standards of advertising are maintained, that the salt content of our microwave meals is disclosed or that the shiny new car we are about to buy is roadworthy. Nevertheless, he warns: 'The problem of commitment is difficult, and there are no other agents sufficiently accountable or credible to secure it. Government is the commitment agent of the last resort, and frequently of the first resort as well.'[24]

Perhaps the most innovative feature of his work is to locate market exchange within the wider world of acknowledgement, attention, approbation and friendship (both personal and political), what Offer terms an 'economy of regard'.

> Market transactions, even when they benefit both sides, are adversarial and potentially stressful, and advertising attempts to win trust with a simulation of intimacy. Cues of intimacy such as facial communication, testimonial and non-verbal gestures bypass the filter of reason. They are compelling even when consciously disbelieved. By saturating the public domain with false sincerity, advertising makes genuine sincerity more difficult. . . . [P]olitics has also embraced marketing technique. In political discourse, as in commerce, the clues of sincerity are used to evoke an emotional response. This exploits the social resource of good faith. (Offer, 2006: 359)

In the concluding chapter of his book, Offer is quite explicit about 'the Great-U-Turn', the growth of inequality in Britain under Thatcher which, although portrayed as necessary to achieve productivity and growth, was in reality driven by class conflict. As inequality grew and incomes stagnated for the less well off, dual-income families became common and, in particular, women were driven to find work. People at the top of the income scale amassed 'positional goods' such as several houses, with the result that many more people were priced out of the market. In the United States, where safety nets were thinner and two-income households were more 'vulnerable to the setbacks of unemployment, divorce and illness', personal bankruptcy exploded.

> Inequality is the reason why the United States, the wealthiest economy, scores so poorly on the indicators of psychological well being . . . [where] high productivity and longer working hours are driven by the risks of degradation like that already suffered by the majority of Afro-Americans. (Offer, 2006: 361)

Offer produces an impressively scholarly and rigorous critique of orthodox theory. Nevertheless, it is very much an economist's critique, one which is arguably too concerned with challenging the logical coherence of demand theory, at the cost of accessibility to the lay reader. It is doubtful whether opaque bits of shorthand like 'hyperbolic discounting' (the tendency to undervalue long-term costs and/or benefits) and 'commitment technologies' (described above) help illuminate the author's main argument. While undoubtedly staking out new and progressive political territory, Offer makes little use of classical political economy or sociology. The spectres of 'capital' and 'labour' may lurk in the wings, but we are denied the opportunity of observing these old adversaries struggle on centre-stage.

In this chapter, I have looked at some of the critiques offered by economists and other social scientists of 'consumerism'. In the chapter that follows, I return to the empirical evidence. In particular, I am interested in the fact that greater inequality adversely affects not just the lower half of the income distribution, but reaches up into the fifth, sixth and higher deciles, the traditional domain of middle-class Britain and America. If this is true and growing inequality is indeed corroding the American dream of rewarding hard work by upward mobility, the ideology of meritocracy – and particularly the version repackaged in Britain under New Labour – is in deep trouble.

6

What About the Middle Class?

In order to gain and to hold the esteem of men it is not sufficient merely
to possess wealth or power. The wealth or power must be put in evidence,
for esteem is awarded only on evidence.

Veblen ([1899]1998: 35)

Inequality and the Middle Class

Today, even the young professional (unless he works in finance) finds it
difficult to buy a home in New York or London. For Marx, there was little
to distinguish 'workers by hand and by brain'; just as the factory worker has
only his labour power to sell, so too has the bank clerk or the doctor, and
all workers must ultimately join forces against the system. In practice, of
course, workers who occupy quite different rungs on the social ladder are
unlikely to see their common interests. They may be victims of an ideology
which blinds them to their long-term interests – suffering from 'false con-
sciousness' as a rather crude version of Marxism circulating fifty years ago
might suggest – but we now realize just how strong ideology can be. Until
relatively recently, we could never have imagined that middle-income
groups – those worthy burghers of Middle England so assiduously courted
by New Labour – could see any element of communality between their
interests and those of the industrial proletariat.

Times have changed. There are fewer proles these days, and far more self-
employed, from white van men to lifestyle consultants. Moreover, starting
under Thatcher, some of them leapfrogged into trading in the City, property speculation or whatever, so that today they have 'loads of dosh' – more
than your average white-collar worker or middle-level manager with a university degree. In today's jargon, the upper middles (and some of the lower
middles too) are becoming super rich while the traditional middle class is
being 'hollowed out'. Significantly, the most recent book by the American
economist, Robert H. Frank, is entitled *Falling Behind: How Rising Inequality
Harms the Middle Class.*

As Peter Wilby recently put it, it's a bit startling when the headline in the *Daily Telegraph* business section reads: 'The backlash has started against income inequality', or the *Daily Mail* decries: 'billionaires who contribute so little to Britain'.[1] Inequality is an issue which will not go away and even Prime Minister Brown will need to accept that inequality is not merely about poverty. New Labour's fear that Middle England will recoil at the mere mention of the world 'redistribution' is being overtaken by events. One has only to look at America where the middle classes' perceived loss of status has burst on to the political stage. In the words of Barbara Ehrenreich:

> [W]hile blue-collar poverty has become numbingly routine, white collar unemployment – and the poverty that often results – remains a rude finger in the face of the American dream. In 2003, . . . unemployment was running at about 5.9%, but in contrast to earlier economic downturns, a sizeable proportion – almost 20% or about 1.6 million – of the unemployed were white-collar professionals.[2]

American Middle-class Woes

Psychologists are fond of telling us that the pain of taking a 25 per cent cut in income is perceived as far outweighing the pleasure of a 25 per cent gain. Nowhere is the phenomenon of middle-class anxiety more visible than in the United States where the self-identified middle class is proportionally far larger than in the UK. Figure 6.1 shows the growth in family income inequality (as measured by the Gini coefficient). Since the late 1970s when inequality in the USA was at a level comparable to the core EU states today, inequality has risen steadily. The inequality story in the USA is not exclusively, or even primarily, about the poor getting poorer; it is primarily about the rich getting very much richer and leaving the middle class (and those below it) far behind. Since 1969, while the proportion of families below the US poverty line ($20,000 for a family of four at 2006 prices) has risen only very slightly, the proportion of families earning twice the median or more – or roughly earning $100,000 or more at 2003 prices) has risen by 55 per cent. Moreover, inequality has risen far more within the group earning $100,000 per annum and above than for those earning less than $100,000.

In *relative* terms, therefore, there has been a decline in the income position of the middle-class family – roughly defined as a family of four earning between $40,000 and $100,000 at today's prices. Nor should it be forgotten that a large number of American families live above the poverty line but below the middle-class 'threshold'; i.e., have a family income of between

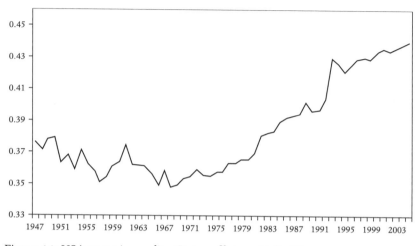

Figure 6.1: US income inequality, Gini coefficient, 1947–2005
Source: Figure 1L from: L. Mishel, J. Bernstein and S. Allegretto (2007)

$20,000 and $40,000. The sociologist Katherine Newman calls these the 'missing class' or the 'near poor' and estimates that there are some 57 million Americans in this category, more than twice as many as those living below the poverty line.[3] Anxiety is a defining characteristic of the 'near poor'; given the paucity of America's social safety nets, it takes only a costly illness or a job loss to plunge them into poverty. And, as the job market changes, anxiety is spreading up the income scale into the heart of America's traditional middle class.

Many American adults can remember a time when economic life seemed to be better. In his book *The Great Risk Shift*, Jacob Hacker recalls an era of an American middle class which had yet to confront downsizing and outsourcing, the days when factories did not relocate abroad and technology seemed less intimidating. People were laid off from time to time, but most workers did not expect redundancy to be permanent.[4] And when Americans looked for jobs, they generally found jobs with decent benefits.[5]

> Today, however, the social fabric that bound us together in good times and in bad is unravelling. Over the last generation, we have witnessed a massive transfer of economic risk from the broad structures of insurance, including those sponsored by the corporate sector as well as by government, onto the fragile balance sheets of American families. (Hacker, 2006: 5–6)

Many Americans share Hacker's concerns. In Flint, Michigan, the closure of eleven General Motors' plants and the loss of over 30,000 jobs during the Reagan years upended the lives of workers who aspired to, and had attained, middle-class economic status. Corporate America's lack of concern, expressed in the soulless jargon of managerial prerogative, is portrayed with folksy wit in Michael Moore's biting documentary, *Roger and Me*. Further east, in Rochester, New York, the few remaining employees at Kodak look back to the days when companies provided in-house health programmes, profit-sharing, company housing, and even generous pensions.

Of course, anxiety about the economy is nothing new. In all capitalist countries, economic downturns have caused people to hark back to older, more secure ways of life. What is most striking about today's anxiety is that it has emerged despite a robust economy. Americans have worried in times of 8 or 10 per cent unemployment, but why at 5 per cent or less? A Gallup survey published in March 2006 reported that 'Americans continue to resist giving the nation's economy positive ratings.' According to one report, in 2005 three times as many Americans were afraid they would lose their jobs than during the recession in the early Reagan years.

During the US Congressional elections in November 2006, jobs, the economy and health care ranked high amongst the key electoral issues; it was not just Iraq, but economic insecurity at home, which helped the Democrats to victory. In Washington, Congress is apparently eager to address these worries; the Democratic majority is critical of the Republicans' 'ownership society' and wants to raise the minimum wage. Charles Rangel, the Democratic chairman of the House Ways and Means Committee, derided the White House plan to move responsibility for health care from employers to individuals. The Republican Senator, John McCain, has warned: 'My children and their children will not receive the benefits we will enjoy. That is an inescapable fact, and any politician who tells you otherwise, Democrat or Republican, is lying.' In the 2008 race for the White House, the economy will be a prominent theme. Economic populism is back with a vengeance.[6]

The Republicans' 'personal-responsibility crusade' which produced measures like Health Savings Accounts, giving families greater discretion in their health-care spending, and which supports the partial privatization of Social Security, has not empowered the middle class by granting them a sense of greater control or wider choice. On the contrary, many Americans perceive such measures as increasing their general anxiety.

While Americans have profited from a housing boom, house prices are now falling and those extra mortgages are proving difficult to repay. Share prices in early 2007 may have been at an historic high (although not after adjusting for inflation), but the top 10 per cent of income earners account for 80 per cent share ownership and the paper profits can easily vanish.

Middle-class investors are only too aware of what happened in 2001. Middle-class America today suffers a sense of ever-increasing financial risk, exacerbated by neo-liberal measures that result in still more insecurity. At the core of this anxiety lies the fact that US labour productivity growth since 1973 has grown faster than median family income. Real average hourly earnings have declined by 3 per cent over the past thirty years, and Americans have made up for this by working longer hours.

Pensions are another worry. Two decades ago, more than 80 per cent of larger firms in the USA provided 'defined-benefit' plans, i.e., traditional pensions. These days, less than a third do. When individuals are responsible for their own retirement (as are most Americans), they confront the ups and downs of the economy on their own. Neither tax-advantaged plans like 401(k) – a tax-deferred retirement plan dating from 1980 sponsored by private employers much like the 'Stakeholder' plan introduced in the UK in 2001 – nor company stocks are insured, and investors can lose nearly everything, as shareholders in Enron learned.

US advocates of the ownership society often point with pride to the fact that the average holding in a 401(k) account is $47,000. But the median figure – that is, for the typical participant in such plans – is a far less impressive $13,000. Believing they will eventually see high returns, investors willingly accept the loss of their old pension guarantees. Employers encourage pension privatization in order to shed obligations, and Wall Street has been delighted to oblige. The amount of money invested in private 401(k) pension plans rose from $400 billion in the 1980s to $2 trillion at the end of the 1990s.

But perhaps the most important reason for middle-class dissatisfaction is that, as middle-class incomes have become more volatile, the American dream of 'economic security' has receded. In Hacker's words:

> Economic insecurity isn't just a problem of the poor and uneducated, as most assume. Increasingly, it affects . . . educated, upper-middle-class Americans – men and women who thought that by staying in school, by buying a home, by investing in their 401(k)s, they had bought the ticket to upward mobility and economic stability. Insecurity today reaches across the income spectrum, across the racial divide, across lines of geography and gender. It speaks to the common 'us' rather than to the insular, marginalized 'them.' [7]

Is Inequality just about Skills and Education?

Take the case of Bill and Terry Will, described in a piece in *USA Today*.[8] Together they earn about $70,000 a year; a tidy sum which places them solidly in the ranks of the middle class. Nevertheless, they find it a struggle to provide for their family and pay off their credit card debt. Terry, forty-four, is a nurse and Bill, fifty, manages a warehouse that ships food and supplies to other countries.

The Wills have five children living at home, aged two to seventeen. They budget every penny and have no savings, no college fund and no retirement nest-egg. Like many middle-class families – often broadly defined as those earning $40,000 to $99,999 at current prices – the Wills have little room to manoeuvre if something unexpected comes up. They barely survived when Bill's job as an oil company sales manager was eliminated in 1999. They came close to losing their home and nearly ended up in bankruptcy before they went to a non-profit credit counselling agency for help. What happened to the Wills is being repeated in legions of middle-class homes across the USA. With personal bankruptcy at an all-time high, it's mostly the middle class that gets trapped: according to a recent study 92 per cent of the record 1.6 million personal bankruptcies in 2003 were middle class.

> 'Costs are rising quickly, and benefits that used to be provided by employers now must be provided by workers themselves, including health insurance and retirement,' says Christian Weller, an economist at the Economic Policy Institute. The average employee contribution toward health insurance premiums was $2,412 for family coverage in 2003. Housing also is eating up more of the average family's budget. About 80 per cent of low- and moderate-income homeowners spent more than half of their income on housing in 2001 Moreover, middle-class families are taking on ruinous mortgages just to find a home in the right ZIP codes.[9]

A much-repeated 'explanation' for growing inequality in the USA (and to a lesser extent in the UK) is that the 'new economy' requires a higher level of 'human capital', that is, a more educated workforce. According to this argument, the growth in inequality is no more than a reflection of the growing gap between the skilled and the unskilled; the latter are increasingly unable to compete in today's environment and are therefore paid less. Right-wing pundits typically add that inequality is about inadequate personal responsibility. If individuals 'make the wrong educational choices', it is hardly surprising that they fail to share the rewards offered by the new economy.

There are good reasons to be sceptical about such arguments. First, although the 'new economy' is commonly associated with the rise of IT in the 1990s, the period in which inequality first started to soar was under Reagan in the 1980s when technological change (measured as labour productivity growth) was no faster than it had been in the 1970s.

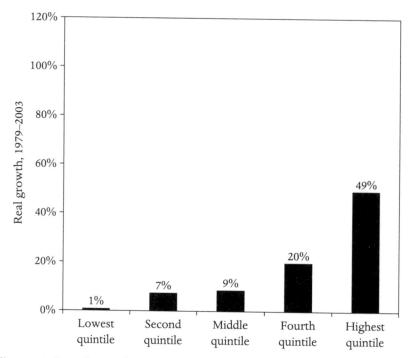

Figure 6.2: Growth in real US household income, 1979–2003
Source: Figure 10 from: L. Mishel, J. Bernstein and S. Allegretto (2007)

Moreover, while it is generally true that technological change is associated with a greater demand for education and skills, technological change took place continuously over the twentieth century as did the educational upgrading of the workforce. The 'technology requires skills' explanation does not tell us why inequality fell for nearly thirty years after the Second World War and subsequently rose again.

> [The] notion that technology has been bidding up the wages of the skilled relative to the unskilled does not accord with many of the basic facts . . . The wages of skilled men, [whether] defined as white-collar, college educated or 90th percentile workers, were flat or in decline from the mid-1980s to the mid-1990s . . . The dramatic fall of entry-level wages for all college graduates in the early 1990s, for both men and women, reinforces this point.[10]

What's Happened to Middle-class Incomes?

One of the most authoritative sources on what has happened to income and employment in the United States is the Economic Policy Institute's series of

Period	Productivity	Median family income
1947–73	103.7%	103.9%
1973–2004	75.7	21.8
1995–2000	13.2	11.3
2000–05	16.6	−2.3

Figure 6.3: The growth of real US median family income, 1947–2005
Source: Table 1.4 from: L. Mishel, J. Bernstein and S. Allegretto (2007)

publications entitled *The State of Working America*.[11] Figure 6.2 shows that between 1979 and 2003 – roughly the period from Ronald Reagan's election to that of Bill Clinton – the growth in real household income in America was very poorly distributed. Families in the top fifth of the distribution (highest quintile) saw their incomes grow by nearly 50 per cent on average, while the bottom quintile experienced insignificant growth. (By contrast, in the period 1947–73, real income of the bottom fifth grew by 3 per cent annually, compared to 2.5 per cent for the top quintile.)[12] Taking the 'middle quintile' (middle fifth) as most typically middle class, then the 9 per cent real increase in income over the thirty-year period translates into an annual growth rate of only 0.3 per cent. Note that the middle quintile spans the approximate household income range of $46–70,000 (in 2005 dollars), with the median household in this quintile earning just over $50,000.[13] For the population as a whole, median household income in the USA was approximately $46,000 in 2005.

Figure 6.3 shows that real US median family income grew less quickly than labour productivity after 1973 than in the post-war period. Strikingly, in the first five years of the new millennium, productivity rose by 16.6 per cent while median family income fell by 2.3 per cent. Although US labour's output per hour rose, the fruit of that labour went elsewhere. This is what is meant when one says that America has experienced a 'decoupling' of wages and productivity. The median family – the one exactly halfway between the top and bottom families – was worse off in 2005 than in 2000. Moreover, when median family income growth is adjusted for changes in family size, although this explains the negative growth in 2000–05, the overall result shows an *annual growth rate of less than 1 per cent* since 1973. At this rate it would take about seventy-five years for the median family to double its real income.

Has the US Middle Class Become Less Productive?

In Figure 6.4, the middle column shows the annual rate of income growth for a family in the middle fifth – the middle 20 per cent – of the income distribution, bearing in mind that average family size has fallen somewhat over the period. Even allowing for this fact, year-on-year growth of income for the median family in America is low. The family at the very heart of the middle class has done poorly. Note that a fall in family size, although generally associated with increased income, can take place as a result of *decreased* income too, i.e., where both parents work in order to generate sufficient income, the cost of having more children rises, and of course raising more children in middle-class America generally involves substantial extra outlays on education.

A further feature of America at the start of the new century is that, since the recession in 2001, recovery has not been accompanied by a strong fall in unemployment. Unlike previous recessions in which jobs and incomes recovered reasonably quickly, incomes – at least for the middle class – have not recovered and the pace of job recovery has stagnated. While many commentators have attributed 'jobless recovery' to the rapid increase in US labour productivity figures in the recent past, Mishel et al. (2005) find this too mechanical an explanation since, if output is growing and jobs are stagnant, productivity must be growing by definition. The key feature of the current period is that productivity gains have not been going to workers; rather, they have gone almost exclusively to income earners at the top of the distribution.

Between the end of 2001 and mid-2004, not only have there been few jobs created but real hourly wages have stagnated. An analysis of expanding and contracting industries since 2001 reveals, worryingly, that expanding ones generally pay lower wages than the latter.[14]

> Another major indicator of the unbalanced pattern of growth during this downturn and recovery comes from the fact that capital incomes (profits and interest) has grown very quickly by historical standards, while total compensation has been flat. . . . the vast majority (84.6%) of the real income growth in the corporate sector since the first quarter of 2001 has accrued to capital income, a hugely disproportionate share when considering that capital income comprised just 16.6% of total corporate income when the recession started in early 2001.[15]

In everyday language, while McJobs have increased, corporate bosses generally have been downsizing and outsourcing while paying themselves the extra rewards.

Growing Middle-income Anxieties

Not only have middle-income families in the USA been falling behind in relative income terms, but they face other problems too. Fewer employment

Period	Unadjusted for family size*	Adjusted for family size**	Difference (adjusted minus unadjusted)
1967–73	2.2%	2.8%	0.6%
1973–79	0.0	0.5	0.5
1979–89	0.2	0.5	0.3
1989–2000	0.6	0.6	0.0
2000–04	−0.6	−0.5	0.1

Figure 6.4: Annual US family income growth for the middle fifth, unadjusted and adjusted for family size, 1967–2004
* the other tables in the book, we use the CPI-U to deflate income here to be consistent with the size-adjusted measures, which also use that deflator.
** Annualized growth rate of family income of the middle fifth, divided by the poverty line for each family size.
Source: Table 1.5 from: L. Mishel, J. Bernstein and S. Allegretto (2007)

opportunities mean that there is unemployment for some and fewer hours for others. Since 1979, middle-income families had been working more than in the past. Between 1979 and 2000, married couples with children in the middle-income fifth worked 500 hours more per annum, the equivalent of 12.5 more weeks per year, i.e., more family members – particularly wives – have spent more time in some form of employment.[16] The growing disparity between average weekly hours for all workers and average weekly hours worked by middle-income families with children is seen clearly in Figure 6.5. Taking 1975 as the reference year (index = 100), although the average weekly hours put in by all workers varied somewhat over the period 1975–2003, the figure remained relatively stable. However, it rose by about 10 per cent over the period for all families, while middle-income families put in about 25 per cent more hours over the period. Of course, this result might simply reflect increasing family size, but since we know that family size was falling over the period, it follows that more family members (particularly wives) were putting in longer hours. Middle-income families – striving to maintain middle-class consumption norms – were putting in the longest hours.

There are several other dimensions to growing middle-class anxieties worth mentioning: notably, the fact that it took the median family far longer to recover from a recession at the end of the century than in the 1950s, the rise in debt as a proportion of disposable income, the erosion of health care and pension provision in the private sector and, closely associated to the latter, the decline in trade union membership and in union bargaining power (affecting both blue- and white-collar workers), and the perception of growing job insecurity.

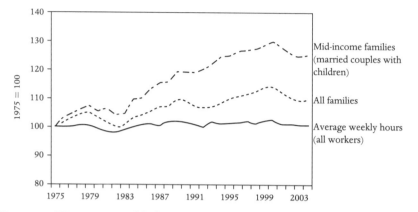

Figure 6.5: US average weekly hours compared to family work hours, 1975–2004
Source: Figure 1W from: L. Mishel, J., Bernstein and S. Allegretto (2007)

Figure 6.6 shows the length of time taken for the median family to recover its initial real income position after a recession. Income losses over downturns in the 1950s and 1960s were quickly made up in two to three years. But starting in the late 1970s until today, recovery has been taking far longer; following the income peak in 1989 and the subsequent recession, it took until 1996 (seven years) for the median family to recover in real terms. Since the income peak in 2000 and the subsequent recession, the 'jobless' upswing means that the recovery this time may take even longer. At the time of writing, median family income has still not recovered in real terms; meanwhile, growth of the US economy is faltering and recession looms.

The period 1979–2003 also saw a decline in private-sector, employer-provided health insurance and pension coverage. For all workers, the proportion in the private sector benefiting from employer-provided health insurance coverage fell from 69.0 per cent in 1979 to 56.4 per cent in 2003; for middle-income earners, the fall was from 74.7 per cent to 62.0 per cent over the same period. Employer-provided pension coverage for all private sector workers was 50.6 per cent in 1976 and 45.9 per cent in 2003; the corresponding figures for middle-income earners were 52.3 per cent and 48.6 per cent . One should bear in mind too that over the same period, the proportion of workers in public sector employment (where health insurance and pensions are nearly universal) fell. Equally, health insurance grew more expensive in real terms, while pension benefits were squeezed.[17] Debt levels as a part of household disposable income in 2003 were at an all-time high.

> All debt rose from about 20% of disposable income at the end of World War
> II to over 60% by the early 1960s. Overall debt levels then remained roughly

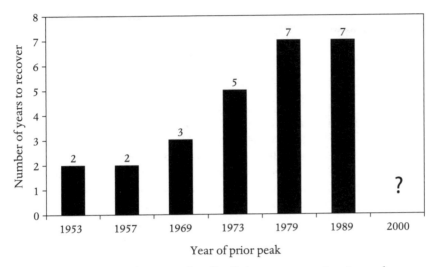

Figure 6.6: Years it took for US median family income to regain prior peak
Source: Figure 1C from L. Mishel, J. Bernstein and S. Allegretto (2007)

constant through the mid-1980s, when they began to increase rapidly again. By 2003, overall debt was 114.5% of annual disposable income.[18]

A further factor in the growth of middle-class insecurity has been the fall in trade union membership in the USA over the past thirty years. The percentage of the workforce represented by unions in the 1970s was just under one-quarter; it began to decline in the early 1980s and has continued to do so until, today, it stands at about 13 per cent or half of its historical level. This fall has affected unionized and non-unionized labour alike, since higher union wages have the effect of pulling up wages for non-union workers as well.

The 'union premium' relates not merely to wages but to non-wage benefits, i.e., health insurance, pensions and holidays. Unionized workers in the USA are 28 per cent more likely to be covered by employer-provided health insurance than their non-union equivalents, and benefits coverage is generally broader with fewer deductibles and extending into retirement. More than 70 per cent of union workers in the USA have employer-provided pensions (versus 44 per cent of non-union workers), and these pension plans are far more likely to be of a defined-benefit nature. Union workers also get longer holidays, and they enjoy 14 per cent more paid time off than their non-union counterparts.[19] Of course, union membership is more strongly associated with blue-collar than white-collar occupations, but there is little doubt that the decline of unions has – if only through the 'union premium' effect – had a negative impact on white-collar workers.

> Attitudes towards job security in the USA have been measured by polling data over the years. A typical indicator is the share of workers who answered 'not at all' when asked about whether they worried they might lose their job within the next 12 months. Whereas in 1978, 71% of workers thought is extremely unlikely they would lose their jobs, by 1996 the figure had fallen to 60%, with much of that drop coming in the 1990s, and the figure rose still further with the recession at the beginning of the new century. Moreover, there appears to have been a considerable increase in the number of workers feeling pessimistic about finding a comparable job if they should lose their present job. Between 2000 and 2002, the number of workers who felt that it would not be at all easy to find comparable work if they lost their current job rose from 29% to 39%.[20]

The changing nature of job insecurity is well-summarized in a recent study by Kusnet, Mishel and Teixeira who find that employees at every level are concerned not just about hanging on to their job and whether they will find another one:

> For most people today, their greatest anxiety is not that they will lose their job and be unable to find another, and their greatest hope is not that they will be able to get and keep a job. Instead, they have more complex concerns: Will their jobs be outsourced to a subcontractor or off-shored to another country? Will a full-time, permanent job be converted into a part-time or temporary job? Will their health insurance be cut back or their premiums or co-payments increased? Will they receive regular raises or earn merit raises? Will they be able to stretch their paychecks to cover their family's expenses? Will their employer continue to provide pensions that offer guaranteed retirement benefits? And can they keep their skills current so that they can hold onto their current job and qualify for a promotion or for a new and better job? These uncertainties are more complicated than what worried their parents and can be summarized as a concern about both regular wages and other aspects of 'job quality.'[21]

How Does the US Middle Class Compare Internationally?

Figure 4.3 in chapter 4 compared Gini coefficients in selected high-income countries while figure 4.4 ranked countries by the ratio of 90th percentile (rich) income to 10th percentile income. The USA and the UK scored poorly

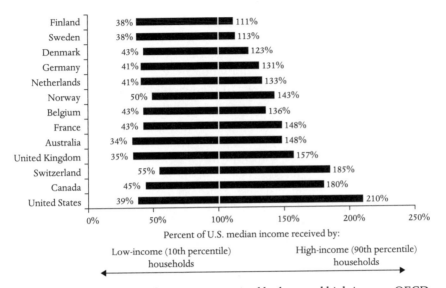

Figure 6.7: Share of US median income received by low- and high-income OECD households, 2000
Source: Figure 8D from: L. Mishel, J. Bernstein and S. Allegretto (2007)

on both measures of inequality, whether in comparison to all OECD countries or in comparison to the EU-15.[22] Figure 6.7 considers US median income in relation to low-income and high-income households, not just for the USA but for thirteen other industrialized countries. Implicitly, US median family income is being taken here as the 'middle-class norm' for all the countries shown. (Income comparisons use official exchange rates.)

In 2000, low-income (10th percentile) households in the USA earned an income of only 39 per cent of the median household income; by contrast, high-income (90th percentile) households earned 210 per cent that amount. When US median income is taken as the basis of comparison for the other thirteen countries, the results are revealing. Canada, for example, has a slightly lower income per capita than the USA, but the 10th percentile household – i.e., the household 10 percentage slices from the bottom – earns 45 per cent of US median household income. Of the countries shown, only in Britain and Australia does the 10th percentile household earn less than its counterpart in the USA. At the other end of the scale, however, high-income households (90th percentile) in the USA earn over twice as much (210 per cent) as the median household.

This is not the case elsewhere. For the countries shown, the 90th percentile household income is generally about 1.4 times as high as US median household income. This is true not merely because other countries have a lower income per capita; in Norway, for example, per capita income is slightly higher than the USA. In general, then, it would appear that for most countries, lower-income households (i.e., those between the 10th decile and the median) are closer to the US 'middle-class norm' than are low-income households in the USA itself. One should bear in mind, too, that this comparison does not take account of the fact that most of the countries shown provide higher levels of social and economic support (e.g., health coverage, pensions, unemployment benefit) to their residents than does the USA.

Looking at trends in income distribution in the period 1980–2000, Mishel et al. (2005) find it equally interesting that the most regressive shift has come in the USA and the UK, where the Gini coefficients have risen by 0.05 and 0.078 respectively over the period, i.e., the income distribution has become less equal. While the USA and the UK are not alone in experiencing growing Gini-inequality, the same is not true of all OECD countries; Germany, France, Spain and the Netherlands all show a fall in Gini-inequality over roughly the same period.[23]

One counter-argument used by the right is that while inequality in the USA (and the UK) may have grown, so too has social mobility. In other words, while the distance from the basement to the penthouse may be greater, anybody starting out in the basement has a better chance of making it to the top. Unfortunately, the evidence does not bear out this claim.

Figure 6.8 records US evidence gathered over three decades – the 1970s, 1980s and 1990s – by Bradbury and Katz (2002), as reported in Mishel et al. (2005). Looking at the top left-hand cell, this cell says that 49.4 per cent of households who started out in the bottom fifth of the income distribution in 1969 were still in the bottom fifth a decade later in 1979; similarly, looking to the right (top row), we see that 27.8 per cent and 24.8 per cent of families starting in the second and middle quintiles respectively in 1969 were still there a decade later.

What is notable from these figures is that, as we go down the columns, in each successive decade the proportion of people starting and finishing in a given quintile rises. If you started the decade of the 1970s either very poor or very rich – or somewhere in the middle – the probability that you would stay that way increased during the 1980s and 1990s. The conclusion is that, for the United States over the period in which inequality was increasing, economic mobility was decreasing.

Quintiles	Bottom	Second	Middle	Fourth	Top
Quintiles in 1969	49.4%	27.8%	24.8%	27.4%	49.1%
Quintiles in 1979	50.4%	31.5%	25.0%	27.6%	50.9%
Quintiles in 1989	53.3%	36.3%	28.3%	31.1%	53.2%

Figure 6.8: US family income mobility over three decades
Source: Adapted from table 1.14 in L. Mishel, J. Bernstein and S. Allegretto (2005)

The Paradox of Consumerism

So far, the picture given of the middle class in the USA is pretty bleak. And yet Europeans often complain about importing 'turbo-consumerism' from the USA where shopping is considered a form of therapy and 'luxury fever' a sign of status. To repeat, one of the difficulties with the familiar accusation that modern capitalism makes mindless shoppers of us all is that it misses the fact that inequality is a key driver of consumption. The American economist, Thorstein Veblen, made this point when writing about 'conspicuous consumption' at the end of the nineteenth century.[24]

Another American economist, Robert H. Frank, coined the term 'luxury fever' nearly a decade ago to describe the growth of consumerism in the United States since the early 1990s.[25] The reason Americans buy ever more elaborate consumer goods, Frank argues, cannot conceivably be because they do the job ever more efficiently. More elaborate goods may in some cases be more efficient, but rarely is this in proportion to the rise in their price tag. Rather, it is because as the income distribution becomes more skewed, the spending patterns of the super rich are spreading to an ever wider public.[26]

Whereas in the 1950s the average American middle-class family might have been satisfied with a three-bedroom house with a carport, by the 1990s only four to five bedrooms would do and a two-car garage was essential. The American generation of the 1990s may have owned more cars than their parents, but they did not have more children. Yet the average American house built at the end of the 1990s was nearly twice as large as its 1950s counterpart. The average American car in 1999 cost 75 per cent more in real terms than a decade earlier. Americans, whatever their social status, find it increasingly difficult to 'keep up with the Joneses', and this concerns everything from the sums spent on weddings to the price of a house in an area with a good school, to the university fees which must be paid if the children are ever to find jobs at a salary commensurate with the lifestyle to which their parents have taught them to aspire.

Crucially, says Frank, there is a price to pay:

> All of us, rich and poor alike, but especially the rich – are spending more time at the office and taking shorter vacations; we are spending less time with our families and friends; and we have less time for sleep, exercise, travel, reading, and other activities that help maintain body and soul. Because of the decline in our savings rate . . . a rising number of families feel apprehensive about their ability to maintain their living standards during retirement. At a time when our spending on luxury goods is growing four times as fast as overall spending, our . . . public infrastructure [is] deteriorating. . . . Poverty and drug abuse is on the rise . . . A growing percentage of middle- and upper-income families seek refuge behind the walls of gated communities.[27]

Frank's reference to growing insecurity is resonant with ILO-based work by Guy Standing on labour market insecurity.[28] But Frank makes greater use of the conventional economic notions of cost externalities and market failure. An individual's decision to buy this house or drive that car almost always has an effect on the rest of us, often negative and unintended. My decision to drive to work instead of taking public transport – bearing in mind the woeful state of public transport in the USA and the UK – may result in a negligible addition to congestion or pollution, but if most of my neighbours decide to do so as well that day, the result is a situation for the collective which none of us could foresee. Similarly, I may decide quite sensibly to take out an extra mortgage to move up to a large detached house, but if everybody gets in on the act, house prices rise, there is greater pressure on urban infrastructure, less green area and so on. In short, what may be a sensible decision taken in isolation turns out to be costly and unjustifiable from the point of view of the community. This 'paradox of isolation' is one of the fundamental problems of market-based choice. This is why markets often need to be regulated and collective decisions need to be made through representative political institutions rather than at an individual level in the market.

In much the same vein, Juliet Schor at Harvard has written on why we increasingly want what we don't need.[29] Schor's key point is that our reference groups are widening and that today comparisons are made over a much broader range of goods and services. Two generations ago, the typical middle-class family tended to view its consumption status in relation to that of the Jones's next door, or perhaps by looking slightly further afield at the lifestyle of the local doctor or bank manager. That appears to have changed: the revolution in the media, in advertising and the rise of celebrity culture means the same family now looks further up the income ladder.

Consumption status is conferred by a far wider range of goods and services; the phrase 'aspirational goods' (aka, lifestyle items) has entered common usage. It is no longer enough to have a detached house or a nice family car in an age where virtually everything you buy – including where you have your hair cut or take your holidays – is scrutinized. And it is not just adults who compare themselves to others; children are subject to intense peer pressure about what designer jeans they wear or whether they sport the coolest brand of trainers or sneakers. As Schor notes, 'when the children of affluent suburban and impoverished inner city households both want the same Tommy Hilfiger logo emblazoned on their chests and top-of-the-line Swoosh on their feet, it's a disaster'.[30]

The change in people's aspirational goals is reflected in survey evidence which relates the level of household income considered 'desirable' to that actually enjoyed. Clearly, very poor households report that they need more money to live properly. What is surprising is that aspirations rise in proportion with income, so that even the rich feel they need more money to enjoy a truly comfortable lifestyle. The aspirational lifestyle is defined by the consumption pattern of those further up the income ladder. As the income ladder is extended ever further upward, so the pressure to earn and consume more increases. It is this fact above all, Schor argues, that helps explain the demand side of the debt-fuelled consumer boom in the USA and the UK, to which we turn in chapter 9. Before looking at the macroeconomic pictures, though, I want to consider the 'costs of inequality' in more detail.

7

The Rising Cost of Inequality

> Except for homicide, Britain has overtaken the United States in most types of crime. Other disorders abound: family breakdown, addiction, stress, road and landscape congestion, obesity, poverty, denial of health care, mental disorder, violence, economic fraud, and insecurity.
>
> Avner Offer (2006: 2)

The New Inequality

I use the term 'new' inequality with caution, for there is surely nothing new about it. What is new is that inequality has reasserted itself so strongly and is characterized (at least in America and Britain) by stagnant incomes for the many and undreamed of wealth for the few. What matters today in these same countries is not just *absolute* but *relative* deprivation. The extent to which income differentials have widened as well as the ensuing spread of runaway consumerism has been explored in previous chapters. Pundits on the right – which includes much of the parliamentary Labour Party in Britain – claim that as long as the poorest are provided for, the fact that the rich get richer is 'glorious'; it provides jobs and attracts great wealth to the UK, thus boosting growth. Or at best, some apologists would argue, it carries no great cost.

To be sure, the poorest have not been provided for. In his book entitled *The New Inequality*, published in 1999, the American economist Richard B. Freeman wrote:

> Falling or stagnating incomes for workers and rising inequality threaten American ideals of political 'classlessness' and shared citizenship. Left unattended, the new inequality threatens us with a two-tiered society – what I have elsewhere called an 'apartheid economy' – in which the successful upper and upper-middle classes live lives fundamentally different from the working classes and the poor. Such an economy will function well for a substantial number, but will not meet our nation's democratic ideal of advancing the well-being of the average citizen. For many it promises the loss of the 'American Dream.' (Freeman, 1999: 2)

Whether one uses the 'hourglass' or the 'apartheid' metaphor, what is surely evident is that exclusion corrodes social cohesion and breeds crime, whether one is speaking of the USA, Britain, France or other OECD countries. The example of crime in America has already been cited. According to a report published in 2003, the USA incarcerates about 700 people per 100,000 of its population (over 60 per cent of which are blacks and Hispanics); the UK rate is 140 per 100,000, while in France it is about 80. Meanwhile, Bill Gates and Warren Buffett have between them built up fortunes equivalent to nearly a third of US household assets and the top 5 per cent of Americans now own more than all the rest put together.

Much of the conventional work on income distribution stresses the measurement and characteristics of poverty. The term 'inequality' stresses the fact that it is not just absolute poverty which matters, but our income status relative to that of our reference group. Indeed, in a pioneering work written half a century ago, the political sociologist W. G. Runciman[1] insisted on the importance of understanding 'deprivation' as stretching across the income hierarchy. Relative deprivation occurs where individuals or groups see themselves as unfairly disadvantaged with respect to other members of their reference group having similar attributes, and feel they deserve similar rewards. Such a situation contrasts with the condition of absolute deprivation, where biological health is impaired or where relative levels of wealth are compared based on objective differences.[2]

Sociologists, criminologists and others have long recognized the relative nature of discontent. They criticize theories linking absolute deprivation to crime by pointing out that many poor countries have low rates of violent crime while the wealthy United States has a comparatively high rate.[3]

A century ago, poverty was still defined in absolute terms and the poor died of malnutrition or were swept off by epidemic diseases. As Europe grew richer during the years of post-war reconstruction, better infrastructure, higher wages and new welfare provisions rescued most people from the threat of absolute deprivation. Writers on health and social policy speak of the 'epidemiological transition' – a term coined by Richard Wilkinson – meaning that as countries grow richer, the traditional 'diseases of the rich' such as stroke and heart disease reverse their social class incidence and become associated with the poor. A most striking example today is that of obesity, a condition once associated with wealth but now with 'junk food' poverty. And as absolute deprivation shrank, so poverty itself began to be redefined in relative terms.

Poverty itself is now increasingly defined in relative terms. Today, for example, the household 'poverty line' in EU member-states is set at 60 per cent of median household income; by contrast, in the USA it is an absolute threshold; it is defined as the cost of the basic bundle of necessities for a family of four adjusted annually, and its current value is roughly $20,000. (If the USA used the EU standard, the threshold would be about $28,000 in 2006 dollars.) This means that in the EU – and to a more limited degree in the USA – as growth takes place, and assuming the rewards of higher productivity to be reasonably equitably distributed, so too the poverty threshold rises. Nevertheless, the reappearance of sumptuous private affluence is associated not just with greater neglect of economic and social infrastructure and declining social cohesion, but a variety of social ills now being catalogued under the new label of 'social epidemiology'.

Health Costs

It may appear paradoxical that, looking at within-country and between-country data, there is a significant relationship between health (as measured by life expectancy) and per capita income in the former case, but little relationship in the latter. Hence, although the income disparity between rural Bangladesh and the Harlem district of New York City is huge, infant mortality (indeed, at most ages) is higher in the latter than the former.[4] The apparent paradox is resolved if we accept that what affects health is not absolute income, but income relative to others – a key marker of social status in society.

The observation that growing prosperity is not accompanied by growing 'happiness' is now so widely recognized as to have become little more than a cliché. There is ample evidence that the growth in inequality – the rise of the super rich about which New Labour has been so intensely relaxed – is associated with poor health, high rates of violence and low levels of social capital. Richard Wilkinson, the social epidemiologist, cites various studies showing the difference in life expectancy (measured from age sixteen) between rich whites and poor blacks in the USA is about sixteen years for both sexes. The studies quoted cover twenty-three different areas; in all cases, differences in area incomes are closely associated with differences in death rates. Wilkinson suggests that health inequalities related to different socio-economic status may deprive the average poor person of 20–25 per cent of the length of life enjoyed by the rich. He adds: 'What would we think of a ruthless government that arbitrarily imprisoned all less well-off people for a number of years equal to the average shortening of life suffered by the less equal of our own societies?' (2005: 18). Nor is this phenomenon associated purely with poverty: the finding holds within classes – for example, within the US middle class as a whole – and across all classes, while the slope of gradient varies from one country to another and across time. In short, statistically speaking, how long you live depends not just on whether you can afford food and medicine, but on your *relative* social position in a particular country.

For the UK, in a well-known longitudinal study of the civil service, Rose and Marmot (1981) took a large sample of male office employees (almost all of whom would call themselves middle class) and found that death rate from heart disease among those of low status was four times as high as among the highest ranks. Donkin, Goldblatt and Lynch (2002) report that whereas in the early 1970s the difference in life expectancy between social class V (unskilled manual) and social class I (professional) was about five years, by the early–mid-1990s the difference was nine and a half years for men and six and a half for women. In Britain at the moment, Dorling reports, the gap between infant mortality for working-class parents and for the population as a whole has risen steadily between 1998 and 2006.[5] In general, as Wilkinson observes:

> Inequality promotes [social] strategies that are more self-interested, less affiliative, often highly anti-social, more stressful and likely to give rise to higher levels of violence, poorer community relations, and worse health. In contrast, the less unequal societies tend to be much more affiliative, less violent, more supportive and inclusive, and marked by better health . . . more unequal societies tend to have higher rates of violent crime and homicide, and . . . people living in them feel more hostility, are less likely to be involved in community life, and are much less likely to trust each other; in short, they have lower levels of social capital. (Wilkinson, 2005: 24)

Social Capital

In this context, Robert Putnam's well-known study *Bowling Alone* shows the decline of community bonds – what he calls 'social capital' – in the USA after the 1950s–1960s, a period of growing inequality. As Wilkinson has noted, Putnam's work suggests that in the more unequal parts of the USA, where participation in community life is lower, it is particularly the poorer people who have ceased to participate. Where there is more income inequality, poorer people are more likely to feel out of place participating in community groups, more likely to feel ill at ease and to think that they will make fools of themselves and be looked down upon.

One expression of the retreat from community life is the decline of trust. Data on the fifty American states suggest that people living in less egalitarian states are most likely to believe that others 'will take advantage of you if they get the chance'. A 1997 study by Kawachi and Kennedy showed striking differences in levels of trust. In the most equal states, only 10–15 per cent of the population felt that they could not trust each other; in the least equal states, the proportion rose to 35–40 per cent.[6] Much the same result emerges from cross-country comparisons, too, although one must bear in mind that in this case strong historical and cultural differences play a role. Figure 7.1, from Rothstein and Uslaner (2005), shows the result of mapping forty-three country observations of 'trust' from the World Values Survey against country inequality. In countries like Sweden, Denmark and Holland, which are relatively egalitarian, about 60 per cent of people think they can trust each other; in highly inegalitarian countries, such as Brazil, Colombia and South Africa, the figure falls to below 20 per cent. Why is 'social trust' important? As the authors observe:

> One reason for the interest in social trust is that, as measured in surveys, it correlates with a number of other variables that are normatively highly desirable. At the individual level, people who believe that in general most other people in their society can be trusted are also more inclined to have a positive view of their democratic institutions, to participate more in politics, and to be more active in civic organizations. They also give more to charity and are more tolerant toward minorities and to people who are not like themselves. (Rothstein and Uslaner, 2005: 41)

But there is an apparent paradox here. Again, a quote from Richard Wilkinson is apposite:

> If – as the data show – social capital is lowest in the most deprived areas . . . then politicians may be tempted to believe that it is not more money that people in these poor areas need but better social relations. Although such a misunderstanding may well explain why social capital is an attractive concept to some on the political right, the truth lies exactly the other way around. What the relationship with inequality actually demonstrates is that societies that tolerate the injustices of greater inequality will almost inescapably suffer their social consequences: they will be unfriendly and violent societies recognised more for their hostility than their hospitality. (Wilkinson, 2005: 35–6)

Or, again, as Richard Titmuss observed of the Second World War in his book *Essays on the Welfare State*, securing the cooperation of the masses in the war effort required 'flattening the pyramid of social stratification'.[7] In consequence, it was noted that during the war income differentials narrowed, taxation became far more progressive and full employment reigned.

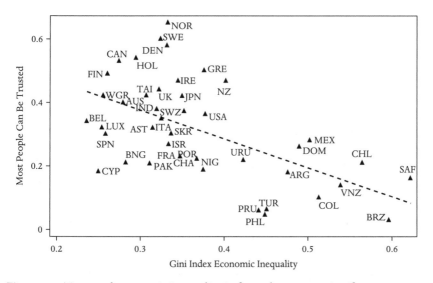

Figure 7.1: Trust and economic inequality in forty-three countries (former communist countries excluded)
Source: B. Rothstein and E. M. Uslaner (2005: 49)

Civilian death rates fell quite substantially, and, as a matter of folk memory, the period 1940–5 in Britain is generally remembered as one in which class barriers were eroded and social solidarity greatly increased.

Not only does growing inequality appear to erode social cohesion and the degree to which people trust each other, but inequality is associated with cuts in social spending. This link provides a feedback mechanism which helps further erode social institutions. A paper by Swabisch, Smeeding, and Olsberg (2004) on income distribution and social expenditure in the USA assembles data from several different sources to examine the cross-national effects of inequality. The authors find that inequality between the middle and top ends of the income distribution (measured by the 90/50 percentile ratio) is associated with a large *reduction* in social spending. As the rich become more distant from the middle and lower classes, they find it easier to opt out of public programmes and to buy substitutes for social insurance in the private market. This implies that 'over time rising inequality will erode support for social institutions and social spending that provides insurance against income loss, upward mobility for the disadvantaged, and equality of opportunity for all citizens'.[8]

This finding mirrors the observation that in Britain, as the National Health Service becomes increasingly fragmented and privatized and a growing proportion of the new middle class in Britain opts for supplementary private health cover, support for public provision declines. In the words of Rothstein and Uslaner:

> In low-trust societies with high degrees of economic inequality, universal programs are likely to fail for lack of political support. Even when such policies are adopted, there is a strong possibility that they will fail in the implementation process. Education, health care, and social insurance benefits (as well as the police and the courts) may very well become commodities for sale . . . Parents 'buy' their children's way into good schools, especially universities, and then pay even more for good grades. Extra 'gift payments' to doctors are routine in countries with high levels of economic inequality. Police will stop drivers for invented traffic infractions and pedestrians for attempting to cross in the middle of traffic and demand payments in lieu of tickets. Each of these actions subverts trust in government and thereby the notion that they could implement universal social policies in a fair and equal way. (Rothstein and Uslaner, 2005: 56)

Religious Revival in an Insecure World

Moving to a different context, a decline in social capital in the USA may help explain the rise of Christian fundamentalist communities to a greater degree than we realize. Like millenarian movements in general, Christian fundamentalism is a reaction to (and a form of managing) social decline. This is particularly true in America with its ever-larger and boxed-in working class, and where the struggle for status and pay grows harsher by the day. In the words of one observer:

> It schools the downwardly mobile in making the best of their lot while teaching them to be grateful for the food pantry and day-care over at the church. At the same time, taking advantage of existing currents of anti-intellectualism and school-tax resistance, it removes from the pool of potential scientists and other creative professionals vast numbers of students, who will have had their minds befuddled with creationism and its smooth-talking cousin, intelligent design.[9]

Why does fundamentalism thrive in the world's richest country? In a fascinating article, Malcolm Gladwell has described the *modus operandi* of the Californian religious entrepreneur, Rick Warren, founder of the Saddleback Church.[10] Warren, an expansive and amiably populist character, started out as a penniless itinerant preacher in 1979 when he first arrived in Orange County, a fast-growing middle-class area south of Los Angeles. Two decades later, he had a congregation of 20,000 members and a 50-acre 'university' campus. He is probably best known for a book entitled *The Purpose-Driven Life* which since 2001 has sold nearly thirty million copies, making it one of the best-selling non-fiction hardbacks ever published. Warren has published half-a-dozen more titles in the 'purpose-driven' series, all revolving around the same core message that God loves you and (with your help) all will be well. Just to get the flavour, the best-seller begins with the words: 'This book is dedicated to you. Before you were born, God planned this moment in your life. It is no accident that you are holding this book. God longs for you to dis-cover the life he created for you to live-here on earth, and forever in eternity.' Like Gates and Buffett, Rick Warren is not personally ostentatious – he has been personally philanthropic, and has founded a number of international charities, *inter alia*, for combating HIV and AIDS and alleviating world poverty. *Forbes Magazine* has said that were the Saddleback Church a busi-ness, it would be compared with Dell, Google or Starbucks.

In order for a church business like Warren's to grow it needs to speak to people's problems, be accessible and inclusive, while at the same time retaining a strong distinguishing identity. It cannot afford to become yet another large, anonymous organization like so many other fundamentalist churches founded in the 1970s and 1980s. In Gladwell's phrase – which could easily have come straight out of an MBA textbook – Saddleback needed to combine low barriers to entry with a well-differentiated product. And it is here that Saddleback has excelled, for it is based on the notion of a 'cellular community': a church built on a network of cells, each group numbering perhaps half-a-dozen people, who meet in each other's homes to work and pray. The author adds a quote from Robert Putnam, who has researched Saddleback: ' "Orange County is virtually a desert in social-capital terms . . . The rate of mobility is really high. It has long and anony-mous commutes. It's a very friendless place, and this church offers serious heavy friendship.' "

The small group – pioneered in the early twentieth century by such orga-nizations as Alcoholics Anonymous – provides an extraordinary vehicle of commitment. To pursue the analogy, just as an alcoholic might sacrifice his job and even his family because of drink, once embedded in a tightly knit social-support group he could change. Gladwell estimates that cellular reli-gious communities such as Saddleback now attract some forty million Americans. One might conclude from Gladwell's piece that Robert Putnam, instead of arguing that community was on the decline in America, should have argued that as wages stagnate and jobs become more insecure, so the prosperous secular communities of the 1950s and 1960s have been replaced by faith-based mutual support systems. An old opiate has reappeared in new bottles.

Apartheid Schooling

Unlike Britain where comprehensive secondary schools first appeared in the late 1960s, America has always prided itself on offering free, non-selective secondary education to all its citizens. Its public schools – the equivalent of state schools in Britain – have traditionally aimed at setting a high standard. Everyone who has ever travelled in the United States will recognize the ubiquitous yellow bus which fetches children each day to school from city streets and far-flung rural areas alike. They are an iconic part of the American dream of equal opportunity for all. Indeed, the great civil rights struggle of the 1960s focused on the right of all Americans, of whatever colour, to learn together and ultimately to grow up and share the same rights and responsibilities together. The civil rights movement sought forever to abolish the segregationist principle of 'separate but equal', the principle first challenged in 1954 in the landmark *Brown* ruling of the USA Supreme Court. That is what the great majority of Americans believed then, and what they still believe today. Sadly, the reality of American secondary education is otherwise.

For well over a decade, secondary education in America has been re-segregating, as the educational writer, Jonathan Kozol, shows in his latest book, *The Shame of the Nation: The Restoration of Apartheid Schooling in America*. Figures for the academic year 2002–3 reveal that in Chicago, 87 per cent of inner-city public school enrolment comprised of children from black or hispanic ethnic minorities.[11] For other major cities the figures are equally revealing: Detroit, 96 per cent; Washington, DC, 94 per cent; Baltimore, 89 per cent; Los Angeles, 84 per cent; St Louis, 82 per cent; Philadelphia and Cleveland, 79 per cent; New York City, 75 per cent. In America's main cities, public schools have been deserted by 'white' children. The overwhelming majority of the white middle class – much of that great bulge which once distinguished the US income pyramid from all others – today sends their sons and daughters to 'white' public schools, or else to private schools of one sort or another. Social and economic segregation starts at school.

Poorer students go to rundown schools where teachers are underpaid. In the late 1990s, the New York Board of Education spent about $8,000 per head on schooling in the Borough of the Bronx; in wealthy suburbs, such as Manhasset on Long Island where students are overwhelmingly white, a comparable figure was $20,000. If the same child was sent to one of New York's many private schools, the parents might expect to pay fees closer to $30,000 per year. And money spent on schools is used to pay teachers' salaries, where the same gradations are evident. In the late 1990s, the median teacher's salary in a poor neighbourhood was just over $40,000, while 10 miles away in a rich suburb it would be $80,000. While a decade later teachers' salaries are higher, the differentials remain the same.

If primary and secondary education is segregated, so too is education at crèche and pre-school level. Unlike some European countries where pre-school facilities are ubiquitous and free or generously subsidized, the USA has no such system; the children of the poor will await entry to primary school at age six. In contrast, for those who can afford the fees, there is a highly competitive market for pre-school places. A private pre-school in New York City can easily cost $25,000 per annum; moreover, competition for admission is so intense that wealthy parents will retain private tutors for their four-year-old at fees as high as $200 per hour. Pre-schooling of this sort will ensure success for the middle-class child when, at the age of eight, he or she sits a battery of standardized exams to determine 'aptitude', i.e., the child's likely educational trajectory. This state of affairs stands uneasily alongside the official rhetoric of equal opportunity, level playing field and, most of all, that in today's knowledge-based economy, parents are accountable for making the right 'educational choices' if their children are to find good jobs.

As educational apartheid in the USA deepens, deprived schools have introduced new strategies to cope with these new realities. Some innovations will be distressingly familiar not just to US teachers, but to their counterparts in Britain:

> [These include] relentless emphasis on raising test scores, rigid policies of non-promotion and non-graduation, a new empiricism and the imposition of unusually detailed lists of named and numbered 'outcomes' for each isolated parcel of instruction, an oftentimes fanatical insistence upon uniformity of teachers in their management of time, an openly conceded emulation of the rigorous approaches of the military and a frequent use of terminology that comes out of the world of industry and commerce . . . Although generically described as 'school reform,' most of these practices and policies are . . . responses to perceived catastrophe in deeply segregated and unequal schools. (Kozol, *Harper's Magazine*, September 2005:47–8)

In its extreme form, educational discipline is imposed using methods inspired by B. F. Skinner; notably, rote-and-drill curricula where the teacher is the 'stimulus' and the student merely responds. Kozol's description of the harsh disciplinary regime he encounters when sitting amongst a class of ten-year-olds at Public School 65 in the South Bronx is illuminating if chilling:

> My attention was distracted by some whispering among the children sitting to the right of me. The teacher's response to the distraction was immediate: his arm shot out and up in a diagonal in front of him, his hand straight up, his fingers flat . . . all the children in the classroom did it too. 'Zero noise,' the teacher said, but this instruction proved to be unneeded. The strange salute the class and teachers gave each other, which turned out to be one of a number of such silent signals teachers in the school were trained to use, and the children to obey, had done the job of silencing the class. . . . 'Active Listening' [the teacher] said. 'Heads up! Tractor beams!' which meant, 'Every eye on me.' . . . Since that day at P.S. 65, I have . . . visited schools in six different cities where the same Skinnerian curriculum is used. The signs on the walls, the silent signals, the same curious salute . . . became familiar as I went from one school to the next. . . . Among the missions of [one school visited] was 'to develop productive citizens' who have the skills that will be needed 'for successful global competition,' a message that was reinforced by other posters in the room. Over the heads of a group of children at their desks, a sign anointed them BEST WORKERS OF 2002. (Kozol, *Harper's Magazine*, September 2005: 48–9)

Or again, Kozol quotes the response of the head of a Chicago school when criticized for turning children into robots. 'Did you ever stop to think that these robots will never burglarize [sic] your home? . . . will never snatch your pocketbooks . . . These robots are going to be producing taxes.' Drill-based methods are part of the 'Success for All' programme first introduced in urban areas in the 1990s. The methods and their complementary systems of assessment were signed into law by the Bush administration in 2002 as part of the No Child Left Behind programme.

Since the programme was adopted, it is reported that the number of standardized tests children must take has more than doubled. In general, few voices have been raised in the USA against such teaching methods, the assumption being that rote-learning and military discipline are essential if children from ethnic minorities and poor neighbourhoods are to learn anything at all. Yet the USA evidence suggests otherwise: between the 1960s and 1980s the achievement gap between black and white children is reported to have narrowed as segregation decreased. The gap widened once again in the 1990s, following the gradual judicial dismemberment of key measures designed to implement the *Brown* decision of 1954.[12]

If growing inequality in education is one facet of growing economic and social inequality, it must not be thought that the USA is unique in this respect. While educational segregation in not nearly as marked in Britain as in the USA nor schools as regimented, teachers and parents in Britain will be aware of the similarities, particularly concerning the explosive growth of testing and performance targets of all kinds in UK state schools, often directly borrowed from the USA. And, if segregation by ethnic group is less visible, social class is no less important. A casual reading of the press suggests that middle-class Britain under New Labour has become obsessed with living in the right school catchment area (aka, the postcode lottery), avoiding 'bog standard' comprehensive schools and lamenting the much-trumpeted 'decline in standards' national exams while celebrating their children's glowing GCSE and A-level results.

At the same time, Britain has one of the worst records for sixteen-year-olds dropping out of education despite government attempts to persuade students to stay on. According to a recent OECD report, only Greece, Mexico, New Zealand, Portugal and Turkey have worse figures for the proportion of seventeen-year-olds continuing in education. A quarter of UK pupils leaves education at sixteen, 8 percentage points lower than the OECD average.[13] For those who finish school, the percentage of eighteen-year-olds going on to university correlates closely with where they live. In London, for example, it is 41.5 per cent in middle-class Harrow but 12.9 per cent in working-class Hackney, while Barking, Dagenham and Tower Hamlets all have 15 per cent or less of their school-leavers entering full-time higher education.

And, of course, educational mobility correlates with social mobility. Once again, research suggests that both the USA and the UK do badly here as well. In a recent report published by the LSE Centre for Economic Performance, comparing eight European and North American countries, Britain and the United States were found to have the lowest social mobility. Social mobility in Britain is lower than in Canada, Germany, Sweden, Norway, Denmark and Finland; moreover, social mobility in Britain has declined whereas in the USA it is stable. Part of the reason for Britain's decline has been that the better off have benefited disproportionately from increased educational opportunity.

Comparing surveys of children born in the 1950s and the 1970s, the report finds that the decline is in part due to the strong and increasing relationship between family income and educational attainment. The opportunity to stay in education at age sixteen and age eighteen benefited those from better-off backgrounds disproportionately. For a younger cohort born in the early 1980s the gap between those staying on in education at age

Total Employment	1983	2000
Netherlands	—	1371
Norway	1485	1380
Germany	1674*	1463
France	1672	1500
Denmark	—	1504
Belgium	1684	1530
Switzerland	—	1568
Italy	1694	1619
Sweden	1520	1625
Ireland	1910	1690
UK	1713	1707
Portugal	—	1708
Finland	1787	1727
Spain	1912	1814
USA	1824	1834

Figure 7.2: Annual hours worked per full-time person in active labour force: 1983, 2000
* 1983 figure for West Germany
Source: OECD *Employment Outlook*, Annexe Table F., OECD 2003; ILO (1999),
'Americans work longest hours among industrialized countries', *ILO News*, Monday 6
September 1999

sixteen narrowed, but inequality of access to higher education has widened further: while the proportion of people from the poorest fifth of families obtaining a degree has increased from 6 per cent to 9 per cent, the graduation rates for the richest fifth have risen from 20 per cent to 47 per cent. The report concludes that the strength of the relationship between educational attainment and family income, especially for access to higher education, is at the heart of Britain's low mobility culture.

An apt summary is provided by the British journalist Nick Cohen: 'The greatest myth of the free-market right is that its policies allow the poorest child to go from rags to riches; socially mobile societies have very few people living in either rags or riches.'[14]

Working Ever More

As top earners pull in more, so too, those on the lower rungs of the ladder of riches demand more, skewing the income distribution even further. But growing inequality entails many other costs; these include working more hours, retiring later, saving less and becoming more indebted.[15]

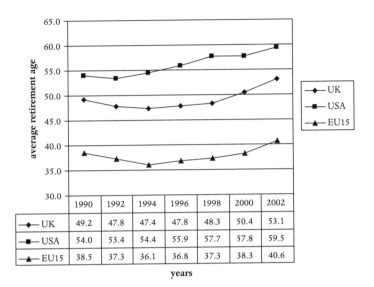

	1990	1992	1994	1996	1998	2000	2002
◆— UK	49.2	47.8	47.4	47.8	48.3	50.4	53.1
■— USA	54.0	53.4	54.4	55.9	57.7	57.8	59.5
▲— EU15	38.5	37.3	36.1	36.8	37.3	38.3	40.6

years

Figure 7.3: Selected employment rates for group 55–64
Source: OECD Factbook 2006: Economic, Environmental and Social Statistics

To earn the money needed to meet their aspirations, American and British families are putting in longer working hours, and the single-earner family is being replaced by one in which both partners have a job. This trend is born out by a comparison of annual hours worked and female labour-force participation rates. Americans, followed by Britons, work the longest annual hours, and women work more, than in other industrialized countries.[16] In America, moreover, the proportion of workers remaining in the workforce after sixty and indeed well beyond retirement age is greater than in most European countries. US workers put in the longest hours on the job in industrialized nations: 1,834 hours per capita in 2000.

Based on OECD and ILO data, the US pattern of increasing annual hours worked per person, which totalled 1,824 in 1983, contrasts most sharply with those of European workers, who are spending progressively fewer hours on the job, particularly in countries such as Norway and the Netherlands where hours worked in 2002 were, respectively, 1,371 and 1,380 per year. In France, full-time workers put in 1,500 hours in 2002 versus nearly 1,700 in the 1980s. In Germany, average working hours for 2002 were 1,463 versus 1,674 in 1983. Workers in the United Kingdom, who put in 1,707 hours annually in 2002, appear to have neither gained nor lost much free time since 1982 when they worked 1,713 hours.

Not only do Americans work more per year, they appear to remain in employment longer. Figure 7.3 contrasts the trend over 1990–2002 in average employment rates for workers aged fifty-five to sixty-four in the USA, the UK and the EU-15. In 1990, 54 per cent of American workers in this group were in full-time employment compared to 49 per cent in the UK and 39 per cent for the EU as a whole.[17] While the trend is upward in all cases, today nearly 60 per cent of older American workers are in full-time employment, considerably more than the proportions in the UK and the EU-15 overall. While this state of affairs might have worrying implications for pension provision in some EU countries, it does support the argument that Americans not only work longer hours but enjoy fewer years of retirement.

Unequal Politics

Perhaps the most serious problem created by growing inequality is that it facilitates the reproduction of the politics and ideology of inequality. The USA and the UK are both countries that pride themselves on a long-established democratic tradition. But in recent years the perception has grown that, regardless of which party is in power, it is the rich who increasingly dominate politics. At a time when ownership of the media is becoming ever more concentrated, and elections more expensive, politicians appear not merely to serve the interests of the rich but to do so unapologetically. In London, the Blair years began with Bernie Ecclestone's £1 million 'donation' to Labour and ended with the 'money for peerages' scandal. In Washington, the Bush administration has hardly disguised its favours to the rich and powerful – fat contracts for cronies, large tax cuts for the top decile – to the detriment of any notion of 'public good'.

It costs money to get elected. Admittedly, the British electoral system with its short general election campaigns and strict rationing of television time is a good deal cheaper to run than its American counterpart, but money still counts. In 2006, the Labour Party was reported to be in debt to the tune of £27 million, about one-third less than the opposition Conservatives; these disclosures follow upon the apparent cover-up of loans to all the main parties. Labour, although less indebted than the Conservatives, needs to pay the money back more quickly (by the beginning of 2008); the party thus has a serious cash-flow problem.

The Labour Party has traditionally been funded mainly by the trade unions and from membership subscriptions, but a combination of shrinking party membership and union membership plus New Labour's conversion to the neo-liberal creed has forced the party since the late 1990s to look elsewhere – notably to a number of very rich individuals – for funds. It emerged after the 2005 general election that Labour had secured nearly £14 million (and the Conservatives £16 million) in the form of short-term loans which, under existing legislation, were not subject to the same disclosure standards as donations. Disclosure standards have subsequently been tightened and a Commission under Sir Hayden Phillips has suggested increased public funding and caps on electoral spending; however, it appears that the room for cross-party consensus is narrow and the success of reforms may be limited.

All this is nothing compared to the sums of money that are poured into presidential and congressional electoral coffers in the USA. In 2001, Michael Bloomberg spent an estimated $74 million to become mayor of New York; it is reported that his mailings alone cost more than his opponent was able to spend for his entire campaign. According to the Washington-based Center for Responsive Politics, in 2006 the average cost of winning election to the House of Representatives is nearly $1 million, while a Senate seat costs $7.8 million – about ten times the amounts spent in the mid-1970s. A study of the 1992 Congressional election reveals that candidates who spent less than $250,000 did not win a single seat; those spending in the range $250–500,000 won one race in four, while those spending over $500,000 could expect to win half the time.[18] In the 2006 Congressional election, the candidate who spent the most money won in 93 per cent of the House races and 67 per cent of the Senate races. (Of course, not only does money help candidates to win, but likely winners will attract more money.) And, while lobbyists in Washington are banned from giving meals, trips and gifts to members of Congress, there is no ban on pointing politicians towards those private interest groups most likely to help fund their campaigns – and taking a fat fee for so doing. According to one report, the prospect of earning high fees was the main reason why nearly half of those politicians who left Congress in 1998 subsequently returned to Washington as lobbyists.[19]

The influence of lobbyists on politics in Washington is hardly new, but it is difficult to understate. Take the Bush administration's push to privatize pensions; the main cheerleader has been Wall Street, which stands to make a packet from privatization in the USA (and elsewhere).[20] Hillary Clinton's attempt to enact health-care reform during her husband's first term in office was successfully opposed by the health-care industry which spent an estimated $235 million on lobbying. In 2001, shortly after 9/11, the US airline industry received a $15 billion bailout, but none of this money went to workers for health care, job insurance or retraining. Nor was Congress moved to allocate money for modernizing US secondary schools – the average building is today more than forty years old. Or take the US chemical industry in the wake of 9/11. The Environmental Protection Agency once had the authority to require action to improve chemical plant security. But between 1995 and 2002, the American Chemistry Council spent more than $80 million in political contributions and lobbying fees to fight chemical plant inspection. Following 9/11, the Bush administration transferred that authority to the Department of Homeland Security; the department does not routinely inspect plants but, instead, relies on information that chemical manufacturers submit voluntarily. More generally, it is estimated that in 2001, the nine largest corporate sectors in the USA together spent $1.25 billion on buying Congressional influence, nearly fifty times as much as the combined lobbying expenditure of the US trade union movement.

Consider taxes. In 2001, George W. Bush's first round of tax cuts were estimated to be worth $1.6 trillion; the additional tax cut passed in 2003 cost a further $1.5 trillion. While the tax cuts currently save an average of nearly $100,000 per annum for households earning more than $1 million per year, there is no tax relief for households earning under $10,000 a year. During the 2001 debate on repealing the US estate tax (inheritance tax), critics noted that the measure would save heirs of Vice-President Cheney up to $40 million, the heirs of Treasury Secretary O'Neill $50.7 million and those of Defense Secretary Rumsfeld up to $120 million. By contrast, when the Clinton administration in 1993 just managed to push though a slight increase in the top rate of tax, Congress responded by pushing through budget cuts that severely limited the government's ability to audit the tax returns of the very wealthy. A subsequent study carried out at Syracuse University showed that over the course of the 1990s, audit rates on America's richest 2 per cent dropped by 90 per cent; for the first time, the relatively low-income households were more likely to be audited than rich households.[21] To make matters worse, the Bush administration is currently proposing to privatize the collection of tax arrears.[22]

The best-known attempt to reform the financing of US election was in 1974, in the aftermath of Watergate, when strict limits were placed on political spending and on donations by individuals and political action committees. But, in 1976, the Supreme Court ruled limits on spending unconstitutional – a candidate had the right to spend whatever he or she wished. But while this ruling did not overturn limits on contributions to candidates, candidates could accept contributions of any size for 'party building', or what became known as 'soft money' contributions. In 2000, it is reported that Republicans and Democrats between them raised nearly half a billion

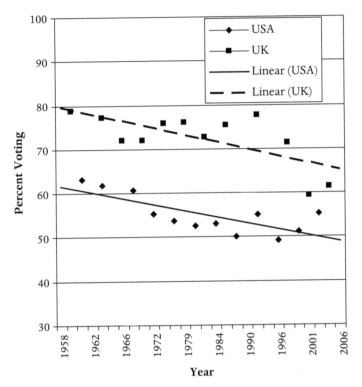

Figure 7.4: Turnout in US and UK general elections, 1958–2005
Source: D. Sanders, H. Clarke, M. Stewart and P. Whitely (2005), The *2005 General Election in Britain*, Report for the Electoral Commission, Colchester: University of Essex., p 4; *National Voter Turnout in Federal Elections*: <http:www.infoplease.com/ipa/A0781453.html>; trend lines by author

dollars in soft money, 90 per cent of which were from corporations or very wealthy individuals.[23] In the wake of the Enron scandal, in 2002 Congress passed new legislation (the McCain–Feingold Bill), attempting to place limits on soft money.

Far more than in Britain, the role of big money in US politics illustrates the case for the public funding of elections and closer regulation of what can be spent by whom. Doubtless, part of the reason for the growing cynicism about politics in Britain and America is the deeply corrosive effect of sleaze, the manner in which politics has become commoditized and is now packaged, advertised and sold like everything else. It is well known that voter turnout in both the UK and the USA has been falling in the past half century. Figure 7.4 shows the trends in voter turnout for UK general elections and US presidential elections respectively over the past fifty years.[24] In the USA, only half of eligible voters turn out; judging by the trend it may soon be the same in the UK. In the words of Paul Skidmore:

> [In Britain] *political* inequality has also been growing. The difference in voter turnout between the highest social classes and the lowest is probably wider now than at any point since the abolition of property requirements. . . . at the same time as social inequality increased in the 1980s and 1990s, the level of political mobilisation has declined. The decline of trade unions has weakened one of the institutions best-placed to mobilise the least well-off into politics.[25]

Mainly, those who abstain from the electoral process are the poor and the unorganized, the lower half of the hourglass society who feel powerless and alienated from the system. The 'absent' electorate is overwhelmingly drawn from the lower half of the household income distribution. In Britain at the 2005 general election, 71 per cent of those in the top social classes voted versus 54 per cent of those in the lowest social class, a gap of 17 per cent compared to a 7 per cent gap in 1960. The same is true of 'interest in politics'; a study by the Institute of Public Policy Research reports that between 1981 and 1999, interest in politics fell across all social classes, but most strongly for the lowest social classes where it fell by half.[26]

The problem is not merely that politicians are beholden to money – it is rather that the electorate itself, at least in the USA, is increasingly becoming a rich man's club. Paul Krugman's reflection, made a decade ago, is apposite:

> The reason why government policy has reinforced rather than opposed this growing inequality is obvious: Well-off people have disproportionate political weight. They are more likely to vote – the median voter has a much higher income than the median family – and far more likely to provide the campaign contributions that are so essential in a TV age.
>
> The political center of gravity . . . is therefore not at the median family, with its annual income of $40,000, but way up the scale. . . . So never mind what politicians say; political parties are competing to serve the interests of families near the 90th percentile or higher, families that mostly earn $100,000 or more per year.[27]

Krugman might well have added that what is increasingly true of political parties is true of the media as well. In Britain, the Blair government assiduously cultivated the support of big media owners such as Rupert Murdoch, the Rothermere family, Richard Desmond and (until his disgrace) Conrad Black. As Paul Whiteley has noted:

Politicians frequently worry about the effect on the voters of newspaper editorials endorsing rival political parties during a general election campaign. Harold Wilson, for example, was said to be obsessed by the press coverage of his government and the likely electoral consequences of it. Similarly, the current prominence of spin-doctors and the growth of media advisers in government demonstrate the importance of having favourable media coverage in the modern never-ending election campaign.[28]

Murdoch, in particular, has been a regular visitor to Downing Street, first under Thatcher and most recently under Blair and Brown; successive governments have deregulated cross-media ownership in a way which has allowed the News International empire to flourish in the UK, where it owns Sky television and five Fleet Street papers (including the The Times and The Sunday Times, and London's News of the World and the Sun), accounting for nearly 49 per cent of Britain's readership. Much the same has happened in the USA where Murdoch's interests range from newspapers, publishers and advertising to the Fox News channel; recently he picked up the Wall Street Journal. More generally, the growth of ownership concentration in America has been documented in a variety of studies. In the early 1980s, ownership of major media outlets was distributed between about fifty major players. Twenty years later, mergers had reduced that number to five.[29]

In 1949, a Royal Commission on the Press took the view that the press is more than just another business. It has a public task and a corresponding public responsibility, being the 'chief instrument for instructing the public on the main issues of the day':

> The democratic form of society demands of its members an active and intelligent participation in the affairs of their community, whether local or national. It assumes that they are sufficiently well-informed about the issues of the day to be able to form the broad judgments required by an election, and to maintain, between elections, the vigilance necessary in those whose governors are their servants and not their masters ... Democratic society, therefore needs a clear and truthful account of events, of their background and their causes; a forum for discussion and informed criticism; and a means whereby individuals and groups can express a point of view or advocate a cause.[30]

But as the late Hugo Young said when his former paper, The Sunday Times, was taken over by Murdoch: 'Very little space is any longer available for the discussion of poverty, inequality, injustice or anything which might be recognisable as a moral issue. If there is an ethic at work, it is an unvarnished version of the business ethic.'[31]

This chapter has focused on the social and political costs of inequality and relative deprivation. The following chapter considers what might be termed the 'macroeconomic cost' of ever-expanding consumption driven by inequality, and particularly on the finance of consumer spending in the USA and its sustainability. Can the consumption binge continue? The short answer is that it cannot. It is widely recognized that market forces are leading to a major recession in the USA; such an outcome could have very grave consequences for the world economy. Tackling inequality is thus important for us all.

8

Is the Consumption Binge Sustainable?

This is a system in which global recession is temporarily averted essentially by expanding the consumption of relatively rich populations in industrial countries, in this case, principally in the United States. And this excessive level of consumption is financed by increasing levels of U.S. external debt, both public and private.

McKinley (2005: 12–13)

Help! We Can't Make Ends Meet

An excellent illustration of the dilemma facing growing numbers of Americans (and Britons) appears in an article in *The New York Times* describing the finances of a young couple with two children.[1] The Smiths (not their real surname) between them take home $66,000 a year (significantly higher than the median household income), have an average size home and an average lifestyle. But here's the rub! They have a mortgage of $90,000, a home equity loan of $70,000 and debt of over $20,000 spread over a dozen credit cards. That's a total debts of $180,000; even assuming a low interest rate of 5 per cent, they would need to pay $9,000 a year in interest alone merely to tread water. They are not alone. It is estimated that in 2006, the average American family spent one-seventh of its income simply servicing debt.

The Smiths may spend half a lifetime paying off their debt. At the moment, they can only make ends meet by judicious juggling; namely, taking the right decisions about when to pay it, when to let it build and how best to consolidate it by taking advantage of credit-card consolidation schemes promising low initial interest rates. To stay afloat, they must avoid bank and credit card penalties incurred for late payment, usurious interest rates of up to 30 per cent and above all keep track of their finances on a daily basis. A few weeks before, Mrs Smith had used a debit card rather than a credit card to make nine purchases totalling just over $200 – but had failed to note that the purchase would tip her over her bank's overdraft limit. In consequence, she faced a $32 penalty on each purchase, or a total of $288 – considerably more than the total value of the purchases.

And, of course, they avoid thinking about how they would cope if either of them incurred a high medical bill or was off work for a protracted period. Mrs Smith describes how one of their neighbours was a couple of weeks' late in renewing his medical insurance premium when he fell and broke his arm; that mistake had cost their neighbour $25–30,000, say the Smiths.

The growth of easy credit may have helped some families to buy a first home or get through a bad patch, but the range of credit instruments has increased so much that many families find it difficult to make sense of a bewildering array of interest rates, financing charges and penalties hidden in the small print. An average American family has a mortgage, a home equity loan, a range of credit cards, a car loan and perhaps a student loan still outstanding. Before the US courts loosened financial regulations in 1996, most credit cards charged the same interest and penalty rates; today, interest rates vary widely as do penalty charges and every day the morning post contains new promises of cheap credit. Measured in constant dollars, US credit card debt is estimated to have trebled since 1990. In 2006, it totalled nearly $1 trillion, with penalty fees alone coming to over $17 billion.

Although Britain provides stronger and wider social safety nets, things don't always feel better to families who can't make ends meet. Consider the story of a forty-year-old woman raising a young son and working as a UK immigration officer. One day, her husband left her. Suddenly, she had to manage the family finances on a single salary; as her debts increased, she became increasingly ashamed of her situation and could tell nobody – until, two years later, her world came crashing down. She tells the story of her personal bankruptcy as follows:

> My debts gradually crept up. The bank had refused to give me an over-draft and the interest rate on my credit card was massive. My bosses kept making me work on weekends and in the evenings, which meant my childcare costs rocketed. It all came to the crunch last March. I owed £32,000 and was completely desperate. Bankruptcy has been one of the most horrible experiences of my life . . . I thought going bankrupt meant all my debts would be wiped clean, but they're making me pay £579 a month for the next three years . . . Because I have no access to direct debit or standing orders, I have to pay everything in cash. Bills have to be paid in a single lump sum, instead of spread evenly over the months, and because I can only take £200 a day out of my account I have to make sure I know exactly when each bill is going to arrive so I can get to the bank – which is on the other side of town – enough times beforehand to take out

all the money. Then I have to take time off work to get to the post office or council tax office, with hundreds of pounds in my bag, to pay the bill. I'm desperate to avoid ever owing any money again, but instead of helping me, going bankrupt has made my life much more difficult. I'd never advise anyone to go bankrupt. It's hell.[2]

Just as in America, Britons are increasingly falling into debt. According to a Bank of England study in 2006, the average person has debts that total 150 per cent of their annual income, half as much again as in 1997. The Bank believes around one million households face problems coping with debt repayments. A report from Citizen's Advice said 770,000 mortgage borrowers had missed at least one mortgage repayment over the past year, while two million homeowners said they were concerned their finances would not stretch to cover their debts. According to the government's Insolvency Service, the numbers becoming insolvent in the second quarter of 2006 reached 26,000, a 66 per cent rise on the same period in 2005.[3]

More Economic Theory

There are a number of ways to theorize the growth of income inequality, and a short digression into relevant economic theories will be useful. For today's neo-classical economists – a term which covers a far wider spectrum than 'neo-liberal' – the most widespread explanation derives from 'endogenous growth theory', a piece of jargon made famous by Gordon Brown when Chancellor. Endogenous growth theory says that – particularly in advanced economies – growth depends not just on equipping workers with machines but on investing in 'human capital', i.e. , in education and training. In consequence, those who miss out on the educational 'input' are left behind. Neo-liberals, particularly in America, tend to add that if some people remain poor, it is that they have made the wrong 'choices' about investing in education.

The problem with this argument is that it is trivial. A more educated workforce is self-evidently a good thing, and, while low levels of education may correlate with low wages, the growth of inequality we observe today is more about the explosion in rewards at the top. Top managers may have more education, but education is certainly not the main driver of inequality. If it were, top CEOs would all have PhDs.

So far, I have treated the present increase in inequality as one result of the neo-liberal restoration of the 1980s which helped restore profitability in the UK and the USA. In addition, it is no coincidence that the politics and economics of this process have swung most to the right in those advanced industrial countries where profits were squeezed most. This is hardly a new thesis: the original version was first set out in a pioneering book by Glyn and Sutcliffe published over thirty years ago, and recently updated and extended in Glyn (2006). In somewhat different form, the argument reappears in Desai (2002).[4]

Inequality is more than a temporary aberration of modern capitalism. Theories that see inequality as *central to capitalist growth* have a long pedigree in classical and development economics. In Ricardo's theory of distribution, labour was paid only what was needed to ensure its survival. Ricardo believed in what economists refer to as Say's Law (after Jean-Baptiste Say): namely, that supply creates its own demand and thus a capitalist economy can never suffer from deficient demand. Ricardo's famous correspondent, John Malthus, argued that any rise in the real wage would soon be offset by rising population growth, leaving workers as poor as they were before. (Although Malthus was deeply conservative, he did fear that capitalism might stagnate as a consequence.) Nearly 125 years later, Keynes and others showed Say's Law to be logically flawed.

For Marx, it was the existence of a large pool of unemployed – his 'reserve army' – that held down the wage and prevented any squeeze of profits. Marx's capitalists, unlike Keynes's, suffered no lack of animal spirits. On the contrary, they endlessly reinvested their surplus – but Marx added that as production became more capital intensive, the rate of profit would fall.

Post-war development theory later incorporated Marx's 'reserve army' by way of Sir Arthur Lewis's seminal article which argued that Britain's industrial revolution was made possible by drawing a large pool of unproductive rural labourers into manufacturing; i.e., equipping them with machines. The result was to make labour far more productive while its wage remained constant, thus enabling the capitalist to invest the surplus in more machines to speed growth. But could growth continue indefinitely? According to Marx, it could not. Marx's 'tendency' for the profit rate to fall, a tortuous argument which rested on an early version of the capital–labour ratio (the 'organic composition of capital'), is today conveniently forgotten. But even Keynes was sceptical about the prospect of sustaining capitalist growth in the long term.

To be sure, a few Marxists (including Rosa Luxemburg) have argued that deficient demand drives capital to search for new markets, to 'globalize' as we would say today. Keynesians, in contrast, have tended to argue that poverty constrains aggregate demand, and therefore that higher wages lead to growth; i.e., that '*measures for the redistribution of incomes in a way likely to raise the propensity to consume* [my emphasis] may prove positively favourable to the growth of capital'.[5] Note that Keynes did not speak of redistributing income in a more egalitarian manner, but writing in the context of the Great Depression this is doubtless what he meant.[6]

Be this as it may, the classical argument – whether in the form of Marx's 'reserve army' or of Lewis's 'unlimited labour supply' – has survived relatively unscathed. In modern parlance, wages can rise – but only as long as labour productivity rises faster. This enables the capitalist to gain a surplus and to invest in newer machines, in turn ensuring that productivity will continue to rise. If wages rise too quickly, profits will be squeezed.

The relevance of this simple principle should be obvious. We are observing not just a redistribution from poor to rich, from wages to profits as it were, but a world where there appears to be an excess of savings over investment, and the excess is flowing broadly speaking from high-saving Asia to low-saving North America. Marx's 'reserve army' labours at subsistence wages in India, China and elsewhere to produce wage goods for export to the rich countries, thus keeping international inflation (and real wages everywhere) low. The globalization of trade and financial services permits capital to relocate centres of profit, and allows surpluses to be recycled towards the world's financial centres.

But there is a further element: under-consumption. Say's Law has long been dismissed, and Marxists, Keynesians and Monetarists all agree that aggregate demand (or in the latter case the money supply) can constrain capitalism at less than full- employment output. One of Milton Friedman's useful insights was to reintegrate the Pigovian 'wealth effect' into consumption; i.e., to assert that, as our assets grow, so too will our consumption. And it appears that this wealth effect has become a major driver of consumption. In both the United States and Britain where assets values have boomed, negative household savings help sustain consumer spending and economic growth. Domestic investment and consumption in turn has been sustained by an inflow of foreign savings from those countries (like Germany, Russia and China) which have a large trade surplus; i.e., whose exports exceed their imports.

To be sure, these surplus countries are quite different from one another. Russia (like the Middle East) is an energy exporter. Germany has traditionally kept the lid on domestic demand – though with high incomes and good public services – through tight monetary policy designed to facilitate the country's export drive; China has massive household savings, while many other countries attempt to be domestically frugal under the tutelage of the IMF. The point to note is that the Anglo-Saxon consumption boom is sustained by rest-of-the-world savings; a drying up of foreign savings for whatever reason would almost certainly provoke a global recession.

How Money Flows Uphill

There's hardly an international economist or financial journalist who has not written about the US external deficit and the dire implications for the world economy if faith in the almighty dollar were to collapse. Everyone agrees that the US overseas indebtedness cannot continue growing indefinitely. But they disagree about the causes and the remedies and, most importantly, about the likelihood of catastrophe. Just as with global warming, anybody rash enough to suggest that a radical change in policy is required to avoid global meltdown is deemed to be a Cassandra. [7]

For some years now, the USA has run a large (and growing) external deficit; i.e., a surplus of imports over exports. To pay for this deficit, the USA has borrowed money, a process greatly helped by the willingness of the rest of the world to hold dollar denominated debt. The conventional view in the OECD countries is that the US deficit is sustainable and will gradually be corrected by market-led exchange-rate movements. On this reading, governments need merely pursue prudent fiscal and monetary policies to bring their own external account into balance or surplus.

In reality, though, it is illogical to suggest that all countries should aim for current account balance or surplus since, to the extent some run savings surpluses, others must run savings deficits. Moreover, one would expect low-income, capital-poor countries to be running deficits in order to finance their development, and rich countries to be financing them. In practice, the opposite is true: the world's richest country runs the largest deficit, one financed by surpluses in less rich countries. [8] The US deficit is many times larger than current official aid flows to poorer countries. In today's topsy-turvy world, capital flows uphill – from poor countries to rich countries. [9] The direction of flow should not be interpreted as meaning that the USA is 'causing world poverty'; quite the contrary, the danger is that if there is a run on the dollar, world trade might be badly hurt in the ensuing recession, and it is the world's poor countries that can least afford world economic disruption. It is vital that this financial imbalance be righted without killing the patient or infecting everyone else.

In essence, the argument presented below is that the long US consumer boom is unsustainable, but that its cure cannot be left to the market. Devaluation alone will not do the trick; indeed, the widespread expectation of very substantial devaluation may lead to a run on the dollar with detrimental consequences for the world economy. A package of coordinated policy measures is needed. The main elements of such a package are managed revaluation of the major non-dollar currencies and, crucially, the reflation of the EU economy. EU reflation is seen as a necessary counterweight to any US deflation needed to re-establish a sustainable external balance.

The relatively favourable growth record in recent years of the USA (compared to, say, the Eurozone) is largely explained by a long consumer boom financed by growing household borrowing and, after the stock-market collapse in 2000, helped along by a large government budget deficit and a long rise in house prices. In explaining the consumer boom which followed the recession of 1990–1, it is worth recalling that, while Bill Clinton was busy balancing the public accounts, net private sector savings in the USA (i.e., firms plus households) fell from 6 per cent of GDP at the beginning of the decade to *minus* 6 per cent, adding an extra $1.25 trillion to aggregate demand. The net borrowing of the private sector over the same period rose to nearly 14 per cent of GDP in 2000, of which about half was financed from abroad. When the stock-market bubble burst early in 2001, the budgetary surplus inherited from Clinton enabled the Bush administration both to loosen monetary policy and to boost the economy fiscally by cutting taxes and increasing defence-linked spending. If tax cuts for the rich worked, it is in part because many better-off households joined the consumption binge and in part because the fiscal stimulus was so large. It is estimated that the US Government pumped an extra $700 billion into the economy – 2 per cent of GDP every year – between 2000 and 2003.

Today one hears much about the US 'twin' deficit; in reality it is a 'treble' deficit encompassing the household, government and external balances. Both the government and the private household sectors spend more than they save, and this gap is reflected in an external deficit on current account equivalent to 6.5 per cent of GDP that must be financed from abroad. In 2006, the USA spent about 50 per cent more than it earned in the world market. The resulting gap represents by far the largest current deficit ever recorded, and it is growing.

In the period 1996–2006, the US current account deficit – the broad balance of trade in goods, services and payments with the rest of the world – rose by over $500 billion to reach a new record of nearly $850 billion. To get some idea of the magnitude of this sum, if we add the external deficits of the poorest third of the world's 168 countries, the resulting figure represents barely one-twentieth of the US deficit. The US trade deficit is over eight times the size of total official development assistance

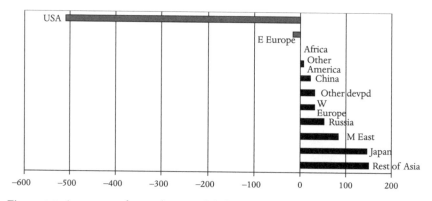

Figure 8.1: Average trade surpluses and deficits, 2000–2004 (US$ million nominal)
Source: Irvin and Izurieta (2006)

(ODA) from all donors in 2005, which stood at $108 billion and included aid to Iraq and Afghanistan. As can be seen in figure 8.1 – and in more detail in figure 8.3 later in this chapter – the US trade deficit has been financed by trade surpluses elsewhere, chiefly those of Asia, the oil-exporting countries and Germany.[10] Moreover, US trade deficits in 2005 increased with every major area of the world, including China (34 per cent), OPEC (18 per cent), Africa (15 per cent), Europe (15 per cent), Mexico and Canada (13 per cent combined), Latin America (12 per cent), and all Asian countries besides China (5 per cent).[11]

As Terry McKinley of the International Poverty Centre in Brasilia has put it:

> Basically, the rest of the world – including current-account surplus countries such as Japan, Germany and Switzerland – have compensated by maintaining large surpluses . . . Up until 1998, developing and transition countries were running sizeable current account deficits; thereafter, however, they swung rapidly into surplus. . . . In Asia, two-thirds of the swing from deficits into huge surpluses occurred during 1996–1998, as a result of the financial crisis that swept the region. Developing Asia's current account surplus had reached US$103 billion in 2004, with China alone accounting for US$70 billion. Countries in the Middle East have also begun to rapidly generate current account surpluses because of the rise in oil prices. In 2004, their aggregate surplus was about US$113 billion. Saudi Arabia has had the largest surplus among this group. Another major current-account surplus region is the Commonwealth of Independent States. Russia, which is about US$60 billion in surplus,

dominates the regional aggregate. The only developing region . . . that is running an aggregate current account deficit is sub-Saharan Africa. Its deficit position, e.g., about US$10 billion in 2004, is little changed from 1997. Instead of running a deficit, South Asia achieved a small current account surplus by 2004, with India leading the grouping with a surplus of about US$2 billion. So some poor regions have recently joined the capital-exporting band wagon. [12]

Why is this deficit a problem? After all, the rest of the world by definition must be able to finance it, since deficits and surpluses must balance for the world as a whole. Equally, if the USA were investing large amounts of overseas money in expanding productive capacity, we might expect the deficit to cure itself. Such investment in turn would add substantially to world demand and would be consistent with economic development elsewhere. But this is not the case: the overseas inflow finances current consumption and the acquisition of financial and residential assets.

Since the amount of US government savings is negative and the government deficit has been rising, it must be financed largely by sales of US securities to foreigners. But foreign governments – particularly low- and middle-income developing countries who hold an estimated $1.8 trillion in reserves – become less interested in holding dollar-denominated paper as its value depreciates against other currencies like the euro; equally, rising interest rates raises the burden on the US government of financing official debt.

US government budget deficits in the past have been offset by US household and corporate savings, but US households now spend more than they earn to a degree that offsets net corporate savings. Whereas, historically, the household sector was a net lender to the tune of about 2.5 per cent of national income, today's households have become net borrowers of about 6 per cent of national income.[13] Clearly, any fall in household borrowing would cause the economy to contract unless offset by more spending elsewhere; e.g., by government. If financial markets worry when there is an external deficit, they worry even more when there are government and private deficits as well.

Admittedly US expansion has acted as a Keynesian 'motor' of the world economy, particularly in the 1990s when financial markets were buoyant. Nevertheless, there is growing anxiety about whether deficit-fuelled growth is sustainable. Since the US private and government sectors have ceased saving, it is foreigners who must save – chiefly by lending their savings to the USA. As foreigners use their surplus dollars to purchase US assets, the USA has moved from being a net creditor to a net debtor to the tune of roughly $4 trillion. The stock of overseas investment in the USA (i.e., US liabilities) at the end of 2006 reached about $14 trillion, slightly more than the country's GDP. Servicing US net indebtedness is beginning to add to the country's current deficit.

Most importantly, the deficit has increased despite a nominal devaluation of more than 40 per cent, or a *real effective* devaluation of about 20 per cent over the five-year period 2002–7. If adjustment is sought by recourse to devaluation alone, then it is clear that much larger effective devaluation is needed. This is mainly because the burden of adjustment must come from expenditure cutting (rather than switching) for devaluation to work. But large-scale expenditure cutting would most likely be accompanied by a US – and thus a world – recession. Such a recession would hardly provide a climate conducive to US export growth. What economists fear is that if financial markets become convinced that the USA deficit is unsustainable, the prophecy will be self-fulfilling.

The Deflating Housing Bubble

A key factor underlying the growth in US and UK household debt has been the liberalization and growth of the financial market. The stock-market boom of the 1990s morphed into the real-estate boom of the current decade, with low interest rates, rising asset prices, mortgage withdrawal and unsecured credit card debt helping to fuel faster growth in private spending. Household savings have disappeared because spending has grown faster than household income. Unlike the asset-market bubble before it, the US house-price bubble has flattened rather than collapsing all at once.

In the past if you wanted a mortgage, you needed a reasonable income, a good credit rating and a deposit. But during the last decade's far more liberal financial markets in the USA and UK, obtaining a mortgage has been nearly as easy as getting a credit card. Mortgage brokers make their money by issuing credit, often using artificially low initial rates of repayments to entice their customers. New mortgages are immediately 'bundled' and sold on the secondary market, so brokers can pass on the risk and thus have little reason to worry about whether the buyer can meet the payments. As long as house prices rise, new buyers don't carry much risk either. If your income is too low to meet the monthly payment, you can draw new equity from the appreciation on your home. As a result, foreclosure rates remained low until recently. But, as prices flatten and credit tightens, the person who bought a mortgage when interest rates were 2 per cent may find him/herself in deep trouble if rates rise to 5 or 6 per cent (as many Britons discovered during the 'negative equity' crisis of the early 1990s). This is just what's been happening in the USA since the Fed began raising interest rates early in 2004; in 2007, nearly a million homes were reposessed in the USA. To quote Dean Baker, head of the Washington-based think tank CEPR:

> [D]elinquency rates began to soar in 2006. More than 10 per cent of the subprime adjustable rate mortgages issued last year (the most risky category) were already seriously delinquent or foreclosed within 10 months of issuance. . . . The investors who bought up these mortgages in the secondary market are now refusing to lend more money. Credit is drying up for both the sub-prime and the Alt-A market, which is a notch above sub-prime in creditworthiness. These two segments of the housing market together accounted for 40 per cent of the mortgages issued in the last two years. If 40 per cent of potential homebuyers suddenly have problems getting credit, it has to have a large impact on the housing market. Throw into the mix that the inventory of unsold homes is 25 per cent higher than at the same time last year. And, the number of vacant units up for sale (normally an indication of a highly motivated seller) is up more than 40 per cent compared to last year. . . . That is the story of a collapsing housing bubble. . . . the politicians pushed policies that persuaded many moderate-income families to buy overvalued homes that they could not afford. And the mortgage brokers made a fortune selling bad mortgages.[14]

As Paul Krugman once said, stock markets may deflate with a bang, but house markets emit a slow hiss.[15] In 2006–7, the hiss speeded up. The US real-estate market flattened in 2005 and economic growth has since slowed substantially. Figures issued in mid-2007 showed new home prices in the USA to be falling at an annualized rate of 11 per cent, the biggest decline since 1970. In Britain, although annual house price inflation has remained positive until recently, successive interest rate hikes and the recent credit crunch have slowed its impetus. The problem is that slowing down the US economy while avoiding recession is a difficult balancing act. The Fed can tighten monetary policy in small steps while hoping the financial market doesn't get too jittery; otherwise the Fed will need to inject credit into the economy quickly. Failure to calm the markets might lead to a worldwide credit crunch and financial market turmoil, possibly provoking a US recession. Because of the highly interconnected nature of world financial markets, contagion in the USA can quickly spread to the UK and continental Europe, as illustrated dramatically by the 2007 sub-prime lending crisis.[16]

Sub-prime Blues

Those who worry about the close connection between negative household savings in the United States and world economic instability need look no further than the 'sub-prime lending' crisis of 2007, an instructive lesson in how quickly a set of apparently unrelated factors can combine to produce the threat of financial meltdown. In early September 2007, small savers in the UK queued up for days outside the branches of Northern Rock in scenes reminiscent of the Great Depression. Northern Rock is one of Britain's many building societies which (much like a US 'thrift') specialized in mortgage lending. Until the crisis, it had been one of Britain's most dynamic mortgage lenders, achieving a high average annual growth rate and holding little bad debt. But in the course of a few days, depositors withdrew nearly £20 billion, and the company's share price plummeted by 80 per cent, making it ripe for takeover. In 2006 the company's chairman, Adam Applegarth, had paid himself a modest £1.4 million; as one journalist noted, unlike Jimmy Stewart in *It's a Wonderful Life*, he did not appear at the door of the bank offering to repay customers from his own money.

Ironically, the run on Northern Rock appears to have been precipitated by factors which have little to do with the institution's financial integrity, but rather were caused by the 2007 summer credit crunch in the US market. Indeed, what is most worrying about this episode is that contagion has crossed the Atlantic and could so easily spread to financial institutions in the UK. The US Fed and the European Central Bank have poured billions into keeping financial markets solvent, the former $70 billion and the latter €150 billion in July and August of 2007. The Bank of England followed in recognizing – perhaps a trifle late – that the damage needed to be contained quickly, given the central role of the City of London in the world's money market. To reassure the market, in mid-September 2007 the UK government guaranteed the savings of all Northern Rock clients and injected £10 billion into the money market. In the USA, the Federal Reserve has reversed course and cut interest rates in an effort to avoid recession. Financial confidence is shaky, the outlook for 2008 is bleak and further bailouts will be needed. How did all this come about?

A generation ago when the world of finance was still relatively simple, mortgage banks took in savers' deposits and used these to make long-term loans, making their profit from the spread between the interest rates paid to lenders and by borrowers. Loan outflows are a bank's assets and deposit inflows are a liability; hence the traditional golden rule of banking – lend short and borrow long – is meant to keep the inflow of maturing loan repayments well ahead of the outflow of liabilities to depositors. A banker's worst nightmare is that the bank's creditors – traditionally, thousands of small savers – will all turn up at once demanding their money back, thus precipitating the bank's collapse. Ostensibly, mortgage banks defy gravity because their loans are all long term; hence, the supreme importance of lending only to those who can repay and whose collateral is quite literally 'safe as houses'.

Several things have happened over the last generation to change the picture. First, the rapid development of financial markets, and particularly that for short-term funds (the international 'money market'), has made access to credit nearly instantaneous and investors are more reliant on such credit. Equally, central banks today are more conscious of their obligation to act as lender of the last resort if a private sector bank cannot meet its cash obligations from its own funds or from the money market. Also, flexible mortgages mean that if interest rates rise, a mortgage bank can pass the rise along to borrowers. Perhaps of most importance, banks need no longer carry risky mortgages which, if unpaid, would be classed as a 'non-performing asset'. Instead, mortgages can be bundled up ('securitized' in the jargon – see figure 8.2), segmented by their degree of risk, and sold in the market just like any other commodity.[17] In short, banks can unload risk on to whoever buys these 'asset backed securities' (ABSs); buyers might be any institution looking to diversify its asset portfolio, including other banks.

In the United States, one of the factors fuelling the housing bubble was the eagerness of banks to lend for house purchase and for the remortgaging of existing property, reflecting the ease with which banks could pass on mortgage risk to the secondary market. Initially, banks granted mortgages to high- and middle-income clients; such mortgages, when bundled into bond-like assets, were given a 'prime' rating by valuers such as Moody's Corporation and thus considered virtually risk-free. As the momentum behind the housing boom grew and interest rates remained low, banks extended their services to low-income clients eager to join the consumption spree – often using bait-and-switch tactics to lure them in, then charging them above-prime rates. Since such clients were vulnerable to any rise in interest rates, the resulting mortgage pools were deemed to be sub-prime. But when sub-prime mortgages were bundled together with prime mortgages, the resulting mortgage pools could still be bought and sold in the world money market like any other financial product.

Starting in June 2004, the Federal Reserve repeatedly pushed up the federal funds rate from a low of 1 per cent to 5.25 per cent by late 2006, in effect nearly doubling the burden of mortgage repayments on the finances

> An ABS is a type of bond or note based on a pool of assets; the pool can be made up of any type of receivable such as mortgages, car loans, credit card payments and so on. The advantage of bundling such receivables is that it spreads risk; i.e., while buying a single $1mn mortgage would be risky (since a default might greatly wipe out the value of your asset), in principle a financial institution would be happy to buy a bundle of 100 mortgages each worth $10,000 since a default or two would hardly affect the asset's anticipated cash flow.

Figure 8.2: Asset backed securities (ABS)

of an average family. Predictably, one result was a dramatic rise in the default rate on mortgages granted to sub-prime borrowers. Banks and other institutions holding fully or partially sub-prime ABSs now found it difficult to sell these in secondary markets and, as the assets lost value, so too did the asset sheet of their holders who, in turn, tightened credit. Because the world money market is today so large and electronic trading is ubiquitous, a wide variety of institutions rely on the money market for short-term credit needs. By mid-2007, what had started as a rise in the default rate on sub-prime mortgages in the USA turned into worldwide credit crunch. The world's leading central banks may have talked tough about the moral hazard of bailing out overexposed institutions, but faced with the prospect of world recession they flooded the market with liquidity.

By late 2007, the world liquidity crisis appeared to have been temporarily contained. But the consumer spree of the past two decades, first facilitated by financial deregulation and driven by the booming stock market and then by the housing market, seemed to be drawing to a close. Indeed, the IMF's *World Economic Outlook* for 2007 was specifically concerned with how far the US slowdown would affect the world economy.[18] The danger is that the world financial system is already quite fragile; a further crisis could send the world economy into a tailspin. More generally, the contagious nature of the liquidity crisis is a further sign that unfettered free markets do not guarantee economic stability and prosperity, nor do they give rise to an income distribution that underwrites social stability and individual well-being.

Unsecured Debt

The long US consumer boom has been not merely about rising house prices and shaky mortgages; it has been about expanding consumer credit, both secured and unsecured. According to figures released by the US Federal

Reserve, between 2002 and 2006 total seasonally adjusted consumer credit outstanding rose from $2.0 trillion to $2.4 trillion, an annual rate of just over 5 per cent . In March 2007, consumer credit increased at an annual rate of 6.75 per cent.[19] These figures cover most short- and intermediate-term credit extended to individuals (mainly credit card and car loan debt), but they exclude loans secured by real estate. US consumer debt has reached staggering levels after more than doubling over the past ten years; in 2006 it stood at approximately $20,000 per household; or approximately two-thirds of personal annual disposable income.[20] Over the period 1990–2003, while the number of people holding charge cards grew about 75 per cent – from 82 million in 1990 to 144 million in 2003 – the amount they charged grew by a much larger percentage: approximately 350 per cent, from $338 billion to $1.5 trillion.

In 2004, it is estimated that the credit industry mailed out about 5 billion card solicitations in the USA – about seventeen per head of population – and the figure for 2006 is thought to be 8 billion. Several reports by the US think tank Demos (not to be confused with Demos in the UK) examine the explosion in credit card debt which took place in the decade of the 1990s and since.[21] Indeed, Draut (2005) argues that credit cards have been a substitute for the traditional household savings cushion. During the 1990s, average household credit card indebtedness rose by over 50 per cent – but it rose particularly quickly for the bottom three quintiles of the income distribution and even for the fourth quintile; i.e., right up to middle-class families with incomes of $100,000. This rise in debt reflected the squeeze on families whose incomes stagnated while costs rose, particularly the cost of health care and housing.

Equally important has been the effects of financial deregulation. Two Supreme Court rulings in 1978 and 1996 were particularly important; the first struck down usury laws capping high interest rates while the second moved supervision from the federal to the state level. Banks began to market credit cards far more aggressively, mainly through direct mailing; they trebled the amount of credit offered to customers, and lowered minimum payment requirements while increasing late payment fees to penal levels. Further liberalization enabled cards to be marketed not just by banks, but by businesses working in conjunction with the finance industry. In consequence, today, everyone from your favourite airline to your local supermarket issues credit cards. The credit card business has become one of the most profitable sectors in the financial services industry.

The story of soaring unsecured debt will be familiar to Britons as well. Like the USA, the UK deregulated the financial services industry during the

Thatcher years. Today, the UK is responsible for one-third of all unsecured debt in Europe; in 2005, net lending on credit cards, loans and overdrafts was £215 billion versus £600 billion for the EU combined. The average European family has credit card debt less than half the size of its British equivalent. There are an estimated 50 million credit cards circulating in the UK, accounting for about 33 per cent of unsecured debt; the corresponding figure in France is just 1.6 per cent and even lower in Germany. A Treasury select committee has voiced concern at total household debt in Britain passing the £1 trillion mark in 2005, while a *YouGov* survey in 2006 found that one in five adults – or 8 million Britons – had unsecured debts of more than £10,000.[22]

Is 'Slightly Slower Growth' Sustainable?

Although the growth in US household spending in the past decade has been relatively painless, and has thus appeared sustainable, rising asset values ('real balance effects') do not automatically translate into extra income. Until recently, holding gains have been turned into ready cash because of the ease of remortgaging, and low interest rates have kept financial markets well-lubricated. But, looking beyond the credit crunch, there are at least four reasons why this pattern cannot persist unchecked.[23]

First, any slowdown in asset appreciation tends to generate uncertainty about the sustainability of future gains, and hence lead to a further slow-down. Slowing asset gains translates into slowing private consumption. Second, although the value of asset growth may slow or even reverse, consumer liabilities remain the same; i.e., the mortgage loan for the new car or the children's education must be repaid. Moreover, under conditions of very low inflation, the value of household debt erodes only slowly. Figure 8.2 illustrates how US private residential investment has burgeoned in the past fifteen years and with it the burden of personal debt.

Third, although a slowdown in private spending can be offset by an increase in government spending, the scope for such counter-cyclical policy has been reduced by the Bush administration. When the stock-market bubble burst in 2001, Washington responded by lowering interest rates, granting swingeing tax cuts and (in the wake of 9/11) switching to security and military expenditure. Washington's monetary stance has since tightened, thus providing scope for renewed loosening. But the fiscal giveaway had two key drawbacks. For one thing, tax cuts were poorly targeted and had minimal growth-stimulating effects; tax cuts cannot easily be clawed back, and this narrows the scope for government to prime the pump in future. For another, a powerful industrial lobby on Capitol Hill drives the continuous expansion of 'security'-related' expenditure, draining money from other forms of government spending such as the maintenance of economic and social infrastructure.[24] In short, if the private household sector cuts its own spending and returns to a sustainable savings path, government must run ever-growing deficits to sustain aggregate demand at a time when the scope for so doing has greatly diminished.

Of course, the US economy might be rescued by increased investment in the corporate sector. But this escape route is blocked by two factors. One is the prospect of slackening domestic demand deterring the growth in new investment – and, with it, the growth of labour productivity.[25] And, even assuming domestic demand is not a constraint on investment, another problem is that the ownership of US corporations is increasingly in foreign hands. As the US external deficit is recycled and used to purchase US assets, the flow of repatriated profits (i.e., the required yield on those assets) will increase, constituting a growing leakage out of US income, in turn resulting in a smaller investment multiplier; i.e., a smaller boost to the economy from each dollar invested..

Nor is protectionism the answer. Populist measures to increase barriers to trade and capital flows would slow the world economy, or invite retaliatory measures from trade partners (such as China) sending the dollar into a tailspin. In short, the increased probability of a weaker dollar and the prospect of a US slowdown is not merely the mechanical outcome growth in the US trade gap.

Why Market Forces Cannot Correct the Problem

The response of the Bush administration to growing external debt has been confused. The Treasury Secretary appears to believe in a solution sustained by increases in productivity resulting from a synergy between the foreign capital keen to invest in the USA and the resilience of 'corporate America'. The Federal Reserve appears keener on market-led exchange-rate adjustment. This response mirrors the IMF traditional view which, succinctly stated, is that a full-employment growth path is sustainable as long as governments practice fiscal and monetary restraint and prices – chiefly the prices of foreign exchange and labour – are allowed to adjust freely. While the precise degree of devaluation required is not stated, the unofficial view in Washington for some years now is that a real effective dollar devaluation of about 20 per cent would suffice to restore overall trade balance. Relative to the dollar's peak against the euro in 2002, the dollar had already fallen by

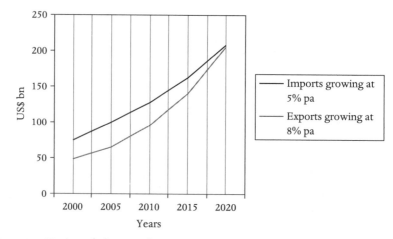

Figure 8.3: Projected closure of US current account gap by 2020
Source: Irvin and Izurieta (2006)

far more than this amount at the time of writing (late 2007). An influential paper by Obstfeld and Rogoff (2005) has suggested that a real depreciation in the range 35–50 per cent is required. And although the US trade balance in 2007 improved slightly relative to the position twelve months earlier with exports growing slightly faster than imports, in late 2007 there was still no sign of a major reduction in the trade gap. Indeed, Reuters reported an ex-economic aide to the Bush administration saying that a weakening dollar might 'make things worse'.[26] Or, again, McKinnon and Schnabi (2006) say:

> William Cline estimates that a 28% real effective depreciation of the U.S. dollar would reduce the U.S. current account deficit from a projected 7.5% of GDP to 3% of GDP . . . We conclude that the impact of massive dollar devaluation on the U.S. trade deficit would be ambiguous, but that the macroeconomic stability of the world economy could be seriously undermined.[27]

There are several reasons why exchange-rate adjustment *alone* cannot restore balance. First, a number of US trading partners (e.g., China, Malaysia, Hong Kong) have effectively pegged their currencies to the dollar – the modern version of the competitive devaluations of the 1930s – and are unlikely to be persuaded to accept the slowdown in export-led growth that currency revaluation would entail. Second, these countries have ample foreign-exchange reserves, enabling them to follow the dollar downward. Third, as numerous analysts have pointed out, the real fall in the dollar relative to the 1990s has not led to a significant improvement in the external account position. This may be due in part to the fact that dollar depreciation has a perverse 'wealth effect'. When the value of the dollar falls, US holders of (say) euro-denominated assets find that the value of their portfolio, when calculated in dollars, has risen. In consequence, they feel richer and continue spending. This effect could in principle be amplified by the fact that non-US holders of dollars would experience a concurrent 'holding loss' discouraging spending, and thus weakening US export demand.[28] More importantly, though, devaluation may have become less effective because of the 'Richistan effect', i.e., the fact that a growing share of US household spending is accounted for by the super rich who don't reduce or switch their consumption in response to rising import prices.[29]

Most important, the trade gap is simply too large. As shown in figure 8.3, exports would need to grow 3 per cent faster than imports for fifteen years merely to bring US exports and imports to balance. Such a turnaround could not be engineered by price adjustment alone but would require constraining import growth via a slowdown in economic activity. But an adjustment induced by stagnation or recession would be painful not just for the USA; it is undesirable because it would threaten the international economy as a whole. In sum, while exchange-rate adjustment may be desirable, it needs to be accompanied by decreased absorption in the USA and increased absorption in the rest of the world.[30]

A variant of this argument that has gained currency in Washington is that the US trade deficit results not from excessive US consumption but from a 'world savings glut'; i.e., an infelicitous combination of the artificially low exchange rates maintained by some of America's trading partners and the fact that the rest of the world is not consuming enough.[31] On this view, it is the rest of the world, not Washington, which must adjust. One need not dwell on the irony that consumption in the rest of the world is constrained at least in part by policies of fiscal and monetary orthodoxy preached (but not practised) in Washington; i.e., by the universal injunction that all countries should exercise restraint.

The main target of this argument is China whose de facto currency peg enables it to run a huge external surplus and stash away a vast hoard of dollars. Irrespective of how one views China's exchange rate,[32] since China's surplus accounts for only 10 per cent of the US deficit (and less than half this figure if consolidated with Hong Kong's trade deficit), it is hard to see how a 'clean' float of the yuan alone could solve this problem. The Chinese, moreover, are unlikely to tighten their belts in order to accommodate a correction to the consumption habits of the USA. As to growth in the rest of the world, this indeed should be encouraged, but – as argued below – faster growth outside the USA will require major policy changes and institutional reform.

What of Europe?

Continued growth of the world economy has been facilitated because government and households in the USA spend more than they earn. The resulting buoyancy in world demand has been sufficient to allow governments and households in the EU and elsewhere to be 'prudent'. This basic principle is often forgotten in comparing the USA and EU growth records. Although some EU-15 countries are in deficit – e.g., the UK, Spain, Italy, Portugal and Greece – collectively, Europe runs a surplus on current account transactions with the rest of the world, a fact explained largely by Germany's export performance. In 2004 and 2005, Germany overtook the United States in the total value of its exports. Over the past ten years the EU-15's exports to the rest of the world have increased from 7 to 11 per cent of total GDP; in the USA, by contrast, the share of exports in GDP over the same period has stagnated.

In this respect, the UK resembles the USA more than the Eurozone. Like the USA, the UK's growth record over the past decade has been better than that of the Eurozone. And, although Gordon Brown's management of government finances was more prudent than that of his US counterpart, the UK runs a sizeable visible trade deficit which is financed by inflows of foreign capital. Britain's sustained growth in recent years is explained only in part by an increase in expenditure on public services; in the main, it is explained by strong household spending facilitated by house price appreciation. Indeed, as asset price appreciation slowed in 2005, the Treasury's projected GDP growth figures for 2006 and 2007 were immediately revised downward and show growth falling slightly below the Eurozone average. According to the EU Commission in Brussels,[33] in 2007 the Eurozone was forecast to grow at 2.6 per cent and the USA at 2.2 per cent; the IMF expected UK growth to be 2.9 per cent. In light of the sub-prime market troubles of 2007, it is unlikely that even these modest growth forecasts will be met.

The Problem with UK Prosperity

During the French presidential elections in 2007, a recurrent theme in the British press was how much Britain shone as a beacon of prosperity for French voters, or indeed for the EU as a whole. Britain's current Prime Minister and ex-Chancellor, who makes no secret of his admiration for the way things are done in America, never misses an opportunity to admonish Britain's EU partners for their failure to liberalize labour markets, cut back on unnecessary government spending and 'modernize' economic management. But although UK per capita income has grown slightly faster than in the EU core countries (Germany, France and Italy) over the past decade, upon closer examination the UK figures are much less impressive.

Much like America, Britain is a country where aggregate demand has been driven by a spending boom fuelled by rising house prices, cheap credit and cheaper imports. According to the Royal Institution of Chartered Surveyors, house prices in Britain rose 170 per cent over the decade of Gordon Brown's Chancellorship. In late 2007, the average price of a house in the UK was close to £200,000 (€300,000). This is all very well if you want to borrow money against the value of your house, but terrible if you are young or poor (or both) and trying to get into the housing market. Moreover, unsecured household debt (e.g., credit card borrowing not offset by rising net worth) in 2006 reached a total of £1 trillion; the UK accounted for half the credit card borrowing in the EU-15. Little wonder that, to continental Europeans, Britons appeared to be on a permanent shopping spree.

But although Britain's strong currency and powerful financial services industry helps attract foreign capital to London, a strong pound is not good for British industry which must compete with cheap foreign imports. Before Mrs Thatcher, the British manufacturing industry produced about 40 per cent of the country's income; in 2007, industry's share in GDP was just 13 per cent. Industry has not thrived in the past decade; indeed, more than a million jobs have been lost on Labour's watch. This sea-change is reflected not just in the relative decline of Britain's industrial heartlands of the north, but in the UK's trading figures. The trade deficit in 2006 was about 5 per cent of GDP, nearly as large as in the USA. Although a positive balance of trade in services – insurance banking, advertising and so forth – brought the figure down to 4 per cent, Britain today lives on a combination of UK investment income from abroad plus capital flowing into the City of London. In the words of the *Guardian*'s Larry Elliot:

> The Germans may have the engineers, the Japanese may know how to organise a production line, but the Brits have the barristers, the journalists, the management consultants and the men and women who think that making up jingles and slogans in order to flog Pot Noodles and similar products is a serious job. It has the deal makers in the City who make fat fees by convincing investors to launch bids for companies, and the corporate spin-doctors who tell their former pals in financial journalism that tycoon X will make a better fist at running Ripoff plc than tycoon Y.[34]

Back in the 1970s, when industry first started shedding jobs, much of the slack was taken up by public-sector employment. And, although Brown helped revive some areas of public services by increasing spending in the period 2000–5, the period of rapidly growing public spending has been brought to a halt by the government's self-imposed rules of financial stringency over the economic cycle. At the current stage in the cycle, if Britain is not to break the Treasury's 'Golden Rule', a period of severe restraint in the public sector is likely.[35]

The latest gimmick of selling Britain's image as a cutting-edge economy consists in proclaiming that Britain is undergoing a 'knowledge economy' revolution, one in which tomorrow's jobs will all require university degrees in rocket science and atomic particle physics. Yet one survey after another reveals that Britons are amongst the most poorly educated in Europe and that today's university students are more likely to want a degree in media studies or accountancy than in maths, sciences or modern languages. According to Will Hutton's Work Foundation, the iconic jobs of the twenty-first century are hairdressers, celebrities, management consultants and managers. Britain's spending in Research and Development compares poorly with other OECD countries; according to the Department of Trade and Industry, more than half the R&D effort takes place in just two sectors: pharmaceuticals and aerospace. Moreover, as Britain pulls out of European aircraft manufacture to redirect its partnership efforts towards the USA, an increasing chunk of the aerospace business is defence-related; i.e., in weapons-systems manufacture.

Disregarding the knowledge-economy hype, as industrial employment declines, although a few graduates may be fortunate enough to land a six-figure salary in the City, the majority of jobs are generated – and will continue to be generated – at the low-skill end of the service sector. Britain now holds the EU record in the proportion of people employed in such occupations as data entry and call centre reception; there are as many people 'in service' (e.g., nannies, maids, gardeners and the like) as there were in Victorian times.[36]

Restoring World Economic Balance

The question remains: how is balance to be restored to the world economy? The conventional wisdom is that the cheaper dollar will eventually bring about adjustment. While exchange-rate adjustment is necessary, I have argued both that devaluation is a weak and insufficient instrument and that a sustainable and effective correction needs a combination of careful global management and good luck. Like the stock market, the foreign-exchange market depends on sentiment, which is notoriously volatile and can lead to over-adjustment. In place of the current policy of benign neglect of the dollar, international action is needed to move towards a set of exchange rates between the main trading blocs that is compatible with full employment and will result in manageable inter-regional surpluses and deficits.

Price adjustment can only be successful if it is complemented by quantity adjustment. Quantity adjustment is conventionally taken to mean that US consumers must reduce their expenditure on foreign imports – tighten their belts – in order to free resources for exports. But harsh belt-tightening in the USA under conditions of universal fiscal and monetary prudence can only lead to world economic stagnation and possible recession. The essential point is that quantity adjustment needs to be expansionary; i.e., the rest of the world must be able to absorb the US deficit. Since US imports have until recently grown steadily at about $200 billion per year and exports at about $100 billion, a *full* correction of the current account requires the rest of the world to absorb nearly $1 trillion of annual US exports in the near future and perhaps even more in future years. It is difficult to see this happening without significant world economic *acceleration*.[37] In practice, 'adjustment' requires immediate action both to move towards more realistic exchange rates and maintain high levels of aggregate demand for tradable goods. But even if one aims at a partial correction of the US external imbalance, the quantities involved are enormous and will not come about without shaking up current institutions and effecting a change in the US mindset. The reallocation of surpluses and financing to generate demand and employment in the world as a whole may be a difficult balancing act, but it is not impossible.

Figure 8.4 shows the eight largest surplus countries and how the 2006 US deficit of $857 billion was 'financed'. The main surplus countries were China and Japan who together absorbed 41 per cent of the US deficit, with Germany, Saudi Arabia and the former Soviet Union countries together accounting for a further 37 per cent. The FSU countries and Saudi Arabia are large energy exporters, and their surpluses can be treated as resulting from industrial expansion elsewhere; i.e., chiefly the EU and Asia. Since growth in China is already very high, little more need be said other than to express some concern about how long the current rate can be maintained. What of Japan and Germany? In Japan, after fifteen years of stagnation and five of deflation, a looser fiscal and monetary stance seems at last to be producing conditions favourable to sustained growth.[38] By contrast, after five years of very slow growth in Germany and other core Eurozone countries,

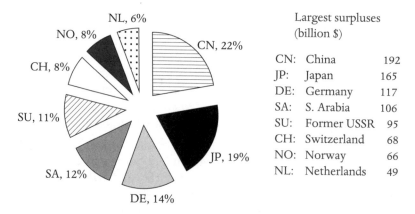

Figure 8.4: Country surpluses as a per cent of the US deficit in 2006
Source: Jomo and Izurieta (2007) and author's own calculations

a slight improvement in performance since early 2006 appears to have produced disproportionate concern about inflation. The ECB raised its key interest rate to 4 per cent in June 2007 for the eighth time in eighteen months and once again warned member-states against budget deficits. And although the ECB has responded to the credit crunch by bailing out the banking system, it has not (at the time of writing) followed the US Fed in cutting interest rates.

Germany's poor growth performance until recently is explained not just by the drag on the economy of sustaining sizeable continued transfers to the East, but also by the dysfunctional nature of the Eurozone arrangements for macroeconomic management. Although there are signs of renewed German and French growth, there seems little doubt that the very slow recovery since 2001 of the core Eurozone countries derives in part from the straitjacket on aggregate demand imposed by the Stability and Growth Pact (SGP), as well as from the European Central Bank's exclusive concern with inflation targeting.

There is a significant and growing literature on how Eurozone macroeconomic policy and institutions might be shifted in favour of expansionary fiscal policy and a more inflation-tolerant monetary policy which I have reviewed in a recent book; in consequence only a few points will be made here.[39] First, the European Central Bank (ECB) currently lacks an exchange-rate policy; it could usefully take the lead in bringing together the USA and its main trading partners to thrash out a medium- and long-term view of sustainable exchange rates for the major trading blocs under different growth scenarios. Second, the Eurozone needs far more robust fiscal arrangements.

If SGP-constrained automatic stabilizers at member-state level have proved too weak to lift the main Eurozone states out of stagnation over the past five years, they provide almost no protection against a large external shock caused by a world credit crunch and/or a run on the dollar. In addition to scrapping the SGP (and concentrating instead on sustainable levels of public debt), the EU budget must be large and flexible enough to play a counter-cyclical role as first suggested in the MacDougall Report.[40]

Minimally, this would mean funding the budget through a combination of progressive taxation, ECB *seignorage* and EU Treasury borrowing; in the longer term, a central fiscal authority would contribute to the fiscal robustness and universality of social insurance and pensions throughout the EU.[41] Most importantly, a long-term investment programme in social and economic infrastructure would provide both a major stimulus to growth and help meet the Lisbon targets; the need for such a programme was clearly envisaged in the Delors White Paper of 1993.[42]

A crucial qualification concerns Europe's finding an alternative to the US and UK growth strategies. 'Anglo-Saxon' growth, as already seen, has been driven by a boom in private spending sustained by rising asset prices. The role of government has been confined largely to keeping interest rates low by capping public borrowing, and to promoting liberalized credit markets, enabling holding gains to be converted to ready cash. Recently, professional discussion has focused on whether or not government (particularly in the USA) has been too discretionary in fiscal and monetary matters, about EU supply-side 'flexibility', about whether the ECB should continue to tighten monetary policy and so on. Almost nothing has been said about the relatively low levels of productive (private and public) investment growth, the decline in manufacturing relative to financial sector activity and the growing household income dispersion accompanying the UK consumer boom. The above suggestions for EU reflation would right this imbalance.

Equally, there is the worry that some Eurozone countries may be moving in the direction of a US-style debt-fuelled growth; e.g., in Ireland, France, Spain (and to a lesser degree in Italy), rising house prices have sparked an increase in spending which appears to be spilling over into the external balance.[43] Moreover, in some countries (e.g., Denmark), the link between financial deregulation and a house-price boom is clear – and potentially more destabilizing than running an 'excessive' government deficit. Asset-inflation-led growth must be distinguished from the classically Keynesian path led by public investment and social provision which facilitates private investment in cutting-edge industries, precisely where comparative advantage can be established and new exports promoted. If slowdown in the USA is to be offset by accelerated growth in the Eurozone, it is vital to consider what constitutes a sustainable growth path.

A New Phase of Instability

The world economy has entered a new phase of potential instability. As Ronald McKinnon of Stanford University has warned:

> the really big incidental negative from a deep nominal devaluation of the dollar is the monetary upheaval associated with debasing the key currency of the international monetary system. Such an event did occur in August 1971 when President Nixon imposed import tariffs in order to force all the other industrial countries to appreciate against the dollar. Because this 'Nixon Shock' was so well telegraphed in advance, the huge flight from dollar assets into foreign monies led to a loss of monetary control both in the United States as well as in Europe and Japan.[44]

The growing deficit in the USA must by definition be offset by growing surpluses elsewhere. Underlying these flows is a burgeoning and volatile world capital market: cumulating stocks of appreciating net assets in whose value is maintained and contested between governments, corporations and households, and an international market for goods and services whose locus of production is drawn towards cheap labour. Since exchange-rate adjustment is today relatively weak and politically constrained, no market mechanism exists for checking world trade imbalances. If world recession is to be avoided, it has become imperative to seek cooperative solutions between trading blocs in which surplus countries accelerate their growth in order to facilitate adjustment by deficit countries. This logic runs counter to the current deflationary orthodoxy.

The debate in the UK about the potentially constraining nature of Gordon Brown's Golden Rule – like the debate in the Eurozone about the constraint on growth imposed by the Stability and Growth Pact – has important implications for the world economy as a whole. European (including UK) growth is required not merely to reduce European unemployment, but to counteract the danger of world recession posed by the US external deficit. World trade deficits and surpluses can only be managed by careful policy coordination between the regions concerned, a role Keynes envisaged for the IMF at the time of its founding in 1944. In practice, this role has been relegated to free markets and to central bankers. But, in today's world, exchange rates must be negotiated and managed with care, and trade flows must not be disrupted by deflationary policies. Most importantly, if it is vital for the Eurozone to grow, it is equally vital that the growth path be more equitable and sustainable than that observed in the USA over the past decade. The European 'social model' is not an optional extra; rather, it is central to the debate over how best to encourage the extra European growth needed to offset the US slowdown.

In this chapter, I have tried to locate the strongly neo-liberal trend in the development of the USA and UK economies in the context of global economic imbalance. Just as annual increments in US GDP (and to a lesser extent UK GDP) are going to the rich, so growth in the world's richest country is financed in good measure by savings from countries which are less well off. Equally, in the same way that the rebalancing of global finance means shifting growth from the USA to other nations, so internal rebalancing means moving towards a more equitable distribution of income within the USA and the UK.

Note that I have carefully qualified the argument by adding that a unilateral slowdown in US growth might precipitate recession which would be bad for the world growth, particularly for the world's poorest countries which are highly trade-dependent. At the same time, the claim should be resisted that greater equality in the USA and the UK is desirable merely because it makes long-term growth more sustainable. Irrespective of the truth of this claim, the case for equality needs to be made explicitly. This matter is addressed in the chapter which follows.

9

In Defence of Equality

Equality of opportunity has long been recognised as a basic principle of social justice, but what is often not understood is just how radical its implications are for the way that our society is currently organised.

David Miller, 'What is social justice?', in Pearce and Paxton (eds) (2005: 10)

'Fair Shares'

Were the Bush 2001 tax cuts 'fair'? Were post-war levels of taxation in the USA or the UK 'punitive', or were they merely designed to redistribute income from the rich to the poor (which they succeeded in doing)? Since the Reagan-Thatcher years, it has become acceptable to use terms like 'fairness' and 'equity' in ways which pervert their meaning, detaching them from any notion of distributive justice. In a letter to the *Wall Street Journal*, arguing in favour of the cuts, the argument was put this way. The top 1 per cent of taxpayers earn about 20 per cent of total income in the USA, but they pay 38 per cent of federal income tax; therefore, it is only 'fair' that they should receive the lion's share of the benefits. Or take another example, this time from the report of the Commission on Social Justice set up by Tony Blair's predecessor, John Smith, which argued that although there was much inequality in Britain, it was inadmissible to return to the 'punitive' high marginal tax rates of the 1970s and that no one should pay more than 50 per cent of his or her total income in tax.[1]

The right-wing press in Britain and America goes on about the inequity of high taxation on a daily basis. But what is a 'fair' share of tax? Is it – as the letter writer would appear to want – a tax rate 'no higher' than that percentile's 'contribution' to national income? If one accepted this argument, then – assuming marginal rates of federal income tax were set by quintile – the richest 20 per cent of Americans would pay a top tax rate of just over 50 per cent, the middle quintile would pay 20 per cent and the bottom quintile less than 5 per cent. Such a scale would be slightly more progressive than the current two-band system, which is presumably quite the opposite of what the letter writer intended. Still, it almost certainly would be insufficiently progressive to change the distribution of income significantly, and might simply result in a lower tax take.

Why cap the top rate of tax at 50 per cent as the Commission on Social Justice wanted? Despite much rhetoric about 'fairness', there is no more justification for capping the top tax rate at 50 per cent than for choosing a cap of 30 per cent or 70 per cent. Even were the top rate 99 per cent, a pay rise for the rich would still make them richer. Unless one has some explicit distributional criterion in mind – for example, to reduce the ratio of the 10th to the 1st decile to 3:1 (roughly the level of Sweden) over twenty years – the choice of a top rate is arbitrary. To say that one is in favour of social justice means justice – starting with equal opportunity – for all, not just for some. As the political philosopher Brian Barry[2] has argued, equal opportunity for all means establishing a level playing field – and it should be clear that, today, the playing field is not merely tilted in favour of the rich, but becoming more so each day. To say that one is in favour of equal opportunities – but that the playing field need not be level – is not merely a retreat to a second-best position, it is illogical.

In Britain, a good example can be found in recent Liberal-Democrat rhetoric. While the Labour Party chose to accept the 40 per cent top rate inherited from their predecessors, the Lib-Dems argued for some years that the top rate should go up to 50 per cent until suddenly scrapping this policy at their annual Conference in 2006. Their Treasury spokesman, Vince Cable, was delighted with the decision and said afterwards: 'The nature of the debate has changed, so it's not now about higher taxes but fair taxes and how we distribute the burden equitably.'[3] That the statement is a *non-sequitur* should be obvious; the current 40 per cent top tax rate in Britain is patently *not* fairer or more equitable than 50 per cent. What Vince Cable implicitly meant was that 40 per cent was 'fairer' for those earning above £100,000 a year, but that would have given away the game.

When the Reagan administration first started cutting top tax rates in the 1980s, the argument was not that such cuts were fairer. Rather, they argued along the lines set out by Arthur Laffer (see chapter 1) that lower rates would, by increasing work incentives, result in higher growth and a maximum tax take. The virtue of such an argument is that, right or wrong, it has some testable empirical basis. If the overriding objective of economic and social policy is to maximize growth while coincidently raising total tax revenue, then a tax system can be devised for this purpose quite irrespective of any concern for distributional justice. The design of the system can be tested and amended accordingly, resulting perhaps in a lower top rate and a lower share of tax in national income. On the other hand, if the main concern in devising a tax system is distributive justice, the purpose can be made clear and one can proceed accordingly. What is quite unacceptable is to devise a system designed to maximize 'efficiency' while pretending that it is based on 'fair shares', that it is the most equitable or that it provides 'equal incentives for all'. And yet this is the sort of rhetoric we hear every day; our willingness to accept the legitimacy of such discourse marks the extent to which neo-liberalism has become deeply entrenched in the UK and the USA.

It is not enough to say that the society in which we live is unjust without providing some alternative benchmark. I shall not attempt here to give more than a crude definition of what I consider a 'distributionally fair' society – crude because it implicitly conflates 'society' with the nation-state (thus ignoring international redistribution) and fails to consider fairness between generations (which would mean looking at the inheritance of wealth, the environment and so on). Clearly, no one, and certainly not Marx, intended that 'distributional fairness' should imply a utopia in which wealth and income are forever distributed in perfectly equal shares. In this sense I agree with the critique of 'simple equality' advanced by Walzer (1983), Bobbio (1996) and others.

The definition of distributional justice offered by the widely respected American political philosopher, John Rawls, in his 1971 book, *A Theory of Justice*, is a good starting point. Rawls's view of a just society makes individual liberty the overriding principle. Crucially, resource endowments are so distributed as to be acceptable to a potential new entrant to society whose social position is unknown to her or him before entry – or behind what he calls the 'veil of ignorance'. Rawls thought that an individual behind such a veil would prefer a society with an egalitarian distribution of initial endowments, although he allowed that a degree of inequality might subsequently emerge. However, Rawls posited a fundamental trade-off between efficiency and equity; moreover, it was for Rawls a sufficient condition of 'fairness' that any improvement in one's position should not leave anybody absolutely worse off, what economists call a 'Pareto improvement'. One should add that Rawls, in contrast to many economists, was not a utilitarian; his notion of distributional justice does not depend on maximizing 'utils' or subjective well-being.

Three points about 'justice as fairness' are far clearer today than they were when *A Theory of Justice* was first published. First, Rawls confined himself to the nation-state; he did not extend his theory to cover international inequality. Second, in a 'knowledge-based' economy, there may be no trade-off between efficiency and equity; indeed, as I have argued, the two are complements, not substitutes. The third and crucial point concerns how much we judge our welfare relative to others, i.e., if one person is made better off, all others will be *relatively* worse off by definition. If *relative* deprivation concerns us – and I have argued that it must – a 'distributionally fair' society must include more than merely reasonably equal endowments and opportunities; it must include a constraint on inequality; i.e., the distribution of wealth and income. If asked to move beyond philosophical speculation and give a concrete example of a 'distributionally fair' society which might be pursued in today's Britain (or even America), the answer would be the Nordic countries.[4]

Rights and Entitlements

When we talk about people's rights, it is important to be clear about what we mean. With the Enlightenment, the medieval notion of separate rights for the nobleman and the common man was gradually replaced by the notion of universal rights. Pre-revolutionary France, in which the 'three estates' benefited from a hierarchy of rights with few rights available to those at the bottom of the social pyramid, would be considered flagrantly unjust by today's standards. More recently, the abolition of slavery or the end of apartheid in South Africa is welcomed for the same reasons. School children in the USA and even the UK will be familiar with the famous phrase (from the US Declaration of Independence) about 'life, liberty and the pursuit of happiness' being the right of every individual.

But of course rights can be defined minimally and maximally. In principle, the notion that 'all men are created equal' means all are entitled to equal treatment under the law. But in practice, slavery was not abolished until the nineteenth century; universal suffrage is largely a twentieth-century product and, even today, discrimination on the basis of colour, gender and religion in still widespread. Or again, minimally, the right to life means that murder is prohibited. In principle, one is protected in law against arbitrary arrest and execution whether by the state or any other agency; but the state is not legally bound to feed and clothe you or provide you with adequate shelter. To be sure, governments everywhere in the West have assumed greater responsibility for providing full employment and enacting minimum wage legislation, but such extensions of 'positive' rights have emerged as a result of the least privileged working through political channels in defence of their interests. At the end of the day, how we view such matters is shaped by the scope for effecting political change.

Such rights have emerged, too, because the ruling class in the twentieth century became more aware that, if the legitimacy of the established political order was to be maintained, greater attention would have to be paid to the demands of the underprivileged. A useful illustration can be taken from the field of disability legislation:

> When Americans talk about the rights of disabled people – say, those who are wheelchair bound – to have access to public places, they do not mean merely that there should be no law forbidding them access. They mean that it should be physically possible, thanks to ramps and elevators, for disabled people actually to get to offices, shops, educational institutions, places of public entertainment, and so on. I shall say that this is the demand not for a right but for an opportunity.[5]

If one accepts the above logic, then the demand for equal opportunities is an extension of the classical demand for equal rights. Moreover, the notion of equal opportunity cannot be reduced to merely legislating against unequal access, unequal treatment before the law, unequal segregated education and so on. If equal opportunity is desired, then – just as in the case of people in wheelchairs or of any other disadvantaged group – the means of access must be provided. Such a definition of equal opportunity, as we shall see, poses a clear challenge to the notion that we live, or at least should live, in a meritocracy.

Meritocracy and Education

'The idea of meritocracy may have many virtues, but clarity is not one of them,' wrote Amartya Sen in an essay entitled 'Merit and Justice'.[6] Clarity in our use of language is a precious gift, as I am often reminded when travelling by air in the United States. American pilots and cabin crews have taken to saying such things as 'We will be taking off momentarily.' What one assumes they mean is 'we shall be taking off *in* a moment'; otherwise, the thought of a fully laden 747 rumbling along at 150 knots and lifting off, stalling and returning to earth a few moments later is decidedly unnerving.

The term 'meritocracy' was coined by Michael Young in the late 1950s, and used to describe a future in which Britain would no longer be ruled by 'democracy' (the rule of many), but by an elite whose advancement depended on merit alone. Young intended the book as a cautionary warning about the power of higher civil servants and other sections of the establishment who wielded disproportionate political power and whose claim to legitimacy in a more modern era could no longer be seen to rest on class privilege and old school ties. Young's intention has been largely forgotten so that in popular usage today, 'meritocracy' is generally thought to be a good thing; indeed, the term has acquired iconic status in the New Labour lexicon and Blair and Brown have missed no opportunity to proclaim the need for Britain to become more 'meritocratic'. Writing in the early 1960s, Michael Frayn brilliantly anticipates (and caricatures) New Labour by imagining the *Modern Living Party* described thus:

> The quality shared by the Party's members was, its leader said: successfulness. By that I mean we are the sort of people who are good at passing exams . . . at winning scholarships to university . . . and in general at doing well for ourselves in a highly competitive world. . . . In short, the sort of people who join the *Modern Living Party* are men and women who enjoy certain natural advantages which they've inherited from their parents, and which they confidently expect to hand on to their children.[7]

The above example, I hasten to add, I owe to Brian Barry whose excellent book *Why Social Justice Matters* inspired my own modest effort in this chapter. The simplest definition of meritocracy is 'advance by merit', or advance on the basis of equal opportunity for individual achievement, always supposing achievement to reflect the qualities of honesty, dedication, hard work and so on. This is the stuff of ideology, what is colloquially know as the American Dream and which, in previous chapters, I have argued is becoming increasingly difficult to realize.

The logical objection to the contemporary concept of meritocracy is twofold. First, merit cannot be a truly legitimate basis for achievement and advancement unless the opportunities for achievement are distributed equally, or at least reasonably so – which they clearly are not in the USA and the UK. Second, if merit is assumed to be based on some sort of inheritable genetic endowment such as IQ, strength of character, determination or whatever, then unless such attributes are distributed randomly and correlate strongly with actual achievement, a 'meritocratic' society is not a just society. This second condition is not met either.

Any discussion of 'equal opportunity' must start with the years prior to becoming an adult. In adulthood, one is supposed to exercise full rights as a citizen as well as to be held fully responsible for one's actions. Childhood is critical because it is in these years – perhaps most strongly in the very first years of childhood – that our potential is moulded. At the heart of these years is 'education' in the broad sense, as well as in the narrower sense of attending school and acquiring a formal education. Whether or not one believes in a distribution of innate talent as measured by IQ or whatever, it is clearly of critical importance that children have environments that are equally conducive to developing their resources to the fullest, thus enabling them as adults to start 'on a level playing field' and to make use of the opportunities which present themselves. In a word, inequalities of adult outcomes are 'fair' as long as they arise from conditions of equal opportunity.[8]

Education and Equal Opportunity

Since this is a book about economic inequality, let us agree to define 'successful adult' in the narrow terms of financial status: rich or poor. It is in early childhood that the process of differentiation between successful and unsuccessful adults begins. The quality of care before and after childbirth is of obvious importance. This category covers a wide variety of services, access to which depends partly or wholly on socio-economic status. A woman is more likely to have a medical examination before childbirth in Britain under the National Health Service than in the USA where medical insurance is far from universal. Parental care includes classes on child care and presumes paid leave, but there is little financial support or leave available in the United States compared to (say) Sweden which provides universal support and where generous paid leave is extended to both parents. Since 1993, US workers in firms of more than fifty employees – about half the workforce – have had the right to twelve weeks of *unpaid* leave; it is reported that nearly two-thirds of workers do not exercise this right because they cannot afford the loss in wages.[9]

Parental time is important not merely in the post-natal phase but throughout early childhood. Here again, social and income status can make a crucial difference. The following extract is as relevant in Britain as in the United States (or anywhere else).

> Some stunningly painstaking and sophisticated American research has shown just how large the gradient of class inequality in talk is: 'The longitudinal data showed that in everyday interactions at home, the average (rounded) number of words children heard per hour was 2,150 in professional families, 1,250 in working-class families and 620 in the welfare families.' There was also a sharp gradient in the complexity of language used.[10]

The early development of good language skills, unsurprisingly, is one of the many ways in which children from well-to-do middle-class backgrounds gain an early lead in the race to find well-paid jobs they will enter after leaving school. A study of over 15,000 children born in the period 2000–2 in Britain shows that by the age of three, children from middle-class families are already twelve months ahead of children from disadvantaged families in their understanding of colours, letters, numbers, sizes and shapes.[11] Moreover, gaining such a lead confers cumulative advantages; these children will consistently outperform their peers in primary school, leading to a greater chance of securing a high place on the secondary school ladder and so on. The crucial point is that, however important investment in education may be, adequate cognitive skills are developed very early in a child's life, largely *before* school age.[12] In the words of Esping-Andersen:

> the very child-centred nature of redistribution in the Nordic welfare states is crucial . . . [these states] have now for decades furnished near-universal day care for pre-school children. With female employment becoming universal, children from economically and/or culturally weaker homes have come to benefit from pedagogical standards and cognitive impulses that are basically the same as for children from privileged backgrounds.[13]

While Britain has the Sure-Start programme which helps parents from poor areas to prepare their children for school, the coverage of Sure-Start has been patchy, and the programme has become increasingly focused on helping to reduce the number of 'workless households'. Worklessness – particularly amongst single parents – is seen by New Labour as a major driver of social exclusion. In the words of *The Millennium Survey; Poverty and Social Exclusion in Britain*:

> As Blair argued in one pre-election television broadcast in 1997, such [workless] households, whether or not headed by a lone parent, failed to instil by example an appropriate work ethic in their children. The policy for reducing poverty among lone-parent families, reducing benefit dependency and overcoming their social exclusion, is primarily a labour market solution.[14]

This is another good example of New Labour 'values': social exclusion is bad not because it disadvantages the children of the poor educationally or otherwise, but because it fails to instil an appropriate work ethic. The solution to such exclusion is not so much to provide such children with compensating resources, but to make sure their parents have the incentive – primarily through Working and Child Tax Credits – to 'get on their bikes' and find a job. The responsibility of the state is to make the poor and the disadvantaged aware of their individual responsibility for overcoming such disadvantages, or quite simply to make them work harder. If this sounds much like the neo-liberal 'responsibility agenda' pursued in the USA, it is because that is exactly where it comes from. As one critic put it:

> Even more worryingly for the left, it seems that Blair has turned Labour supporters against the idea of redistribution. It is almost a truism that Labour is now a middle class party . . . [but] Blair has changed the ideological base of the party's support as well as its social base.[15]

Once a child is in school, the advantages conferred by class background and economic status are unlikely to be offset by remedial programmes, free school lunch programmes and the like, important though these may be. The main difference outside school is the amount of time parents devote to their children. Barry (2005: 55) reports that, in a US study carried out in 2000 on parental time as a determinant of school performance, it was found that children who scored poorly in reading and maths were significantly more likely to have working parents with little or no entitlement to holidays, sick leave or flexible hours. This result emerged even after controlling for differences in family income, parental education and total hours worked. Moreover, a child from a family where one or more parents worked at night was nearly three times as likely to be suspended from school at some stage.

Another factor affecting parenting abilities is job-related stress. There is ample evidence that stress-related anxieties tend to increase as one moves down the social gradient. Poorly paid jobs are generally the least secure jobs where the rate of turnover is high. And in 'meritocracies' where individuals are taught to believe that economic status is determined wholly by one's own effort, just as the wealthy will feel winners, the poor will feel losers. In short, children from poor families not only receive less attention, but the lack of entitlements, low security and high-stress accompanying poor pay means that poorer parents must necessarily do less well at parenting than the better-off.

An experiment carried out in the United States helps make the point. A programme in Wisconsin took seventeen mothers from deprived backgrounds whose IQ score was 75 or below; para-professional care-givers were enrolled to help train both mothers and their small children. The programme was highly intensive, each care-giver spending three to five hours a day for an average of three days a week in the family home. At six to eight weeks, the children were placed in full-time day-care facilities while the mothers received job training. By the age of eight, these children's IQ scores were equal to the national average, and were significantly higher than a control group of children from similar deprived, low-achievement mothers. It should be added that although this programme was part of the welfare-to-work scheme developed in the Clinton years, it involved a substantial investment in resources needed to offset the initial educational disadvantage of the family. It is to be distinguished from other welfare-to-work programmes in which families receive subsistence-level tax credits made conditional on taking any job, however menial and ill paid, and which reduce the time available for parenting.

It should be apparent that if equality of opportunity is to be a meaningful concept – if eighteen-year-olds are to start adult life on a level playing field – then a universal programme of remedial education for the underprivileged, starting before school-age and sustained for many years, is required. Indeed, it is important to have multiple opportunity ladders, so that people who miss out on educational opportunities before eighteen will have further chances to develop their potential. This will be necessary both in the United States, where social exclusion is strongly associated with membership of an ethnic minority, and in Britain where the class divide is still enormous.

Moreover, in the USA and Britain, social mobility appears to be decreasing. In Britain, a study dated 30 March 2004 undertaken by Stephen Aldridge for the Prime Minister's Office, entitled 'Life chances and social mobility: an overview of the evidence', concludes that in recent decades, the expansion of the middle class has virtually stopped. '[A] middle-class child is 15 times more likely to stay in the middle class than a working-class child is to move into the middle class . . . A baby's fate is virtually fixed at 22 months: school is too late. Only the USA has less upward social mobility than the UK among western nations.'[16] Evidence of the same nature for the United States has already been set out in chapter 6.

The Asymmetrical 'Responsibility Agenda'

Neo-conservatives in the United States and Britain like to argue that a 'fair' society is one in which everybody assumes full responsibility for his or her own choices; in their view, 'welfare' merely creates dependency on the state – hence the derogatory term 'nanny' state – instead of placing it squarely on the shoulders of the individual. This was the central message of the Reagan-Thatcher years. The message was taken on board by a good many Clintonites as well who, for fear of being branded 'liberals', promised 'an end to welfare as we know it', a phrase which harks back to the Victorian distinction between the 'deserving and undeserving poor', the latter having to find work if they want support, entirely in keeping with Mrs Thatcher's values and Norman Tebbitt's injunction to 'get on your bike'.

Much the same can be said of New Labour whose rhetoric and policy agenda is so closely modelled on that of Bill Clinton's.

What is objectionable about this view is not just that it is wrong. Although it is clearly misleading, or at best woefully naïve, to argue that the poor remain so only because they fail to work sufficiently hard and make the wrong choices, crucially, the 'responsibility agenda' is inconsistent. The current generation of rich and powerful displays little of the sense of philanthropy and civic duty which their Victorian ancestors allegedly held to be important. In the Unites States, the notion that privilege entails responsibility would have been familiar to such elite political families as the Kennedys and Rockefellers, just as in Britain it is associated with 'one nation' Conservatives in the mould of Butler and Macmillan.

The same cannot be said of the Bush family whose offspring show little concern for anything more than rewarding their cronies, or even of a Labour government which hands out ASBOs to the poor and peerages to the financiers. Today's super rich feel that they deserve their rewards irrespective of the jobs that are lost through downsizing, the deteriorating working conditions entailed by locking out trade unions or the environmental damage resulting from relaxing emission standards and the deteriorating public provision from lobbying for corporate and personal tax breaks.

Or take the example of 'national defence'. Economists call this a 'public good' because it must be provided collectively, but they add that there is usually a 'free-rider' problem with public goods; i.e., the danger that some will avoid their responsibility and get a 'free ride' from society. They rarely add that, in the case of going to war, it is the middle class who are most often the free-riders, obtaining exemption from the draft (conscription) not generally available to the poor. So, while the Kennedys famously served during the Second World War, George Bush sidestepped Vietnam, as did most of his Cabinet appointees. These days – in deference to the middle class whose sons and daughters generally prefer to avoid the battlefield – armies have become 'professional' and it is young people from deprived backgrounds who are most likely to become cannon-fodder. Because the poor 'choose' to become soldiers through the mechanism of the market, the 'free-rider' problem is deemed to be resolved.

Or, again, consider the growing concern expressed in some quarters that the breakdown of marriage may be 'causing' poverty and social exclusion. In 2007 *The Economist* carried a special section on 'Marriage in America', citing a number of recent studies showing a negative statistical correlation between divorce and educational attainment.[17] 'Marriage is a wealth-creating institution,' wrote one academic researcher, arguing that young men (and women) who get married and remain so are far more likely to complete secondary education successfully, acquire one or several degrees, get better-paid jobs and so on. The piece ended by urging government to draw attention to the benefits of marriage, just as it does to the perils of smoking. What is remarkable here is that the implied causality runs from individual attitudes towards marriage to future socio-economic status; i.e., get married and you'll earn more. The notion that the causality might run both ways – much less that socio-economic status may be the prime determinant of whether one can afford to get married, finish school, go to university and so on – goes unmentioned. The message once again is that the poor are the authors of their own misfortune.

In Britain, New Labour's rhetoric may occasionally suggest a concern for providing more resources for the least advantaged, but the reality is little different. A quote from Martin Kettle – a journalist generally sympathetic to the New Labour agenda – is apposite:

> New Labour's strong doctrine of personal responsibility has always made it extremely clear that the poor are expected to make changes, in some cases sacrifices, in order to be able to claim the benefits and rewards of the new opportunity orientated economic policy. But there has never been any equivalent responsibility placed on the rich. Few changes, much less sacrifices are demanded from them in New Labour's moral economy.[18]

Blair was particularly vulnerable on this count since, despite having repeatedly proclaimed his choices to be informed by the highest principle and the deepest sincerity, his main legacy as Prime Minister was one of spin, cover-up and patronage, punctuated by holidays spent visiting the rich and famous. Nor did the responsibility of the state feature notably in this agenda. His 'Vision for Britain', published in 2002, made it clear that he had broken with the social democratic view which, from the 1940s to the 1970s, held that the state had an obligation to provide welfare and security. This was the view of a 'permissive society', he claimed, one which divorced fairness from personal responsibility. Jack Straw, speaking in 1998, is explicit about breaking with the old Left:

> [W]e must acknowledge that the old Left contributed to this culture, too. It failed to argue against the development within the Left in the sixties of a social attitude which asserted that an extension of individual freedom had to mean a licence to do almost anything, and that the State existed as some sort of universal great provider, which made no moral judgements regardless of the merits of those who were dependent upon it.[19]

In 1996, when the US Congress repealed federal income support for parents in favour of the Personal Responsibility and Work Act, sending single mothers out to work was not matched by any sense that the state should contribute to providing free day-care facilities, or that legislation might be needed to endorse more flexible working hours for single mothers, or paid time off or even decent health-care provision. Instead, the Democrats introduced Direct Job Placement, a scheme requiring welfare recipients to accept any job offered to them no matter how low the pay or demeaning the working conditions. As Barbara Ehrenreich writes in *Nickel and Dimed*, her chilling account of trying to survive as a low-paid, unskilled worker in America:

> According to the National Coalition for the Homeless, in 1998 – the year I started the [book] project – it took, on average nationwide, an hourly wage of $8.89 to afford a one-bedroom apartment, and the Preamble Center for Public Policy was estimating that the odds against a typical welfare recipient landing a job at such a 'living wage' were 97 to 1.[20]

The so-called 'responsibility agenda' is simply a further example of the neo-liberal justification for devolving all welfare provision to the private market and returning to a minimal or 'night-watchman' state. Hollowing out the state makes a nonsense of the claim that government should help promote a level playing field. The growing premium on education in the 'knowledge economy', the growing gap in income and wealth between different socio-economic groups, the associated growth of the education and health gaps, the inter-generational transmission and reinforcement of privilege, and the reduction in social mobility: all these factors point in the same direction towards a society in which those at the bottom are increasingly likely to stay there, those in the middle are faced with an ever more precarious existence (including a longer way to fall), while income and wealth becomes increasingly concentrated at the top. Britain and the United States, far from moving towards being 'meritocracies', where the same opportunities are open to all, have become ever more polarized societies in which equality of opportunity is a distant and receding dream. Can this trend be redressed and, if so, how?

Making Taxation Progressive

A few brave souls in the economics profession have suggested that the costs of inequality might best be mitigated by returning to a more progressive structure of taxation. Below are some examples.

The Institute on Taxation and Economic Policy (ITEP) in Washington, DC, has calculated the impact of raising the marginal rate of tax from the current 35 per cent to 50 per cent for projected earnings in 2008. ITEP assumes a 50 per cent marginal rate of tax would apply both to joint incomes of more than $5 million and to unmarried couples each earning more than $2.5 million; this results in an extra $70 billion for the US Treasury. And if a 70 per cent top tax rate were applied instead, the revenue increase would be $105 billion.

Pizzigati has calculated the increase in tax revenue that would be available in the USA if federal income tax schedules were to return to the progressive levels existing under Eisenhower in the late 1950s.[21] In 2007, according to the Brookings Institution Tax Policy Center, the 148,000 taxpayers with America's top 0.1 per cent of incomes earned $5.5 million each before tax, while paying an overall average of 26.7 per cent of their incomes in federal personal tax, adding about $220 billion to government revenue. In 1957, the midpoint of the Eisenhower years, Americans earning over $750,000 – the equivalent of $5.2 million today – paid an average tax rate of 51.6 per cent. If this average rate of tax were applied to today's top 0.1 per cent of income, the US Treasury would collect $420 billion, or an extra $200 billion. How much is $200 billion? It is nearly three times 2007 spending on education and the environment; it is well over half the $354 billion federal budget deficit. It is certainly enough to relaunch the 'war against poverty' briefly attempted and abandoned under Lyndon Johnson. And we are only talking about raising the tax rate for the top one-tenth of 1 per cent of incomes!

Since America today is very much richer than it was then, a return to the 'war against poverty' would have a far greater chance of success, always assuming that such programmes were designed to operate for several generations. As argued above, even the handicap arising from the lack of resources in early childhood is so great that it cannot be overcome in a decade or two. Continuity of effort in establishing greater equality is thus paramount, as suggested by the case of Sweden where a social-democratic government has ruled with brief interruptions for nearly seventy years. But what sort of taxes would be needed?

In chapter 14 of *Luxury Fever*, Robert H. Frank proposes replacing income tax with a consumption tax as shown in figure 9.1. Part I, the left-hand side of the figure, shows a simplified version of Frank's tax scale, rates on consumption rising from 20 per cent to 70 per cent. Part II, the right-hand side, shows tax payable. Thus, if a $30,000 tax threshold is assumed ($7,500 per head for a family of four), a family with an annual income of

Part I Taxable consumption	marginal tax rate	Part II income ($)	savings ($)	taxable consumption ($)	tax payable	equivalent effective rate on income
$0–39,999	20 %					
$40,000–59,999	23 %	30,000	1,500	0	0	0
$60,000–79,999	27 %	50,000	3,000	14,167	2,833	6 %
$80,000–99,999	31 %	100,000	10,000	49,836	10,164	10 %
$100,000–159,999	36 %	150,000	20,000	81,538	18,462	12 %
$160,000–219,999	44 %	200,000	40,000	104,328	25,672	13 %
$220,000–249,999	50 %	500,000	120,000	258,000	92,000	18 %
$250,000–499,999	60 %	1,000,000	300,000	458,000	212,000	21 %
$500,000–999,999	70 %	1,500,000	470,000	654,588	345,412	23 %
$1,000,000 and above	70 %					

Figure 9.1: Illustrative income, consumption tax rates and tax take from Frank's 1999 proposal
Source: Frank (1999: 215)

$50,000 which saved (say) $3,000, would consume $47,000 and, after allowing for the $30,000 deduction, would pay tax on consumption worth $17,000 (minus $2,833 in tax = $14,167). Since the relevant rate of tax is 20 per cent as shown in Part I of the figure, tax payable is $2,833 (20 per cent of $14,167).

The merit of this proposal is that the tax rates proposed are ostensibly quite progressive, and doubtless some simplified form of such a scheme – with steeper rates for higher quintiles and a 70 per cent marginal rate for annual expenditure in excess of (say) $500,000 – would be quite feasible to administer. Frank's rationale for a consumption tax is well known. A tax on consumption does not penalize income and savings, and therefore cannot be objected to on efficiency grounds, a point I return to below.

Nevertheless, there are several problems with Frank's proposal. The first is that most of the OECD countries, with the notable exception of the United States, already have a form of consumption tax, namely value-added tax (VAT).[22] VAT is a flat tax and thus regressive, although some European countries attempt to mitigate this feature by exempting such basic necessities as food and children's clothing. Nor does VAT lend itself to any form of progressive banding since it is designed to be levied at the point of sale. It seems unlikely therefore that (say) the UK would want to replace personal income tax with a personal consumption tax since the latter already exists,

income	MPS	savings ($)	taxable consumption ($)	tax ($)	equivalent effective rate on income
30,000	0.050	1,500	0	0	0 %
50,000	0.075	3,750	16,250	3,250	7 %
100,000	0.100	10,000	60,000	12,954	13 %
150,000	0.150	22,500	97,500	24,225	16 %
200,000	0.200	40,000	130,000	35,000	18 %
500,000	0.250	125,000	345,000	165,800	33 %
1,000,000	0.300	300,000	670,000	377,800	38 %
1,500,000	0.350	525,000	945,000	570,300	38 %
2,000,000	0.400	800,000	1,170,000	690,700	35 %
3,000,000	0.450	1,350,000	1,620,000	1,042,800	35 %
4,000,000	0.500	2,000,000	1,970,000	1,287,800	32 %
5,000,000	0.550	2,750,000	2,220,000	1,462,800	29 %

Figure 9.2: Equivalent income tax incidence of Frank's proposal
Source: Frank (1999: 215) and author's calculations

just as it seems likely that the USA would more readily adopt VAT as a consumption tax than follow Frank's scheme.

A further objection is that, while the nominal rates appear progressive, the equivalent effective rate paid on income is far less progressive as one moves up the income scale. This is apparent from the last column in figure 9.1. A (very rich) family earning $1.5 million a year, while paying consumption tax at a marginal rate of 70 per cent, would pay only 23 per cent of its total income in tax. Moreover, because the marginal savings rate can be assumed to increase with income and because the top rate of tax remains constant beyond $500,000 per annum, the effective overall rate of tax can be shown to flatten (and eventually to fall) as one gets richer.

Figure 9.2 illustrates why this is so. I have simplified Frank's assumptions – notably, using slightly different Marginal Propensities to Save (MPS) and removing the assumption that 'taxable consumption' is already netted for tax. Figure 9.2 shows what happens if one extends a Frank-type consumption tax scheme right up to the top 0.1 per cent of income earners (earning over $5 million annually). These would pay less than 30 per cent of their total income in tax – less if they saved more. Compare this to the figure of 26.7 per cent calculated by the Brookings Tax Policy Center quoted above. The redistributional effect of Frank's scheme would thus appear to be quite small when compared to the current US Federal personal income tax structure.

The crucial objection to Frank's proposal, as indeed to any reform which only affects earnings and/or spending, is that it does not touch wealth. Since the distribution of wealth is the main driver of inequality, some form of wealth tax is imperative. It is important to distinguish between inheritance tax, capital gains tax and a wealth tax. Inheritance tax – what used to be called 'death duties' in the UK and is now called 'death tax' by US neo-conservatives – is levied on inter-generational transfers, while capital gains tax recoups some of the income gains made from asset appreciation. A wealth tax, by contrast, is levied on the individual's reported net worth. Such a tax currently exists in a number of European countries; the rate of tax is typically quite low, ranging from a fraction of 1 per cent in the Netherlands (where it was only introduced in 2001) to 3 per cent in Switzerland. I shall not detain the reader here with a detailed discussion of tax rates on wealth and their redistributive impact since various academic and other studies address this matter. Suffice it to say that, to make a serious impact on today's extraordinarily unequal distribution of income and wealth, it would be necessary to combine a wealth tax with a far more progressive personal income (or consumption) tax schedule.

There are, of course, two further and quite common objections to any reform of the tax system which aims to redistribute income and wealth. The first is that there is a trade-off between equity and efficiency, an objection I deal with elsewhere in this book. The second is that because wealth is increasingly 'footloose' in a globalized world, reform of the tax system, however desirable, is impractical since the rich will simply shelter their wealth in low-tax countries. To a degree, this is of course quite true, particularly in the UK where the rich have a variety of geographically accessible tax-shelters such as Monaco or the Channel Islands. It is less true of the USA, in part because the country is so large, and the arm of the Internal Revenue Service so long, that changing residence and/or shifting money abroad is more difficult. The preferred solution would be for the European Union to harmonize personal (and corporate) tax legislation in such a way as to greatly reduce tax avoidance. But even if one allows that harmonization is some years away, the question is not whether reforming the tax system will lead to tax avoidance, but rather whether it will do so on a scale which leaves the Treasury with less income. Since I don't know of any study suggesting this would happen (indeed, most suggest that the super rich pay very little tax), such an objection cannot be considered fatal to the design of a more equitable tax system.

A Basic Income for All?

Several *very* brave souls have gone well beyond suggesting reform of the current system of taxation on income and wealth. Rather, they assume such a reform feasible, and call for a regular cash grant from the state – a basic income for all – which is neither means-tested nor conditional on being in employment.[23] Rather, in the same way that the NHS in Britain was founded on the principle of universality because of the stigma associated with means-testing, the basic income or 'social minimum' would be universal. Universality would have two further advantages. It would save on the cost of administering a means-tested and/or employment contingent income supplement, and it would remove the 'poverty trap'.

The current Working Tax Credit scheme (supplemented by Child Tax Credit), implemented in 2003 under Labour, is expensive to administer; moreover, nearly 30 per cent of the 7 million people in the UK eligible for benefit do not claim it, and take-up is particularly low amongst ethnic minorities and the disabled: 'For adults, the qualifying conditions for the disability elements of working tax credit are so complicated that it is difficult for claimants to know if they are within the criteria for entitlement or not.'[24]

Moreover, as gross income increases above a certain threshold, tax credits are withdrawn and the recipient becomes subject to paying National Insurance (NI) contributions plus income tax. The combined effect of moving from a negative to a positive income tax plus paying NI contributions is equivalent to a 70 per cent marginal tax rate on extra gross income from employment. Hence, in addition to the stigma of means-testing, the current system still creates a 'poverty trap' in the sense of penalizing those whose earnings may rise above the threshold level. Although the problem can be massaged to a degree, it remains an inescapable property of any supplementary income or 'negative income tax' scheme. And of course, where there is significant variability in a family's earnings, people may find themselves alternately receiving benefits and paying back benefits to which they are no longer entitled. As one news story reports:

> Hina Patel will not be applying for any more government money – even though she is sure she could legitimately claim several hundred pounds a year in child tax credit. The reason? The last time she claimed, the Inland Revenue, recently renamed Revenue & Customs, overpaid her by more than £5,000 – and now she has had to borrow the money to pay it back. . . . They are just one of the 1.8 million families that a committee of MPs recently estimated had been overpaid when they claimed child and working tax credit in 2003.[25]

In short, moving from means-tested benefits to a universal income entitlement scheme would – just as when the National Health Service was launched in 1948 – unquestionably be more advantageous to the poor. Moreover, it would be an important way of tackling the pervasive lack of job satisfaction in contemporary society, particularly amongst the low paid whose bargaining power vis-à-vis their employers would be enhanced since they would enjoy a financial cushion not merely against being made redundant, but against quitting.

Glyn (2006), who supports such a scheme, is perfectly aware of the objections that will be raised – he sees two as fundamental. First, would the public accept the 'free-rider' problem that inevitably would arise if people were free to collect a basic income without working? The problem is a major one; as Philippe Van Parijs has pointed out, even Marx in writing about the first stage of communism believed 'to each according to his work'.[26] One answer would be to redefine the scheme in such a way as to make it conditional on being engaged in some variety of work covering a very wide range, paid and unpaid (including housework and study) as well as retirement, or what has been called the 'participation income' concept. It is almost certain that incorporating such a principle would be politically necessary in order for the scheme to gain political acceptance. One strategy for getting from here to there might be to move from the concept of the minimum wage, now largely accepted, to that of a 'living wage' and ultimately to 'basic income'. Initially, basic income might be quite low and 'conditional' in the above sense; raising the entitlement and loosening conditionality would become both more affordable and acceptable as society became richer.

Second, it might be objected that such a scheme, because it provides a single rate of benefit to all, is regressive. Glyn argues somewhat apologetically that even the relatively well-off would benefit, since there are times in everyone's life when time off work is essential. My own view is that to term the scheme 'regressive' is simply a misnomer. A basic income scheme is 'redistributional' in that it could only be financed at a reasonable level by moving to a taxation scheme whose combined incidence (direct plus indirect) was strongly progressive – in contrast to the current regressive incidence of overall taxation in the UK and the USA. Still, the argument advanced in this book is that, irrespective of whether one accepts the basic income principle at some future date, action to redress inequality is required now.

Welfare Economics and Redistribution

Economics is probably the only branch of the social sciences in which an explicit trade-off is said to exist between equity and efficiency; perhaps this is why Mrs Thatcher renamed the old Social Science Research Council and believed, following Keith Joseph, that all forms of social welfare expenditure should be subject to cost-benefit analysis, a view subsequently adopted by a number of New Labour's economic gurus. In this section I shall argue that the standard theoretical justification for believing in such a trade-off is logically incoherent. (The reader who is put off by a further excursion into economic theory – an understandable reaction at this stage – should go to the next section.)

Textbook economic theory holds that the distribution of income results from the efficient working of the market – more specifically, the labour market in which each is paid his or her marginal value product – and that the market should not be tampered with unless some form of market inefficiency can be shown to exist. The assumption that the labour market functions perfectly is quite a strong one, but let us accept it for the moment. More specifically, welfare economics tells us that there is such a thing as a Pareto optimum: a point at which the optimality conditions are fulfilled by the equation of price ratios with subjective and technical rates of substitution for all pairs of individuals, goods and factors of production (sometimes called the *optimum optimorum*). Such a point is specific to a given set of equilibrium prices, and this set in turn is specific to a given income distribution. Any departure from such a point will, by definition, reduce efficiency and welfare.

Taking matters a bit further, students of welfare economics will be familiar with the Edgeworth box-diagram which, for any pair of individuals A and B, shows the locus of Pareto efficient points for all distributions between them, or what is familiarly known as the 'contract curve'. Any move off the contract curve violates Pareto efficiency conditions and is by definition unacceptable. Any movement along the contract curve, although it changes the distribution of income between A and B, does not violate Pareto efficiency. It follows that, as long as changes in the income distribution take place along the contract curve, we must be indifferent regarding any distribution of income between A and B, equal or unequal.[27] When generalized to all pairs of individuals, the contract curve becomes multidimensional. To any distribution – a member of a very large but finite set of efficient distributions – there corresponds a specific set of efficient prices, such that the set of all such efficient prices must be of cosmological dimensions. A moment's reflection will suggest that the orthodox neo-classical theory of factor rewards is circular; one must assume a distribution of income in order to arrive at a unique set of efficient prices, but if one must first assume an income distribution to arrive at factor rewards, one cannot claim that factor rewards *determine* the distribution.

Economists concerned with public policy have, for the most part, accepted the neo-classical theory of income distribution while acknowledging that in practice, policy changes that affect relative prices and/or the income distribution may not meet the conditions of strict Pareto optimality. A few economists – Hicks, Kaldor and Scitovsky are the best known – have proposed that when policy moves affect the income distribution, one should ask whether 'the gainer can compensate the loser and still be better off'. Such 'compensation tests' may be of theoretical interest, but since economists have never agreed on whether compensation should be hypothetical or actual, such tests are of no practical significance. Others have proposed games theoretical constructs under the banner of establishing a 'social welfare function', but such constructs have proved neither fully logically consistent nor capable of resolving the distributional problem. The best that can be said of welfare economics is that it is theoretically at an *impasse*; few economic courses today bother to teach it. Its applied branch, cost-benefit analysis, was extended in the 1970s in order to explicitly incorporate redistributional ends by means of weighting income gains and losses according to which income class they accrue. But this extension has been so rarely applied as to make it of negligible practical significance.

Consider, too, what recent research on the effect of inequality tells us about equity and efficiency. In welfare theory, any move along the contract curve is a zero-sum game (A's gain is B's loss); since there is no efficiency loss, A and B continue to divide the same total pie. But any move off the contract curve is inefficient in the sense that the pie is reduced in size. Or, put the other way, if we are not on the contract curve, any move back on to it will be Pareto efficient in the conventional sense. But this does little justice to a variety of other possibilities.

Suppose we are to start from a position off the contract curve, a plausible hypothesis in any world where growth shifts the production possibility frontier outward and price adjustment is less than instantaneous. How do we share out the increase in output resulting from getting back on it? Pareto optimality tells us that even if all the extra output is arbitrarily assigned to B, thus leaving A no better off, we can posit a welfare gain. Sociologists and psychologists would cite experimental evidence suggesting that, as a result of A's arbitrary reward, B is *relatively* worse off. Or, again, suppose B initially to be far poorer than A, but in consequence of A's gain the two are made equal. A's gain (materially, in self-esteem and so on) might greatly outweigh any loss of status felt by A, who was previously richer. Or, again, supposing A to have some degree of altruism, he or she might feel more comfortable in a situation where B was lifted out of poverty. We can posit any number of outcomes, some of which will involve a gain in efficiency more than offset by an equity loss (a negative sum game) or both an efficiency and equity gain (a positive sum game). The salient point is that welfare economic theory provides no clear guidance here.

Finally, let us relax the assumption that labour markets are efficient, a step which seems justified both because the neo-classical theory of factor rewards is logically flawed and because it bears little relationship to the empirical evidence cited in earlier chapters suggesting a break in the link between wages and productivity. After all, it is very difficult to defend the efficient labour-market assumption in Britain and America where, for more than a generation, enormous gains have accrued to those at the apex of the income distribution while a quarter of the population lives below the poverty threshold. It should be apparent that we cannot relax this assumption while continuing to claim that greater equality necessarily entails an efficiency loss. The following quote from the introduction of Glyn and Miliband (1994) is instructive, particularly in light of the latter's association with the New Labour project:

> [W]hile it has become conventional wisdom since the late 1970s to assert that advanced industrial societies face a severe 'trade-off' between equality and efficiency, the empirical research suggests that the assumption is at best unproven, and at worst wrong. . . . [W]hilst some redistributive policies may have some disincentive effects, the effect on efficiency is [usually] only a small percentage of the sum redistributed . . . It is perfectly sensible to frame redistributive policies so as to minimise such effects, but it cannot possibly be argued that a priori they undermine egalitarian policies.[28]

Equity as a Survival Strategy

Economists have argued for more than a century about the trade-off between equity and efficiency. The main argument in this book is that inequality damages social cooperation; greater equity, by contract, creates an incentive for greater social cooperation, which favours efficiency, particularly where the 'knowledge economy' becomes increasingly important in an industrialized society. While such an argument may seem to be at odds with the usual *homo economicus* assumption, this inconsistency is more apparent than real. Individuals can as easily be assumed to be partly altruistic as to be entirely selfish.

Another illustration from social psychology is apposite. Consider a game in which A has found a sum of money and he must divide it with B. This game is accompanied by an ultimatum that, if B refuses to play, he will get nothing, nor can the game be repeated. If the players are selfish, A's optimal strategy is to give B as little as possible. B's optimal strategy is to accept, regardless of how much he gets. This outcome, moreover, appears to correspond to a Nash equilibrium. (We owe the notion of an equilibrium outcome in games theory to the mathematician, John Nash.) Nash's basic notion is that if each player has chosen a strategy and no player can benefit by changing his or her strategy while the other players keep theirs unchanged, then the current set of strategy choices and the corresponding payoffs constitute a Nash equilibrium.

Nevertheless, experimental evidence suggests that most givers will give 40–50 per cent of the sum to B, while, when less than 25 per cent is given, B will generally refuse the offer. These results are robust; they appear to hold as much for well-to-do players as for poor ones. Moreover, the results are recorded only when it is clear that both parties know the rules of the game – so 'ignorance of the rules' is not a problem. One might also note that when the experiment is run *without* any ultimatum, instead of A's sharing 40–50 per cent of the money, the typical outcome falls to 30 per cent – not to zero![29]

The interesting thing is that these versions of the game are not simply about 'altruism'; they tell us about the motives of givers and receivers and about more general social norms. Where B refuses, he normally does so because he has in mind some concept of fairness; an 'unfair' offer is one that demeans him, that sets him below the perceived social norm. Refusing the offer becomes a way of 'punishing' A for not abiding by common social norms. In general, what is at work here is not simple 'altruism', but partly a socialization process in which giving and receiving is associated with social norms, position and status. In a pure model of social Darwinism, of course, it might be concluded that a 'selfish' A (who takes 99 per cent of the loot) is more likely to survive and reproduce than a socially sensitive B who walks away from such an offer. But, in fact, people like B do survive, and not just in human societies.

Consider the parable of the hawks and doves. When discovering food, doves will cooperate and share the food while hawks fight over the spoils. The former result is not just more equitable, it is more efficient since time is not wasted, nor blood shed, in fighting over how to divide the spoils. The doves' community of interests survives; the hawks' does not, at least not always. Biologists would speak about the 'evolutionary stability' of a successful community of animals. Such 'evolutionary stability' amongst animals cannot be imputed to rational 'individual decision-making'. Biological equilibrium does not depend on the rational pursuit of individual interests; moreover, it can generate various 'equilibria', or successful evolutionary strategies, some of which will be more cooperative than others. Biologists have done particularly relevant work in showing that amongst some species the offspring of altruistic parents are more likely to survive, and that these in turn are more likely to be altruistic. Why then do hawks survive? The point is that the *coexistence* of cooperative and non-cooperative groups serves the important purpose of sustaining sanctioning mechanisms which make 'equitable' solutions possible and likely.[30]

In his book *The Evolution of Co-operation*, the political scientist Robert Axelrod argued that 'nice' is not just better than 'nasty' but is a successful long-term survival strategy. Avner Offer has made much the same point:

> Regard promotes sociability, and sociability facilitates co-operation . . . 'Reciprocal altruism' is widely observed in animal species and is supposed to confer genetic benefits. It is easy to imagine the capacity for regard as being selected in human evolution for its survival benefits . . . [and even] to assume that the capacity for regard, like the capacity for language, is innate, even if the forms that it takes are culturally specific. (Offer, 2006: 81–2)

Conclusions

I have argued that talking about a 'fair' distribution of income and wealth is part of a wider discussion about 'redistributive justice'. Today, the term 'meritocracy' is used widely, often far too loosely. If the term is to be used at all, then a 'meritocracy' is a society in which advancement is secured by individual effort. But, in keeping with the Rawlsian notion of fairness, no individual or group can be said to advance by merit if the playing field is highly tilted in their favour at the outset.

In Britain and the United States far more than in other advanced countries, a highly inegalitarian distribution of wealth, income and therefore opportunity mocks the very notion of meritocracy, or of 'fairness' – a term I much prefer. After all, when speaking of the developing world, no one would argue that a poor peasant's child living in an African or Indian village has the same 'opportunity' to get ahead in life as the average middle-class member of a rich Western country. Everyone would accept that a child is deeply disadvantaged if he or she is from a village in which there is no electricity and running water, where the nearest clinic or school is several kilometres away and where life expectancy is less than forty years. That is not to say that no individual can ever escape from such an environment, but rather that the probability of doing so is drastically reduced by the initial conditions described. Similarly, it should be obvious that a representative child growing up in Harlem or Hackney is seriously disadvantaged compared to one in Westchester County or in Surrey.

Evidence gathered on mortality, life expectancy, literacy and various other social indices all points in the same direction: the steeper the inequality gradient, the more unequal the playing field. In order to live in a 'meritocracy', young adults must start life with a reasonable chance – note that I say 'reasonable', not 'perfect' chance – of competing successfully, or advancing on the basis of some fortuitous combination of brains, determination and hard work. Not only are such conditions absent in America and Britain, but both societies seem to be moving further away from ever providing 'equal opportunity'. This is true in both a material and ideological sense.

Materially, inequality has grown hugely and now approaches levels last seen in the 1930s. Ideologically, the neo-liberal concept of personal responsibility has served as a means of privatizing the notion of collective action. First under Reagan and Thatcher, and more recently under the New Democrats and New Labour, it has become increasingly common to hear that the poor must be motivated to work, cured of 'welfare dependency', made to get on their bikes and so forth. It should be obvious that the recent version of 'getting on your bike' is not a solution if a growing number of qualified people are competing for a limited number of jobs. In the same vein, 'curing' welfare dependency by making all benefits contingent on being in employment not only assumes that an adequate number of jobs exist, but that the extra income earned can be used to fully offset the deleterious effects of devoting fewer hours to the care of one's children. And, while a more flexible and deregulated labour market is thought to 'encourage' the poor to worker harder, often for lower pay, no such logic is applied to the captains of industry. Far from weaning them off the sort of welfare that a six- or seven-figure salary confers, we are told that growing filthy rich is glorious, that top people need further financial incentives if they are to create shareholder value and that only by continuing to provide these in abundance can the USA and the UK meet the challenge of globalization.

I have argued, finally, that the body of economic theory used to rationalize inequality – centrally, the neo-classical theory of factor rewards and the corollary assumption of a trade-off between equity and efficiency – is empirically flawed and logically incoherent. Strictly speaking, it is not necessary to invoke the principle of 'diminishing marginal utility of income' nor to excoriate consumer demand theory in order to defend greater equity. Equity is fundamental to social solidarity; it lies at the heart of what we understand to be a 'fair' society. At the same time, empirical evidence (or lack of it) is relevant. There is no evidence to support the view that CEO rewards are either determined in some good approximation of a perfect labour market or that their pay reflects marginal productivity. The evidence points almost entirely the other way, namely, to the fact that German and Japanese executives perform at least as well as their American and British counterparts who are paid a great deal more; or, again, to the observation that relatively egalitarian Nordic countries – where welfare standards are high and wage-salary differentials low – are at least as dynamic as the neo-liberal countries.

A major argument of this book is that the Reagan-Thatcher neo-liberal revolution was a response to the crisis of Anglo-American capitalism in the 1970s. That crisis, far from being resolved through the application of neo-liberal strictures, has become worse. Neither America nor Britain can continue to distribute so large a share of the pie to the rich at the expense of the majority, just as neither country can continue to sustain its spending by creating ever greater global financial imbalances.

I said in the introduction that I would not deal with inequality on a world scale. The reader will rightly wonder why a lengthy discussion of the international macroeconomic repercussions of growing consumption inequality in the USA and of 'capital flowing uphill' has not been complemented by any mention of international inequality. This omission is serious, particularly as the various estimates of international (inter- and intra-country) Gini income coefficients (typically in the 0.60–0.70 range) are higher than the Ginis for even the world's most unequal countries such as South Africa and Brazil; i.e., on a world scale the difference between rich and poor is greater than on a national scale. In part, the omission reflects the complexity of the subject: there is a very large literature on international inequality which differs in scope, time-scale and methodology of comparisons and therefore has produced divergent results. In part, too, it is because there is a serious political gap between the view of many anti-globalization campaigners that the past two decades has produced a huge increase in world inequality and the view amongst most academic specialists that it has not.

If there is a consensus amongst academic specialists, it is broadly that while world income distribution worsened over much of the twentieth century, over the period 1980–2000 it has remained stable or improved slightly.[31] This is in part due to the fact that rapid and sustained economic growth in China has pulled so many out of poverty, despite the fact that inequality within China has risen sharply. But China strongly influences the lower-middle end of the global income distribution. What researchers have also noted is that in the past three decades the extreme ends of the global distribution have lengthened: some populations (particularly in Africa) have become very much poorer while others – notably the upper end of the distribution in the USA and the UK – have become much richer. In a word, the gap between the world's richest and poorest 1 per cent has grown. Assets are distributed even more unequally. A WIDER study of the world distribution of net wealth reveals that in the year 2000, the richest 1 per cent of adults alone owned 40 per cent of global assets in the year 2000, and that the richest 10 per cent of adults accounted for 85 per cent of the world total.[32] This book aims to contribute to understanding the political economy of what has happened at the top end of the world income and wealth distribution, particularly since the neo-liberal revolution has been sustained by an ideology which treats all concerns with inequality – whether at national or global level – as unfounded, or at best unproblematic.

Environmental sustainability is another crucial matter that requires urgent attention; I have already said that the issue is not addressed in this book. However, it seems appropriate to point out that how we deal with climate change is linked to collective decisions about achieving greater equality. In particular, climate change is a key dimension of inter-generational equity: the question of what sort of ecological future we bequeath our children is intimately tied to that of the economic future they inherit. One of the most memorable images of inequality – invoked in an exchange between George Monbiot and Clive Hamilton[33] – is that of wealthy Texans turning up their living-room air conditioning in order to better enjoy the comfort of their log fire. This image is readily counterposed to television footage of tens of thousands of Bangladeshi villagers made homeless by the floods caused in part by the unregulated carbon emissions of the rich. Carbon taxes and other emission reduction measures are urgently required, beginning with the OECD countries. It is the poor of the world who are most at ecological risk.[34] Because carbon taxes are generally regressive (i.e., bear equally on the OECD purchaser whether rich or poor), this strengthens the case put in this book for progressive income and wealth taxation in the rich countries.

Clearly, achieving greater equity will require radical tax reform. I have deliberately refrained from suggesting precise tax rates for income and wealth. Suffice it to say that, in the UK, raising the top rate of tax to 50 per cent for incomes above £100,000 is pure tokenism. What is more relevant is to set goals based on explicit political priorities. A plausible target would be that the USA and the UK should return within (say) one generation to the level of equity ruling in the late 1970s, reversing the 'great U-turn' in income distribution that began in the Reagan-Thatcher years. (In the UK, the Gini coefficient for income was at that time close to 0.24, but rose to the much less egalitarian value of 0.34 by the late 1980s, where it remains today.)

Levying new taxes on wealth and income that enabled this result to be achieved within a generation would be a major step forward, but this would need to be accompanied by complementary measures. Establishing a 'level playing field' involves, *inter alia*, a major extension of social legislation and services. Chapter 4 showed that on a wide variety of social indicators (child and old-age poverty, pre-school and formal education, social mobility and so forth) the USA and the UK score far worse than the EU average and the 'best practice' Nordic countries. The crucial test of a future progressive government should be whether targets are to be set and measures adopted which redress this imbalance; measures which would bring us up to current Nordic standards by mid-century.

To achieve such results will require, above all, a change of political direction sustained over a long period. Changes in UK voting arrangements may be part of that process, but such changes will be insufficient. To borrow Gramsci's phrase, a 'war of position' is necessary; the struggle of ideas, the building of alliances in civil society are crucial to effecting change. This is a tall order, although the task is not impossible. In the USA, public pressure is building to reverse extreme income inequality and, more visibly, to bring to an end the neo-conservative hegemony of the Bush years. In Britain, inequality is back on the agenda thanks to pressure from the trade union movement and from a variety of NGOs including new, militant consumer groups.[35] An elected House of Lords is imminent; proportional representation is used in regional and European elections. A change from first-past-the-post to a form of proportional representation, such as recommended by the Jenkins Commission,[36] would in all likelihood result in a long period of centre-left government, always assuming that the Lib-Dems and the Labour Party could agree to a social-democratic programme of renewal along the lines described. Crucially, it is the centre–left – which in Britain includes a large number of people who have become deeply disillusioned with party politics – that must debate and develop these issues if they are to set the new political agenda. Greater equity is not just 'another policy target'; it is part of what we mean when we speak of living in a more civilized society.

Any discussion of equity raises issues of collective choice; i.e., choices which we make not as individual consumers but as citizens in the public sphere. The public sphere, as David Marquand reminds us, is quite distinct from the market sphere of commodity production and exchange, just as both are distinct from the private sphere of love, friendship and personal relations. There is – and in a civilized society there must be – a distinction between private and public interests, between the realms of private satisfaction and of collective interest. I can do no better than to quote him:

> [T]he public domain is both priceless and precarious – a gift of history, which is always at risk. It can take shape only in a society in which the notion of the public interest, distinct from private interests, has taken root . . . De-regulation, privatisation, so-called public-private partnerships, proxy markets, performance indicators mimicking those of the private corporate sector, and a systematic assault on professional autonomy narrowed the public domain and blurred the distinction between it and the market domain. Public functions of all kinds were farmed out to unaccountable appointed bodies, dominated by business interests and managed according to market principles. . . . The dilapidated, overstretched public services of twenty-first-century Britain are the most obvious legacy of this *kulturkampf*, but they are by no means the most dangerous one. Incessant marketisation, pushed forward by the core executive at the head of the most centralised state in western Europe, has done even more damage to the public domain than low taxation and resource starvation. It has generated a culture of distrust, which is corroding the values of professionalism, citizenship, equity and service like acid in the water supply. (Marquand, 2004: 2–3)

Marquand's is an elegant distinction between the public and private – not some superficial mantra about giving consumers greater choice or characterizing 'public choice' as a mere extension of the private domain. For unless the growth of inequality is seen for what it is – as not merely one more injustice but as a cancer eating away at the fabric of society itself – it will prove difficult, perhaps impossible, to create and sustain the change in politics which is required to reverse the damage wrought by nearly thirty years of neo-liberal ascendancy.

Notes and References

Introduction

1 See David Teather, 'Is greed always good?', the *Guardian*, 3 November 2006.
2 Median family (2+2) income in the UK is currently about £20,000 per annum and the 60 per cent family poverty line about £12,000. See 'How the rich keep the poor in their place', leader, *New Statesman*, 3 September 2007.
3 Toynbee reckons the inheritance tax change was worth some £3.5 billion. See Polly Toynbee, 'This was the week that Labour's leaders left social democracy for dead', the *Guardian*, 12 October 2007.
4 See Blackburn (2006: 39).
5 See J. Finch and J. Treanor, 'Britain's soaring boardroom pay revealed', the *Guardian*, 2 October 2006; see also 'Trends in CEO pay 2006': <http://www.aflcio.org/corporate-watch/paywatch/pay/>.
6 See M. Orton and K. Rowlingson (2007).

Chapter 1 Neo-liberalism and the Return of Inequality

1 Max Hastings, 'They've never had it so good', *Guardian*, 6 August 2005.
2 This hypothesis is generally attributed to Simon Kuznets's work in the 1950s.
3 The Washington Consensus is the name given in the early 1990s to the set of orthodox policies pursued by the International Monetary Fund and the World Bank.
4 See, for example, Glyn and Sutcliffe (1973) and Glyn (2006). Another good discussion is Harvey (2005).
5 The 'Big Bang' in the City greatly changed the nature of trading; *inter alia*, fixed commissions on transactions were abolished and electronic trading was introduced.
6 See, for example, Gordon and Townsend (2000).
7 See UK Office of National Statistics (ONS), 'The effects of taxes and benefits on household income, 2005/06', quote from Francis Jones, pp. 2–3. Also see Larry Eliott, 'Inequality is at the same level as under Thatcher', the *Guardian*, 18 May 2007.
8 See Dorling, Rigby et al. (2007).
9 See Pizzigati (2004: 451, 479). A study by Crystal concluded that differences in corporate performance explained only a tiny fraction of differences in corporate rewards; the main explanatory variable was corporate size; see K. Day, 'Soldiers for shareholders', *Washington Post*, 27 August 2000.
10 See J. Freedland, 'Don't be fooled by Europe's mood. Globally, the left is reawakening', the *Guardian*, 9 May 2007.
11 At the time of writing, Ed Balls was Minister for Children, Schools and Families in the Brown government.
12 See Alice Thompson, 'Class doesn't talk as loudly as money', <www.telegraph.co.uk>, 19 April 2007. See <www.telegraph.co.uk/opinion/main.jhtml?xml=/opinion/2007/04/19/do1902.xml>.

13 See Lansley (2006: 205).
14 See <http://www.tgwu.org.uk/Templates/Campaign.asp?NodeID=42437>.
15 See Heather Stewart, 'A bit rich: scandal of the capital's two-tier economy', the *Observer*, 19 November 2006.
16 See, for example, C. Wright Mills (1956); J. K .Galbraith (1958).
17 See Irwin Redlener, 'Orphans of the storm', *The New York Times*, 5 September 2006. For example, one-third of children in US government subsidised shelters suffered from chronic illness. Six months after the hurricane, one in four school-aged children were either not enrolled in school or attended school sporadically.
18 See Editorial 'It didn't end well the last time', *The New York Times*, 4 April 2007.
19 C. Luna 'Political lunacy: three strikes and you're out', *San Diego CityBeat*, 28 March 2007.
20 See Editorial, 'Reaganomics at 25', *Wall Street Journal*, 12 August 2006.
21 An excellent introduction to income, wealth and power in the USA is Domhoff (2001).
22 See Krugman (2004).
23 In economists' terms, the upper tail of the income distribution conforms to a Pareto distribution. Thus, if (hypothetically) the richest, second richest and third richest person are A, B and C, if B were 10 times richer than C, we would expect A to be 100 (10x10) times richer than C. Some economists (e.g., Martin Feldstein) regard this as a normal state of affairs and see no problem with the rich becoming richer as long as the poor are no worse off.
24 See Editorial, 'Life in the bottom 80 Percent', *The New York Times*, 1 September 2005.
25 Following in Meade's footsteps, see Stiglitz (1969) for a model of the relation between patterns of inheritance and the distribution of assets and of income.
26 See Paul Krugman, 'Wages, wealth and politics', *The New York Times*, 18 August 2006.
27 See, for example, Bernstein and Mishel (2007).
28 See Dew-Becker and Gordon (2005), abstract.
29 In the USA, options cashed in by executives become tax-deductible expenses for companies. By the 1990s, the use of options is thought to have cut billions off corporate tax bills (Pizzigati, 2004: 11).
30 See *The Economist*, 'A special report on executive pay', 20 January 2007.
31 In 1999 alone, mergers in the USA totalled $1.75 trillion, ten times the value of mergers in 1990 (Pizzigati, 2004: 171).
32 For current concerns in the UK, see Will Hutton, 'Private equity is casting a plutocratic shadow over British businesses', the *Guardian*, 23 February 2007; also see 'Special report: private equity', the *Guardian*, 24 February 2007.
33 See 'Special report: private equity', the *Guardian*, 24 February 2007.
34 See Piketty and Saez (2003).
35 See Michael H. Trotter, 'Tax plutocrats to restrain their pay', *Daily Report, Law.com*, Tuesday 27 February 2007.
36 Quoted in Trotter, ibid.
37 In Britain, the bottom 10 per cent pay a higher proportion of income in tax than the top 10 per cent. See Dixon and Paxton, 'The state of the nation; an audit of social injustice in the UK', in Pearce and Paxton (eds) (2005).
38 See Brewer, Goodman et al. (2004).
39 See Paul Harris, 'Welcome to Richistan', the *Observer*, 22 July 2007.
40 Recent sources are Lansley (2006); and Pearce (2004).
41 See Dixon and Paxton, 'The state of the nation; an audit of social injustice in the UK', in Pearce and Paxton (eds) (2005).
42 See Cahill (2001) for a heroic effort at piecing together the evidence.
43 See, for example, Serge Haumi, 'US: Republican deficits', *Le Monde Diplomatique*, November 2006.

44 See L. Mishel, J. Bernstein and S. Allegretto (2005).

45 See J. Bernstein (2006).

46 See Special Report, 'Inequality in America', *The Economist*, 17 June 2006: 25.

47 See B. Ehrenreich (2006: 2).

48 See H. Stewart, 'The dream dies on Main Street', the *Observer*, 3 October 2006.

49 See Special Report, 'Inequality in America', *The Economist*, 17 June 2006.

50 See M. Rustin (2007), 'New Labour and the theory of globalisation', <http://www.soundings.org.uk/>.

51 See David Miliband, 'Does inequality matter?'. in Giddens and Diamond (eds) (2005: 40).

52 See 'The super-rich; always with us', *The Economist*, 19 October 2006.

53 See Nettle (2005: 14).

54 See Pahl et al. (2007); Orton and Rowlingson (2007); P. Taylor-Gooby, 'Attitudes to social justice', in Pearce and Paxton (eds) (2005). I owe the ISER reference to an excellent short piece by Wilby; see Peter Wilby, 'The rich versus the very rich', *New Statesman*, 8 October 2007.

55 See R. Chaytor, 'Council worker paid £91,000 to fix the lights', *Daily Mail*, 1 November 2006.

56 See Beverly Goldberg, 'The pain component of inequality: living with less than your neighbors', The Century Foundation, Newsletter, 11 June 2007: <http://www.tcf.org/list.asp?type=NC&pubid=1598>.

57 See R. H. Frank (1999).

Chapter 2 Do We Need Fat Cats?

1 See Polly Toynbee, 'The Farepak scandal lays bare gross inequality', the *Guardian*, 14 November 2006.

2 See Peter Taylor-Gooby, 'Attitudes to social justice', in Pearce and Paxton (eds) (2005).

3 See Andrew Clark, 'US executive pay bill passes first hurdle', the *Guardian*, 21 April 2007.

4 See Lansley (2007).

5 The quote is cited in Lansley (2006: 173).

6 See Lansley (2006: 163).

7 See Cahill (2001: 18–19).

8 See Tom Nicholas, quoted in Lansley (2007: 152).

9 See the discussion on pp. 73–6, in L. Mishel, J. Bernstein and S. Allegretto (2005).

10 Smith used the pin-factory story to illustrate the productivity gain of adopting a factory-based 'division of labour' in preference to artisanal production.

11 See Frank and Cook (1995); they argue that because such markets today have spread to corporate management, investment banking and a variety of other spheres, winner-take-all markets are the main driver of growing US inequality.

12 See Pizzigati (2004: 13).

13 Ibid., p. 11.

14 For a detailed account, see Pizzigati (2004: 25–7).

15 See Citizen Works, Tools for Democracy, 'Corporate Scandal Sheet', <http://www.citizenworks.org/corp/corp-scandal.php>

16 See 'Effects of corporate corruption far-reaching',25 July 2006, <http://www.voanews.com/english/archive/2006-07/2006-07-25-voa50.cfm?CFID=195135586&CFTOKEN=54488734>.

17 See Bethany McLean, 'Is Enron overpriced?', *Fortune Magazine*, Monday 5 March 2001.

18 See Steve Schifferes, 'Enron's trail of deception', 13 February 2003, <http://news/bbc.co.uk/2/hi/business>.

19 See Bank of America Business Capital, ACG/Thomson Financial Dealmakers Survey: 'M&A surge to continue in 2007', March/April, 2007; also see Andrew Verity, 'Private

equity on crest of a wave', Radio Five Live (transcript) BBC News, Business, 26 April 2007.

20 The quote is from Nils Pratley, 'Liberation capitalists are taking over', the *Guardian*, 24 February 2007.

21 See David Teather and Jill Treanor, 'Corporate buccaneers caught in a political storm', the *Guardian*, 24 February 2007.

22 See Polly Toynbee, 'This wild west capitalism is born of servility to the City,' the *Guardian*, 5 June 2007.

23 See Citizen Works, Tools for Democracy, 'Corporate Scandal Sheet', <http://www.citizenworks.org/corp/corp-scandal.php>.

24 See 'Effects of corporate corruption far-reaching', 25 July 2006, <http://www.voanews.com/english/archive/2006-07/2006-07-25-voa50.cfm?CFID=195135586&CFTOKEN=54488734>.

25 See Matt Krantz, 'Private equity firms spin off cash', *USA Today*, 16 March 2006.

26 See GMB, 'Private equity's broken pension promises; private equity companies' links to insolvent pension funds', a GMB Central Executive Council Special Report, 2007; also see N. Mathiason, 'Private equity stole our pensions', the *Observer*, 10 June 2007.

27 Quoted in David Teather and Jill Treanor, 'Corporate buccaneers caught in a political storm', the *Guardian*, 24 February 2007.

28 See Augar (2005: 9–11).

29 See Blackburn (2006: 42).

30 See Augar (2005: 79).

31 Ibid., p. 12.

32 According to a Congressional report in 2001, the proportion of US households owning mutual funds is estimated to have risen from 10 per cent in 1980 to nearly 50 per cent in 2000. See <http://www.house.gov/jec/news/2001/PRESS/2001/11-15-01.htm>.

Chapter 3 The Rise of Neo-liberalism

1 Quoted in Pizzigati (2004: 96).

2 The 'principle of diminishing marginal utility' says that as we acquire more of a given good, the increment in satisfaction (or utility) derived from each extra unit falls. Thus, if you are thirsty, although drinking your first glass of water may bring great satisfaction, by the time you have drunk nine glasses, the tenth may bring little or no extra satisfaction.

3 See Buchanan and Tullock (1962).

4 See Harvey (2005: 19).

5 See Glyn (2006; 5–15).

6 This trend was first identified by Glyn and Sutcliffe (1973).

7 The 'Bretton Woods system' refers to the post-war system of trade arrangements and regulatory institutions agreed at a conference in Bretton Woods, New Hampshire, in 1944; it was here that the IMF, the World Bank and the precursor of the World Trade Organisation were established; in particular, a fixed exchange-rate regime was agreed and countries could only devalue with the approval of the IMF. By the 'collapse of the Bretton Woods system' is meant the collapse of fixed exchange rates.

8 See Reid (2003).

9 See Harvey (2005: 44).

10 Callaghan arguably began Labour's move to the right after he took over from Wilson, long before Blair. He torpedoed the Wilson-Castle attempt to resolve the industrial relations crisis by negotiation, probably destroying the 1964 government in the process, then wrecked the 1974 government by imposing an excessive burden on wage earners in 1978–9. He was also in charge of Northern Ireland when the Wilson government surrendered to the Protestant workers' strike.

11 Thomas Edsall, quoted in Harvey (2005), p. 48.

12 See Harvey (2005: 51).

13 PATCO was the Professional Air Traffic Controllers Organization which, ironically, had broken with the trade union movement by endorsing the Reagan candidacy in the 1979 election.

14 See Harvey (2005: 52).

15 For a detailed analysis of the collapse of the post-war settlement in Britain, see Devine (2006).

16 See Harvey (2005: 59) on whose succinct account I rely heavily in this section.

17 Simon Jenkins (2007), himself an ex-Thatcherite, has written a trenchant critique of New Labour's pursuit of Thatcherite policies.

18 See, for example, Eric Hobsbawm, 'The Forward March of Labour Halted', *Marxism Today*, September 1978.

19 For an excellent account of how Labour's 'commitment' to the National Health Service has in reality undermined its founding principles, see Pollock (2004).

20 An excellent critique is Grieve Smith (2001).

21 See Stuart Hall, 'New Labour's Double Shuffle', *Soundings*, 24 July 2003: 10.

22 See Blackburn (2006: 39).

23 I am grateful to Michael Rustin for making this point in correspondence.

Chapter 4 America, Europe and the Welfare State

1 See, for example, Reid (2004); Rifkin (2004); Haseler (2004); or, in a somewhat different vein, Kagan (2003).

2 Reading *New Left Review* is always instructive on this matter; a recent editorial contribution is Watkins (2005).

3 See Turner (2000).

4 Mike Dixon and Nick Pearce, 'Social justice in a changing world; the emerging Anglo-social model', in Pearce and Paxton (eds) (2005: 10).

5 See D. Dinan (2004: 6).

6 See John Gray, 'For Europe's sake, keep Britain out', *New Statesman*, Monday 19 May 2003.

7 When discussing inequality, one must distinguish between income distribution before taxes and transfers (sometimes called the 'market' distribution) and income distribution after taxes and transfers. It is conventional when comparing countries to use the latter. Until recently, pre- and post-net transfer data was not available for the EU. This has been remedied with the development of the EUROMOD dataset, developed at Cambridge to estimate and compare the effects of taxes and transfers on personal and household income across the EU-15.

8 The Gini calculations refer to the mid-1990s and are based on the Luxembourg Income Study (LIS) household data, 1979–99, the most recent attempt to measure income using a standardized definition. For details, see Smeeding (2002). Gini coefficients for Portugal and Greece, excluded from the Smeeding study, are taken from Papatheodorou and Pavlopoulos (2003) whose data is from the Consortium of Household Panels for European socio-economic research (CHER);.

9 Although Smeeding (2002) uses several measures of income inequality besides the Gini coefficient, I have ignored them since they all give roughly the same country ranking.

10 *Inter alia*, see Smeeding (2002) and Atkinson (2003).

11 See, for example, Atkinson (2003).

12 See Esping-Andersen (2005:14).

13 See Atkinson (2003).

14 See Smeeding (2006).

15 See L. Mishel, J. Bernstein and S. Allegretto (2005: 409), based on Luxembourg Income Study.

16 In France, for example, it is alleged that because employers must pay directly for much of the welfare of their employees, firms become less competitive in the face of globalization. What the argument misses is that 'social contributions' paid by employers are largely offset by lower real wages; i.e., contributions in effect come largely from labour rather than capital.

17 The exceptions were Greece, Portugal and Ireland, but all have figures lower than the USA. See figure 8K, L. Mishel, J. Bernstein and S. Allegretto (2007).

18 See OECD (Organisation of Economic Cooperation and Development) (2001), *Employment Outlook 2001*, Paris: OECD.

19 See Morley et al. (2004); note that there are seventy-one European NUTS-1regions whose average size is approximately the same as the states of the USA. (NUTS, not the best of Brussels acronyms, stands for 'nomenclature of territorial units for statistics').

20 See, for example, Papatheodorou and Pavlopoulos (2003: 15).

21 See, for example, Will Hutton, 'The case for keeping inheritance tax', the *Observer*, 7 October 2007.

22 One can argue that in real terms all pensions are 'pay as you go' in that the goods and services that pensioners consume are produced by the current generation of workers. Saving while you are at work generates a financial entitlement to your retirement consumption, but not the goods to satisfy it.

23 The share of first-time buyers in total housing purchases at present in the UK is falling.

24 See Krugman (1999).

25 See Stiglitz (2007); also see Wade (2007).

26 See Esping-Andersen et al. (2002).

27 See Esping-Andersen (2005: 32).

28 See Esping-Andersen et. al. (2002: 16).

29 Ibid.

30 See Irvin (2006).

31 See Desai (2002); also see M. Rustin (2007), 'New Labour and the theory of globalisation', <http://www.lwbooks.co.uk/journals/soundings/debates/left_futures7.html>.

Chapter 5 Happiness and Pareto

1 See Layard (2005); for a thoughtful and critical review, see Rustin (2007).

2 The HDI was developed in the early 1990s and is used in the annual Human Development Report published by UNDP.

3 Pareto was a 'classical liberal' sympathetic to the Austrian school of economists; in *Les systèmes socialistes*, a two-volume work written in 1902–3, he deemed all forms of socialist doctrine to be logically flawed.

4 See Sen (1987).

5 In this section I rely heavily on the excellent discussion to be found in chapter 1 of Nettle (2005).

6 The notion of 'aspirational' or 'positional' goods is originally from Fred Hirsch (1976); Hirsch further qualifies 'positional goods' as goods in fixed supply which can be 'consumed' only a few times or even once in a lifetime; e.g., a Harvard or an Oxbridge degree, a country mansion, a unique bottle of rare wine and so on.

7 See Frank (1999: 74).

8 See Layard (2005: 48).

9 See Neal Lawson, 'Turbo-consumerism is the driving force behind crime', the *Guardian*, 29 June 2006.

10 I am indebted to Jenny Shaw of the University of Sussex for comments on the 'drivers' of consumerism. For the sake of brevity I have omitted a critical discussion of the notion that the 'range of choice' of public goods should be market-driven, that building super-casinos expands choice and so on.

11 See OECD, *Employment Outlook*, July 2002.

12 For example, see Turner (2001).

13 A recently published variant on this sort of argument is A. Alesina, E. Glaeser and B. Sacerdote (2005).

14 The survey, by Frey and Oberholzer-Gee, is reported in a number of articles and books; I have used B. Schwartz, 'Stop the treadmill', *London Review of Books* 8, March 2007.

15 See Layard (2003c: 16).

16 See, for example, A. Sen and B. Williams (1982), *Utilitarianism and Beyond*, Cambridge: Cambridge University Press; M. Nussbaum (2001), *Upheavals of Thought*, Cambridge, Cambridge University Press.

17 See Arrow (1963).

18 See Axelrod (1984).

19 Some thirty years after the appearance of the textbook written by Little and Mirrlees (1974) recommending the use of a 'free foreign exchange' *numeraire* and explicit intra-temporal distribution weights, the World Bank has adopted the former convention but still not the latter. Nor, to my knowledge, has any national planning authority.

20 See Irvin (1979).

21 The evidence, including the above sources, is set out at some length in chapter 15 of R. H. Frank (1999).

22 See Mental Health Policy Group (2006), *The Depression Report: A New Deal for Depression and Anxiety Disorders*, Project Report. London: Centre for Economic Performance, London School of Economics and Political Science (aka, the 'Layard Report on Mental Health').

23 See Offer (2006: 167–8).

24 See Offer (2006: 358).

Chapter 6 What About the Middle Class?

1 See Peter Wilby, 'Revolt of the middle classes', *New Statesman*, 21 May 2007.

2 See B. Ehrenreich (2006: 2–3).

3 See Newman and Chen (2007).

4 In this section I have drawn on the early section of a recent piece by Amity Shlaes; see, A. Schlaes, 'The politics of middle-class anxiety', *Commentary* 123/3, March 2007.

5 See Schmitt (2005).

6 All quotes are from A. Schlaes, 'The politics of middle-class anxiety', *Commentary* 123/3, March 2007.

7 See Hacker (2006: 6).

8 Christine Dugas, 'Middle class barely treads water', *USA Today*, 15 September 2003.

9 Ibid.

10 See L. Mishel, J. Bernstein and S. Allegretto (2005: 210); here and in subsequent sections of this chapter I have drawn extensively on both the 2004/5 and the 2006/7 editions; for the full references, see Bibliography.

11 See L. Mishel, J., Bernstein and S. Allegretto (2005); a previous edition was issued by the Economic Policy Institute in 2002. The authors acknowledge their improved analysis of income distribution owes much to the pioneering analysis by Piketty and Saez (2003).

12 Smeeding reported in Esping-Andersen (2005:11).

13 In the USA, the poverty level is defined as 50 per cent of median income (vs 60 per cent in the EU). A somewhat different way of defining middle-income families is to take all

those in the range between half and twice the median. Because the both the proportion of families in poverty and those above 200 per cent of the median have been growing, the middle-income share has fallen from 71.2 per cent of families in 1969 to 60.7 in 2002. See Mishel et al. (2005: 90).

14 See L. Mishel, J. Bernstein and S. Allegretto (2005); 27–8.
15 See L. Mishel, J. Bernstein and S. Allegretto (2005: 31).
16 But since 2001, the extra employment has been harder to find and it appears that the fall in family income is associated partly with a fall in hours worked and partly with taking less well-paid jobs.
17 See L. Mishel, J. Bernstein and S Allegretto (2005: 138–9).
18 Ibid., p. 299.
19 Ibid., pp. 192–3.
20 Ibid., pp. 275–6.
21 See D. Kusnet, L. Mishel and R. Teixeira (2006: 2–3).
22 The OECD includes a number of non-EU countries: i.e., Japan, Canada, Australia and Switzerland, while the EU-15 includes non-OECD countries: Luxembourg, Greece and Portugal.
23 See table 7.13 in L. Mishel, J. Bernstein and S. Allegretto (2005).
24 See Veblen ([1899] 1998: 35).
25 See R. H. Frank (1999) and R. H. Frank (2007); R.H. Frank should not be confused with the journalist, R. L. Frank, author of *Richistan*; see R. L. Frank (2007).
26 An academic study offering a fundamental critique of economists' treatment of consumption is Offer (2006).
27 See R. H. Frank (1999: 5).
28 See Standing (2004).
29 See J. Schor (1998).
30 See ibid., p. 5.

Chapter 7 The Rising Cost of Inequality

1 See W. G. Runciman (1966).
2 See J. Young: <http://www.malcolmread.co.uk/JockYoung/relative.htm>.
3 See, for example, R. G. Wilkinson, I. Kawachi and B. Kennedy (1998), 'Mortality, the social environment, crime and violence', *Sociology of Health and Illness* 20/5: 578–97.
4 See C. McCord and H. P. Freeman (1990), 'Excess mortality in Harlem', *New England Journal of Medicine* 22: 173–7.
5 See Danny Dorling, in Cruddas et al., 'Closer to equality? Assessing New Labour's record on equality after 10 years in government', *Compass*, Southbank House, London, 2007.
6 As reported in Wilkinson (2005: 40–1); see Kawachi et al. (1997), 'Social capital, income inequality and morality', *American Journal of Public Health* 87/1.
7 Titmuss is quoted in Wilkinson (2005: 115).
8 See abstract, J. Swabisch, T. Smeeding and L. Olsberg (2004).
9 See Katha Pollitt, 'Intelligible design', *The Nation*, 3 October 2005.
10 See M. Gladwell, 'Letter from Saddleback: the cellular church', *New Yorker Magazine*, 11 September 2005.
11 This section draws heavily on an excellent piece by Jonathan Kozol, 'Still separate, still unequal', *Harper's Magazine*, September 2005. The material is drawn from his recent book: Kozol (2005).
12 In 1954, in *Brown vs The Board of Education of Topeka*, the US Supreme Court declared that 'separate but equal' school facilities for black and white students was unconstitutional.

13 See S. Cassidy, 'Drop out rate for UK school-leavers is among the worst in the world', the *Independent*, 14 September 2005.

14 Quoted in Sam Pizzigati, *Too Much*, Weekly Newsletter of the Council on International; and Public Affairs, Washington, 14 May 2007.

15 The seminal work on the USA is Schor (1992); note that this work has been questioned by various authors, including B. Bluestone and S. Rose (1997). See too 'The land of leisure', *The Economist*, 2 February 2006.

16 Of course, many women have entered the paid labour force because they seek financial independence, social fulfilment through work, etc.; not just in response to economic pressures

17 It should be noted that the EU-15 average includes the UK; also, the average does not show the considerable variation between different EU countries in employment rates for the 55–64 age group.

18 See Pizzigati (2004: 383).

19 See Joel Bleifuss, 'Outlawing legal bribery', *In These Times*, 4 January 2007, <http://www.inthesetimes.com/article/2964/outlawing_legal_bribery>.

20 See G. Datz (2004). 'Pension privatization and the politics of default in Latin America', paper presented at the annual meeting of the American Political Science Association, Hilton Chicago and the Palmer House Hilton, Chicago, IL, 2 September 2004.

21 For further details on much of the above, see Pizzigati (2004: 382–92).

22 See <http://www.americanprogress.org/issues/2007/05/stop_madness.html>.

23 See Pizzigati (2004: 393).

24 The OLS trend lines are fitted to twelve observations each for the UK and the USA.

25 See Skidmore in Cruddas et al., 'Closer to equality? Assessing New Labour's record on equality after 10 years in government', *Compass*, 2007: 40–1, published by Compass, Southbank House, London

26 See Dixon and Paxton, 'The state of the nation: an audit of social injustice in the UK', in Pearce and Paxton (eds) (2005).

27 See Paul Krugman, 'The spiral of inequality', *Mother Jones*, November/December 1996.

28 See Paul Whiteley, 'Paper chase', the *Guardian*, 9 May 2000.

29 See 'Goliath getting bigger', *American Prospect* 3/8, 6 May 2002; reported in Pizzigati (2004: 399).

30 Quoted from 'Media ownership in the UK': <http://www.cultsock.ndirect.co.uk/MUHome/cshtml/media/mediaown.html>.

31 See <http://www.cultsock.ndirect.co.uk/MUHome/cshtml/media/mediaown.html>.

Chapter 8 Is the Consumption Binge Sustainable?

1 See John Leland, 'Couple learn high price of easy credit', *The New York Times*, 19 May 2007.

2 See A. Hill and L. Bachelor 'Britain in debt: five people tell us their harrowing stories', the *Observer*, 3 June 2007.

3 See D. Prosser, 'Britain's towering debt mountain threatens to crush borrowers', the *Independent*, 28 September 2006.

4 Desai, in contrast to Glyn, finds the resurgence of liberal capitalism on a global scale a positive development, and he presents a strong argument for thinking that Marx himself would have welcomed it; doubtless Marx would have favoured the rapid development observed in India, China and the Asian NICs.

5 See Keynes (1936: 373).

6 The Polish economist Michael Kalecki provided an important clue to the puzzle; his analysis of capitalist crisis entailed assuming that workers consumed their wages while capitalists invested their profits; in his phrase, 'workers spend what they earn and

capitalists earn what they spend'. Kalecki's implicit 'classical' savings function depended on the distribution of income. One might also cite Nicholas Kaldor, a Keynesian who postulated that when savings exceed investment at full employment, re-establishing equilibrium between them might not automatically entail a fall in income and employment – as long as the distribution of income could change in favour of workers.

7   This section is based on Irvin and Izurieta (2006).

8   A detailed analysis appears in T. McKinley (2005).

9   See M. Wolf (2005), 'Flowing uphill: why capital from poorer countries must one day reverse its course', *Financial Times*, 27 June 2005; also see Morrissey and Baker (2003).

10 Because figure 8.1 uses averages, the US deficit is smaller than indicated in the text; equally, surpluses and deficits do not sum exactly to zero.

11 See Robert Scott, 'Current account picture', Washington, DC: Economic Policy Institute, 14 March 2006, <http://www.epi.org/content.cfm/webfeat_econindicators_capict_20060314>.

12 See T. McKinley (2005: 9–10).

13 One must distinguish household consumption from household spending; the latter is defined as consumption plus residential investment. Much of the confusion about financial balances in the US is precisely because most people do not realize that households must borrow if total spending, not merely consumption, is greater than income.

14 See Dean Baker, *The Housing Bubble Starts to Burst*, Washington, DC: Center for Economic Policy Research, 6 March 2007.

15 See Paul Krugman, 'The hissing sound', *The New York Times*, Op-Ed., 8 August 2005.

16 See Larry Elliott, 'Forecasting house prices, let alone averting a crash, is getting ever more tricky'. the *Guardian*, 28 May 2007; H. Stewart, 'UK housing market hits tipping point', the *Observer*, 7 May 2007.

17 The origins of bundling mortgages into collaterized debt obligations is discussed in Michael Lewis's fascinating book, *Liar's Poker*; see Lewis (1989).

18 See IMF (2007).

19 See <http://www.federalreserve.gov/releases/g19/current/default.htm>.

20 See <http://www.myloanandcredit.com/debt/about-debt.html>; also Blackburn (2006: 41).

21 See Draut and Silva (2003) and Draut (2005).

22 See Phillip Inman, 'Britons leave prudence to Europe', the *Guardian*, 27 September 2006.

23 For a comprehensive and prescient discussion of 'sustainability', see W. Godley (1999), *Seven Unsustainable Processes: Medium-term Prospects and Policies for the United States and the World*, Special Report, Annandale-on-the-Hudson, New York: The Levy Economics Institute of Bard College.

24 See, for example, Naomi Klein (2007).

25 One assumes here that 'labour productivity' growth arises from equipping the workforce with more machines under conditions of buoyant aggregate demand.

26 See 'Weaker dollar may make US trade gap worse – ex-Bush aide', Reuters, Wednesday 2 May 2007; <http://www.reuters.com/article/companyNewsAndPR/idUSL0270 311920070502>

27 See R. McKinnon and D. Schnabi (2006).

28 These 'wealth effects' obviously must be netted for the fact that euro-holders will feel richer and buy more US exports and dollar-denominated assets.

29 See R. L. Frank (2007), who claims that the super rich now account for nearly 70 per cent of US household spending.

30 The evidence so far seems to suggest that, while holding gains have a real balance effect, holding losses do not seem to impact negatively on spending with the same force. This may help explain why a strong dollar has not discouraged spending in the US despite a loss of foreign-denominated wealth.

31 See Zanny Minton Beddoes, 'The great savings shift', *The Economist*, 25 September 2005.
32 See Paul Krugman, 'The Chinese connection', New *York Times*, Op-Ed., 20 May 2005.
33 See 'IMF upbeat on UK economic growth', BBC News, 5 March 2007, <http://news.bbc.co.uk/2/hi/business/6421087.stm>.
34 See Larry Elliot and Dan Atkinson, 'Talk is cheap', the *Guardian*, 18 May 2007.
35 The 'Golden Rule' says that over the business cycle, UK Treasury borrowing can only fund capital spending; current spending must balance. Moreover, Brown decreed that public indebtedness must not surpass 40 per cent of GDP.
36 See Elliot and Atkinson, 'Talk is cheap', the *Guardian*, 18 May 2007
37 See W. Godley and A. Izurieta (2004); also see G. Irvin (2006).
38 The Bank of Japan is celebrating the first signs of the end of deflation by announcing a possible rise in interest rates! See J. McCurry, 'Bank of Japan prepares to raise interest rates after five years at near-zero', the *Guardian*, 10 March 2006.
39 See, for example, Irvin (2006); C. A. E. Goodhart (2006).
40 For an excellent discussion of this matter, see Grieve Smith (2005); also see C. A. E. Goodhart (2006).
41 The MacDougall Report (1997) called for an initial federal budget amounting to 2 per cent of EU GDP and rising to 5–7 per cent. A separate commission, reporting in 1993, called for a European Fiscal Transfer Scheme (EFTS) to cushion the currency area from external asymmetric shocks; see European Commission (1993a),
42 See European Commission (1993b).
43 See M. Ball, M (2006), *European Housing Review*, London: Royal Institute of Chartered Surveyors; Ball finds that financial liberalization is one factor contributing to rising house prices, though he finds constrained supply most important. Equally interesting, Ball suggests that rapidly rising house prices are associated with rising income inequality. Also see OECD (2005), *World Economic Outlook* 78, December.
44 See *Financial Times* Forum – Martin Wolf's blog: comment posted by Ronald McKinnon on 15 December 2006.

Chapter 9 In Defence of Equality

 1 Reported in Barry (2005: 7–9).
 2 See Barry (2005).
 3 See Matthew Tempest, 'Campbell wins key conference vote on tax', the *Guardian*, 19 September 2006.
 4 A particularly useful introduction to the 'Swedish model' is Robert Taylor's essay; see Taylor (2003).
 5 See Barry (2005: 20).
 6 See chapter 1 of K. Arrow, S. Bowles and S. Durlaud (eds) (2000).
 7 See Barry (2005: 110); the original is in M. Frayn (1964), *On the Outskirts*, London: Collins, p. 140.
 8 See Barry (2005: 117).
 9 Ibid., p.49.
10 Ibid., pp.50–1
11 See John Carvel, 'Class divide hits learning by the age of three', the *Guardian*, 11 June 2007.
12 See Esping-Andersen (2005: 31).
13 Ibid., p.34.
14 See Ruth Levitas, Emma Head and Naomi Finch, 'Lone mothers, poverty and social exclusion', in Pantazis et al. (2006).
15 See Peter Wilby, 'Thatcherism's final triumph', *Prospect* 127, October 2006.
16 See Polly Toynbee, 'Going nowhere', the *Guardian*, 2 April 2004.

17 See 'Marriage in America: the frayed knot', *The Economist*, 26 May 2007.
18 Quoted in Barry (2005: 145); also see Stuart White (1999), 'Rights and responsibilities: a social democratic perspective', *The Political Quarterly* 70, 166–80.
19 Quoted from: Jack Straw, 'Building social cohesion, order and inclusion in a market economy', speech to the *Nexus* Conference *Mapping out the Third Way*, Friday 3 July 1998.
20 See Ehrenreich (2001: 3).
21 See Sam Pizzigati, 'Taxing the rich, 1957 style', *Too Much*, Weekly Newsletter of the Council on International and Public Affairs, Washington, DC, 13 February 2006.
22 Strictly speaking, VAT is paid on value added at each stage of production and sale; it is only a consumption tax if all output is ultimately consumed and if it leads to no compensating price adjustment downward.
23 See, for example, Van Parijs (1995a); Miller (2005); and Glyn (2006).
24 See *Tax Credit Take-up Resource Pack: Helping Clients to Assess Tax Credits and Manage Their Claims*, London: Citizens Advice Bureau, November 2006, p. 6. <http://www.citizensadvice.org.uk/pdf_debranded_tax-credit-takeup-e-2007-01.pdf>
25 See Ian Pollock, 'I won't claim tax credits again', 30 September 2005, <http://news.bbc.co.uk/1/hi/business/4294444.stm>.
26 See P. Van Parijs (1995b).
27 The basics are to be found in most textbooks on welfare economics, but I have always found Maurice Dobb (1973) to be particularly helpful.
28 See Glyn and Miliband (eds) (1994), Introduction, pp. 2 and 13–14.
29 See L. Rampa (2007), 'Preferire l'equità nuoce all'efficienza?', *Prolusione*, Dipartimento di Economia Politica e Metodi Quantitativi, University of Pavia, 15 January, p. 5.
30 See ibid.
31 The literature and measurement problems of world income inequality are admirably resumed in Sutcliffe (2002).
32 See J. Davies et al. (WIDER) (2006).
33 See Clive Hamilton, 'Climate change wars', *New Left Review* 45, May/June 2007.
34 This argument is admirably spelled out in Monbiot (2006).
35 See Stephen Armstrong, 'Mad as hell', *New Statesman*, 14 May 2007.
36 See Jenkins Commission, *The Report of the Independent Commission on the Voting System*, London: The Stationery Office, 28 October 1998.

Bibliography

Alesina, A. and D. Rodrick (1992) 'Distribution, political conflict and economic growth: a simple theory and some empirical evidence', in A. Cuckierman, Z. Hercowitz and L. Leiderman (eds), *Political Economy, Growth and Business Cycles*. Cambridge: MIT Press, 1992.

Alesina, A., Glaeser, E. and B. Sacerdote (2005) 'Work and leisure in the US and Europe: why so different?', Discussion Paper No 2068. Cambridge, MA: Harvard Institute of Economic Research, April 2005.

Arrow, K. (1963) *Social Choice and Individual Values*. New York: John Wiley & Sons.

Arrow K., Bowles S. and S. Durlaud (eds) (2000) *Meritocracy and Economic Inequality*, Princeton, NJ: Princeton University Press.

Atkinson, A. B. (2003) 'Income inequality in OECD countries: data and explanations', *Working Paper No 881, CESifo* (Centre for Economic Studies, University of Munich), February.

Augar, P. (2005) *The Greed Merchants: How the Investment Banks Played the Free Market Game*. London: Penguin Books.

Axelrod, R. (1984) *The Evolution of Co-operation*. New York: Basic Books.

Barry, B. (2005) *Why Social Justice Matters*. Cambridge: Polity.

Beck, U. (1992) *Risk Society: Towards a New Modernity*. New Delhi: Sage.

Bernstein, J. (2006) *All Together Now: Common Sense for a Fair Economy*. San Francisco, CA: Berret-Kohler.

Bernstein, J. and L. Mishel (2007) 'Education and the inequality debate', *EPI Issue Brief No. 232*, Washington, DC: Economic Policy Institute February 8, 2007,

Blackburn, R. (2006) 'Finance and the fourth dimension', *New Left Review 39*, May–June: 39–70.

Blandon J., Gregg, P. and S. Machin (2005) *Intergenerational Mobility in Europe and North America*. London: London School of Economics, Centre for Economic Performance and The Sutton Trust, April.

Bluestone, B. and S. Rose (1997) 'Overworked and underemployed: unravelling an economic enigma,' *The American Prospect 8/31*, March.

Bobbio, N. (1996) *Left and Right*. Cambridge: Polity.

Bradbury, K. and J. Katz (2002) 'Are lifetime incomes growing more unequal? Looking at new evidence on family income mobility', *Federal Reserve Bank of Boston, Regional Review 12/4*.

Brewer M., Goodman A., Myck M., Shaw J. and A. Shephard (2004) *Poverty and Inequality in Britain: 2004.* London: Institute of Fiscal Studies.

Buchanan, J. and G. Tullock (1962) *The Calculus of Consent: Logical Foundations of Constitutional Democracy.* Ann Arbor: University of Michigan Press.

Cahill, K. (2001) *Who Owns Britain?* Edinburgh: Canongate.

Corry, D. and A. Glyn (1994) 'The macroeconomics of equality, stability and growth', in A. Glyn and D. Miliband (eds), *Paying for Inequality: The Economic Cost of Social Injustice.* London: Rivers Oram, 1994.

Craig, D. (2005) *Rip-Off.* London: The Original Book Company.

Craig, D. (2006) *Plundering the Public Sector.* London: Constable.

Davies, J., Sandstrom, S., Shorrocks, A. and E. Wolff (WIDER) (2006) 'The world distribution of household wealth,' UNU-WIDER, Helsinki, 5 December.

Desai, M. (2002) *Marx's Revenge: The Resurgence of Capitalism and the Death of Statist Socialism.* London: Verso.

Devine, P. (2006) 'The 1970s and after: the political economy of inflation and the crisis of social democracy', *Soundings* 32, March.

Dew-Becker, I. and R. J. Gordon (2005) 'Where did the productivity growth go? Inflation dynamics and the distribution of income', *NBER Working Papers* 11842. Washington, DC: National Bureau of Economic Research, Inc.

Diamond, P. (2006) 'Equality now: Labour's agenda of economic and social reform', *Renewal* 14/3, 2006.

Dinan, D. (2004) *Europe Recast: A History of the European Union*, London: Palgrave Macmillan.

Dobb, M. (1973) *Theories of Value and Distribution since Adam Smith*, Cambridge: Cambridge University Press.

Domhoff, G. W. (2001) *Who Rules America?*, 4th edn, New York: McGraw Hill.

Donkin, A., P. Goldblatt, K. Lynch (2002) 'Inequalities in life expectancy by social class, 1972–1999', *Health Statistics Quarterly* 15 (autumn 2002).

Dorling, D., Rigby, R., et al. (2007) *Poverty, Wealth and Place in Britain, 1968 to 2005*, Rowling Foundation. Bristol: Policy Press.

Draut, T. (2005) 'The plastic safety net: the reality behind debt in America', Report published by Demos, Washington, DC; see: <http://www.demos.org/pubs/PSN_low.pdf>.

Draut, T. and J. Silva (2003), *Borrowing to Make Ends Meet: The Growth of Credit Card Debt in the '90s*, Report published by Demos, Washington, DC; see: <http://www.demos.org/pubs/PSN_low.pdf>.

Duménil, G. and C. Lévy (2004) 'Neoliberal income trends: work, class and ownership in the USA', *New Left Review* 30, Nov/Dec: 105–33.

Easterlin, R. A. (2001) 'Income and happiness: towards a unified theory', *The Economic Journal* 111 (July): 464–84.

Ehrenreich, B. (2001) *Nickel and Dimed: On (Not) Getting By in America*, New York: Henry Holt.

Ehrenreich, B. (2006) *Bait and Switch: The Futile Pursuit of the Corporate Dream*, London: Granta Books.

Esping-Andersen, Gøsta (2005) 'Inequality of incomes and opportunities', in Giddens and Diamond (eds) (2005).

Esping-Andersen, Gøsta et al. (2002) *Why We Need a New Welfare State*, Oxford: Oxford University Press.

European Commission (1993a) 'Monnaie stable – finances saines: les finances publiques de la communauté dans la perspective de l'UEM', *Economie Européene 53*, Brussells.

European Commission (1993b) 'Growth competitiveness and employment' (Delors White Paper), Luxembourg.

Frank, R. H. (1999) *Luxury Fever: Money and Happiness in an Era of Excess.* Princeton, NJ: Princeton University Press.

Frank, R. H. (2007) *Falling Behind: How Rising Inequality Harms the Middle Class.* Berkeley: University of California Press.

Frank, R. H. and P. Cook (1995) *The Winner-take-all Society*, New York: The Free Press.

Frank, R. L. (2007) *Richistan: A Journey Through the 21st Century Wealth Boom and the Lives of the New Rich.* New York: Crown Publishers.

Freeman, R. (1999) *The New Inequality; Creating Solutions for Poor America*, Boston: Beacon Press.

Frydman, C. and R. Saks (2005) 'Historical trends in executive compensation, 1936–2003', Working Paper, Harvard University.

Galbraith, J. K. (1958) *The Affluent Society*, London: Hamish Hamilton.

Giddens, A. and P. Diamond (eds) (2005) *The New Egalitarianism*, Cambridge: Polity.

Glyn, A. (1992) 'The costs of stability: the advanced capitalist countries in the 1980s', *New Left Review 1/195*, Sept–Oct.: 71–95.

Glyn, A. (2006) *Capitalism Unleashed: Finance, Globalisation and Welfare*, Oxford: Oxford University Press.

Glyn, A. and D. Miliband (eds) (1994) *Paying for Inequality: The Economic Cost of Social Injustice*, London: IPPR/Rivers Oram Press.

Glyn, A. and B. Sutcliffe (1973), *British Capitalism, Workers and the Profits Squeeze*, London: Penguin Books.

Godley, W. and A. Izurieta (2004) 'Balances, imbalances and fiscal targets: a new Cambridge view', *Cambridge Endowment for Research and Finance (CERF)*, Cambridge: Judge Institute.

Goodhart, C. A. E. (2006) 'Replacing the SGP?', Draft paper to the Franklin Conference on the Future of Europe, Lugano, 2–4 March.

Gordon, D. and P. Townsend (eds) (2000) *Breadline Europe: The Measurement of Poverty*, Bristol: Policy Press.

Grieve Smith, J. (2001) *There is a Better Way: A New Economic Agenda*, London: Anthem Press.

Grieve Smith, J. (2005) 'Unemployment and fiscal policy in the EU', *European Policy Brief 17*, London: The Federal Trust for Education and Research, November.

Hacker, J. (2006) *The Great Risk Shift*, New York and Oxford: Oxford University Press.

Harcourt, G. C. (1972) *Some Cambridge Controversies in the Theory of Capital*, Cambridge: Cambridge University Press.

Harvey, D. (2005) *A Brief History of Neo-liberalism*, Oxford: Oxford University Press.

Haseler, S. (2004) *Super-State: The New Europe and its Challenge to America*, London: Tauris.

Hills, J. (2004) *Inequality and the State*, Oxford: Oxford University Press.

Hirsch, F. (1976) *Social Limits to Growth*, Cambridge, MA: Harvard University Press.

IMF (International Monetary Fund) *Economic Outlook 2006*, Washington, DC: International Monetary Fund.

IMF (International Monetary Fund) (2007) *World Economic Outloook: Spillovers and Cycles in the World Economy*. Washington, DC: International Monetary Fund, April.

Irvin, G. (1979) *Modern Cost Benefit Methods*, London: Macmillan.

Irvin, G. (2006), *Regaining Europe; An Economic Agenda for the 21st Century*, London: Federal Trust.

Irvin, G. and A. Izurieta (2006) 'The US deficit, the EU surplus and the world economy', *Renewal 14/4*, London.

Jenkins, S. (2007) *Thatcher and Sons: A Revolution in Three Acts*, London: Penguin Books.

Jomo, K. S. and A. Izurieta (2007) 'Global imbalances require inclusive multi-lateralism', address to the Shadow-G8 Conference *Global Economic Imbalances. A Need for Global Governance Beyond the G8?*, Berlin, 6–7 June.

Kagan, R. (2003) *Of Paradise and Power: America and Europe in the New World Order*, New York: Alfred Knopf.

Kawachi et al. (1997), 'Social capital, income inequality and morality', *American Journal of Public Health 87/1*.

Keynes, J. M. (1936) *The General Theory of Employment, Interest, and Money*, New York: First Harvest/Harcourt Brace Edition, 1964.

Klein, N. (2007) *The Shock Doctrine: The Rise of Disaster Capitalism*, London: Allen Lane.

Kozol, J. (2005) *The Shame of the Nation: The Restoration of Apartheid Schooling in America*, New York: Crown Publishers.

Krugman, P. (1999) *The Accidental Theorist*. London: Penguin Books.

Krugman, P. (2002) 'For richer', *New York Times Magazine*, 20 Oct. 2002.

Krugman, P. (2004) 'The problems of inequality', in Stephenson, H. (ed) (2004) *Challenges for Europe*, London: Palgrave.

Krugman, P. (2006) 'Wages, wealth and politics', *New York Times*, 18 August 2006.

Kusnet D., Mishel, L. and R. Teixeira (2006) *Talking Past Each Other; What Everyday Americans Really Think (and Elites Don't Get) About the Economy*, Washington, DC: Economic Policy Institute.

Landsburg, S. (2006) 'Why Europeans work less than Americans', *Forbes Magazine*, 23 May 2006.

Lansley, S. (1994) *After the Gold Rush*, London: Century.

Lansley, S. (2006) *Rich Britain: The Rise and Rise of the New Super-Wealthy*, London: Politico's.

Lansley, S. (2007) 'Britain's wealth explosion', *Soundings 35*, spring: 148–57.

Layard, R. (2003a) 'Towards a happier society', Robbins Lecture, London School of Economics (revised), 24 Feb. 2003.

Layard, R. (2003b) 'Income and happiness: rethinking economic policy', Robbins Lecture, London School of Economics, 27 Feb. 2003.

Layard, R. (2003c) 'What would make a happier society?', Robbins Lecture, London School of Economics, 5 March 2003.

Layard, R. (2005) *Happiness: Lessons from a New Science*, London: Penguin Books.

Levy, F. and P. Temin (2007) 'Inequality and institutions in 20th century America', *MIT Department of Economics Working Paper No. 07–17* (1 May 2007).

Lewis, M. (1989) *Liar's Poker*, New York: W. W. Norton.

Little, I. and J. Mirrlees (1974) *Project Appraisal and Planning for Developing Countries*, London: Heinemann Educational Books.

Marquand, D. (2004) *Decline of the Public*, Cambridge: Polity.

McKinley, T. (2005) 'The monopoly of global capital flows: who needs structural adjustment now?', *Working Paper Number 12*, Brasil: International Poverty Centre.

McKinley, T. and A. Izurieta (2007) 'The gross inequities of global imbalances', *International Poverty Centre, UNDP*, Brasilia, Feb., No. 30.

McKinnon, R. and D. Schnabi (2006) 'Devaluing the dollar: a critical analysis of William Cline's case for a new plaza agreement', *Journal of Policy Modelling* 28/6, September.

Marquand, D. (2004) *Decline of the Public*, Cambridge: Polity.

Millar, J. and K. Gardiner (2004) 'Low pay, household resources and poverty', York: Joseph Rowntree Foundation.

Miller, D. (2005) 'What is social justice?', in Pearce and Paxton (eds), *Social Justice: Building a Fairer Britain*, London: Politico's.

Mishel, L., Bernstein, J. and J. Schmitt (2001) *The State of Working America*, Ithaca, NY: Cornell University Press.

Mishel, L., Bernstein, J. and S. Allegretto (2005) *The State of Working America 2004/05*, Ithaca, NY: Economic Policy Institute, Cornell University Press.

Mishel, L., Bernstein, J. and S. Allegretto (2007) *The State of Working America 2006/07*, Ithaca, NY: Economic Policy Institute, Cornell University Press.

Monbiot, G. (2006) *Heat: How to Stop the Planet Burning*, London: Allen Lane.

Morley, J., Ward, T. and A. Watt (2004) *The State of Working Europe*. Brussels: European Trade Union Institute.

Morrissey, M. and D. Baker (2003) *When Rivers Flow Upstream: International Capital Movements in the Era of Globalization*, Report, Washington, DC: Center for Economic Policy Research, March.

Nettle, D. (2005) *Happiness: The Science Behind Your Smile*, Oxford: Oxford University Press.

Newman, K. and V. Tan Chen (2007) *The Missing Class: Portraits of the Near-Poor in America*, Boston: Beacon Press.

Nussbaum, M. (2001) 'The enduring significance of John Rawls', *The Chronicle Review*, The Chronicle of Higher Education, Washington DC, 20 July 2001.

Obstfeld, M. and K. Rogoff (2005) 'Global current account imbalances and exchange rate adjustments', *Brookings Papers on Economics* 1: 67–123.

OECD (Organisation for Economic Cooperation and Development) (2002) *Employment Outlook*, Paris: OECD, July.

Offer, A. (2006) *The Challenge of Affluence: Self-control and Well-being in the United States and Britain since 1950*, Oxford: Oxford University Press.

Orton, M. and K. Rowlingson (2007) *Public Attitudes to Economic Inequality*, Report, York: Joseph Rowntree Foundation.

Pahl, R., Rose, D. and L. Spencer (2007) 'Inequality and quiescence: a continuing conundrum', ISER Working Paper 2007–22, September, Essex: Institute for Social and Economic Research, University of Essex

Pantazis, C., Gordon, D. and R. Levitas (2006) *Poverty and Social Exclusion in Britain*, Cambridge: Polity.

Papatheodorou, C. and D. Pavlopoulos (2003) 'Accounting for inequality in the EU: income disparities between and within member states and overall income inequality', CHER Working Paper 9, CEPS/INSTEAD, Differdange, G.-D., Luxembourg.

Paxton, W. and M. Dixon (2004) *The State of the Nation: An Audit of Injustice in the UK*, London: Institute for Public Policy Research.

Pearce, N. (2004) 'Income inequality has declined but wealth inequality is roaring ahead', *Prospect* 102, September.

Pearce, N. and M. Dixon (2005) 'New model welfare' *Prospect* 110, May 2005.

Pearce, N. and W. Paxton (eds) (2005) *Social Justice: Building a Fairer Britain*, London: Politico's.

Pew Research Center (2006) *Are We Happy Yet?*, Washington, DC, February 13.

Phillips, K. (2002) *Wealth and Democracy: A Political History of the American Rich*, New York: Broadway Books.

Piketty, T. and E. Saez (2003) 'Income inequality in the United States, 1913–1998', *Quarterly Journal of Economics* CXVIII/1.

Pikkety, T. and E. Saez (2006) 'How progessive is the US federal tax system? An historical and international perspective', CEPR Discussion Paper 5778, London: Centre for Economic Policy Research.

Pizzigati, S. (2004) *Greed and Good*, New York: Apex Press

Pizzigati, S. (2006) 'A most dangerous Yo-Yo'; review dated 19 June 2006, of Jared Bernstein's *All Together Now: Common Sense for a Fair Economy*, San Francisco: Berrett-Kohler, 2006. <http://www.cipa-apex.org/toomuch/articlenew2006/Jun19a.html>.

Pollock, A. (2004) *NHS plc; The Privatisation of our Health Care*, London: Verso.

Price, L. (2005) *The Spin Doctor's Diary*, London: Hodder & Stoughton.

Putnam, R. D. (2000) *Bowling Alone: The Collapse and Revival of American Community*, New York: Simon & Schuster.

Rawls, J. (1971) *A Theory of Justice*, Cambridge, MA: Harvard University Press.

Reid, M. (2003) *The Secondary Banking Crisis; 1973–75*, London: Hindsight Books.

Reid, T. R. (2004) *The United States of Europe: The New Superpower and the End of American Supremacy*, New York: Penguin.

Report of the Commission on Social Justice (1994) *Social Justice: Strategies for National Renewal*, London: Vintage.

Rifkin, J. (2004) *The European Dream*, Cambridge: Polity.

Rose, G. and M. Marmot (1981) 'Social class and coronary heart disease', *British Heart Journal* 45.

Rothstein, B. and E. M. Uslaner (2005) 'All for all. Equality, corruption and social trust', *World Politics* 58: 41–73, October.

Runciman, W. G. (1966) *Relative Deprivation and Social Justice*, London: Routledge.

Rustin, M. (2007) 'What's wrong with happiness?', *Soundings* 36, September.

Sampson, A. (2005) *Who Runs this Place? The Anatomy of Britain in the 21st Century*, London: John Murray.

Schmitt, J. (2005) *How Good is the Economy at Creating Good Jobs?*, Report, Washington, DC: Center for Economic Policy Research (CEPR), October.

Schmitt, J. and B. Zipperer (2006) *Is the US a Good Model for Reducing Social Exclusion in Europe?*, Report, Washington, DC: Center for Economic Policy Research (CEPR), July.

Schor, J. B. (1992) *The Overworked American: The Unexpected Decline in Leisure*, Cambridge, MA: Harvard University Press.

Schor, J. B. (1998) *The Overspent American*, New York: Basic Books.

Schumpeter, J. (1942), *Capitalism, Socialism and Democracy*, New York: Harper & Brothers.

Sen, A. (1987) *The Standard of Living*, Cambridge: Cambridge University Press.

Smeeding, T. M. (2002) 'Globalisation, inequality and the rich countries of the G-20; evidence from the Luxemburg Income Studies (LIS)', paper prepared or the G-20 meeting: *Globalisation, Living Standards and Inequality; Recent Progress and Continuing Challenges*, Sydney, Australia, May 26–28.

Smeeding, T. M. (2006) 'Poor people in rich nations: the United States in comparative perspective, *Journal of Economic Perspectives* 20/1.

Standing, G. (2004) *Evolution of the Washington Consensus: Economic Insecurity as Discontent*, Geneva: International Labour Office.

Stern, A. (2006) A *Country That Works: Getting America Back on Track*, New York: Free Press.

Stiglitz, J. (1969) 'Distribution of income and wealth among individuals', *Econometrica* 37: 382–97.

Stiglitz, J. (2003) *The Roaring Nineties*, London: Penguin Books.

Stiglitz, J. (2007) *Making Globalization Work*, London: Penguin Books.

Sutcliffe, B. (2002) 'A more or less unequal world? World income distribution in the 20th century' (bilingual), *Cuaderno de trabajo de HEGOA* 31, October, Bilbao: Universidad del Pais Vasco.

Swabisch, J., Smeeding, T., and L. Olsberg (2004) 'Income distribution and social expenditures: a cross-national perspective', *Working Paper, Center for Policy Research*, New York: Maxwell School, Syracuse University, <http://www.russellsage.org/publications/workingpapers/incdistsocexpend/document>.

Taylor, R. (2003) 'Sweden's new social democratic model: proof that a better world is possible', London: Compass.

Taylor-Gooby, P. (2004) *Making a European Welfare State*, Oxford: Blackwell.

Torrini, R. (2005) 'Profit share and returns on capital stock in Italy: the role of privatisations behind the rise of the 1990s', Centre for Economic Performance Discussion Paper No 671, January, London: London School of Economics.

Toynbee, P. and D. Walker (2005) *Better or Worse? Has Labour Delivered?*, London: Bloomsbury Publishing.

Turner, A. (2000) 'Growth, productivity and employment', Centre for Economic Performance Discussion Paper, London: London School of Economics, December.

Turner, A. (2001) *Just Capital: The Liberal Economy*, London: Macmillan.

Van Parijs, P. (1995a) *Real Freedom for All*, Oxford: Oxford University Press.

Van Parijs, P. (1995b) 'Are inequalities ever just?', *Documents de travail de la Chaire Hoover* 15 (DOCHs), Louvain: University of Louvain.

Veblen, T. ([1899] 1998) *The Theory of the Leisure Class*, New York: Prometheus Books.

Vidal J., Branigan T. and J. Randerson (2006) 'Could scrapping Trident save the planet?', the *Guardian*, 4 November 2006.

Wade, R. (2007) 'Economic liberalism and the "outward alliance" of big companies, finance and the state: a perspective from the United Kingdom', in P. Bowles, H. Veltmeyer, et al. (eds), (2007), *National Perspectives on Globalization*, Basingstoke: Palgrave Macmillan.

Walzer, M. (1983) *Spheres of Justice*, Oxford: Martin Robinson.

Watkins, S. (2005) 'Continental tremors', *New Left Review* 33, May/June.

Wilby, P. (2006) 'Thatcherism's final triumph', *Prospect* 127, October.

Wilkinson, R. G. (1996) *Unhealthy Societies: The Afflictions of Inequality*, London: Routledge.

Wilkinson, R. G. (2005) *The Impact of Inequality*, New York: Routledge.

Wilkinson, R. G., Kawachi, I., and B. Kennedy (1998) 'Mortality, the social environment, crime and violence', *Sociology of Health and Illness* 20/5: 578–97.

Wolf, M. (2005) *Why Globalisation Works*, London: Yale Nota Bene.

World Values Survey (1990–93), Inter-University Consortium for Political and Social Research (ICPSR), Ann Arbor: University of Michigan.

Wright Mills, C. (1956) *The Power Elite*, New York: Oxford University Press.

Young, M. (1958) *The Rise of the Meritocracy, 1870–2033, the New Elite of Our Social Revolution*, New York: Random House.

Index